D1568317

LINCOLN, LAND, AND LABOR, 1809–60

LINCOLN, LAND, AND LABOR, 1809–60

Olivier Frayssé

Translated by
Sylvia Neely

UNIVERSITY OF ILLINOIS PRESS
Urbana and Chicago

© Publications de la Sorbonne, 1988, loi du 11 mars 1957
English language translation published in 1994 by
the University of Illinois Press under agreement
with Publications de la Sorbonne.

Manufactured in the United States of America
C   5   4   3   2   1

This book is printed on acid-free paper.

Library of Congress Cataloging-in-Publication Data

Fraysse, Olivier, 1953-
    [Abraham Lincoln. English]
    Lincoln, land, and labor, 1809–60 / Olivier Fraysse ; translated
by Sylvia Neely.
        p.   cm.
    Includes bibliographical references and index.
    ISBN 0–252–01979–2 (acid-free paper)
    1. Lincoln, Abraham, 1809–1865—Views on land.   2. Land use—
United States—History—19th century.   I. Title.
E457.2.F78513   1994
973.7'092—dc20
                                3-1569
                                  CIP

CONTENTS

TRANSLATOR'S NOTE

Olivier Fraysse's *Abraham Lincoln: La terre et le travail, 1809–1860* was published in 1988 by the Publications de la Sorbonne in Paris. I wanted to make this work available to American readers, first because it offers an original interpretation of Abraham Lincoln (in itself, a difficult thing to do). Second, it embodies a European perspective on American history rarely encountered by those historians in this country who do not read French fluently. Fraysse, Maître de Conférences in the Department of Anglophone Studies at the Université de la Sorbonne Nouvelle Paris III, brings to his work the sensibilities of a student of language and literature, as well as of economic theory and the global economy. His analysis of Lincoln's relationship to the land, a subject not treated systematically before, draws heavily on Marxist theory and provides a provocative and thoughtful approach to the subject.

Fraysse wrote the book for French readers, and I have not attempted to recast it as if its origins were American, for that would have destroyed much of its value to its new audience. Whenever possible, quotations from French sources have been located in published translations. Where such translations did not exist, I have translated the passages. Fraysse's assistance in the translation of this work has been invaluable. At every stage he has offered advice and made corrections. The translation was, indeed, a collaborative endeavor for which I express my appreciation. For this edition in English, he made a few revisions, adding a discussion on Lincoln and mining. I hope that this publication will contribute to a fruitful exchange of ideas among historians throughout the world and that knowledgeable and serious works on the history of the United States will in future be more readily made available in translation.

—Sylvia Neely

INTRODUCTION

As far back as 1934, Professor James G. Randall, in a well-known article, asked, "Has the Lincoln theme been exhausted?" He showed at that time the immense and unexplored fields of unedited works, of periods and subjects that had never been examined, and concluded optimistically that despite a list of some three thousand works, a survey of historians in the year 1984 would prove that great progress was still possible in Lincoln studies.[1]

Well before that fateful date, and thanks to Randall himself, in 1960 Clyde C. Walton wrote "An Agonizing Reappraisal: 'Has the Lincoln Theme Been Exhausted?'"[2] He pointed out then that most of the 1934 questions had been answered: the whole of Lincoln's work was available; a committee of more than a hundred historians had completed a detailed chronology of even the most minor events of his life;[3] and all the directions for research indicated by Randall, and many others besides, had been followed. "We know more about Lincoln's day-by-day activity than he knew; we know more about his family and ancestors than he knew. Some of our scholars may know more about the details of his life than they know of their own."[4] Walton concluded, however, that Lincoln remained as mysterious as ever and that the path to new interpretations remained wide open.

One of the themes leading to a new interpretation of Lincoln has never been explored on its own, although it is woven throughout all Lincoln studies: his vision of the land and of those who work it.[5]

It is indeed impossible to ignore this aspect of a man who worked the land with his own hands for fifteen years, surveyed it for five, and spent nine-tenths of his life in agricultural areas. As a lawyer specializing in land law, as a politician representing a rural district, he had to pay some attention to the national debate over the future of public lands, to issues linked to real estate taxes, to the relationship between town and country, and to many other problems of importance to those among whom he lived.

Questions spring immediately to mind: What were his relations with farmers, both large and small? How much attention did he pay to agriculture? What place did that occupation hold in his economic views?

These questions cannot be answered independently of one another: the issue underlying them all is the relationship between Lincoln and the rural America of his day, the story of a journey from the log cabin to the presidency. His country origins, his hard-working youth, but also, paradoxically, his social rise in manhood and the break with the land that accompanied it recall the observation of his friend and biographer Isaac Arnold: "Abraham Lincoln was . . . the racy product of American soil and American civilization. No other age, or country, could have produced his counterpart. No other section of his country but the great national Northwest could have produced him."[6]

Yet Lincoln acted upon American civilization as much as he was a product of it: the three historic results of the Lincoln administration (the abolition of slavery, the Homestead Act, and the beginning of the "final solution" of the Indian question) constitute the perspective from which we must look back at the years when Lincoln experienced the growth of the rural society of the Old Northwest, a growth that was a decisive element in triggering the Civil War.

Still to be explained is how this unique being, Lincoln the individual, came to embody, for both history and myth, the soul of an entire nation, how he was able to rediscover on a higher level, thirty years after rejecting them, the American values of land and labor, those values of freedom for which he would become the symbol.

Was the evolution of his thought on slavery the key to the mystery? Indeed, until 1854, Lincoln experienced slavery in his political and professional life in Kentucky and then in Indiana, an experience over which he had no control. After that date, he began to make history by dedicating his life to the struggle against the extension of the peculiar institution, and, by so doing, his personal story merged with American history.

1

KENTUCKY: THE NATIVE LAND

> Abraham, grandfather of the subject of this sketch, came to Kentucky, and was killed by indians about the year 1784. He left a widow, three sons and two daughters.... Thomas, the youngest son, and father of the present subject, by the early death of his father, and very narrow circumstances of his mother, even in childhood was a wandering laboring boy, and grew up litterally without education. ... he removed to what is now Spencer county Indiana, in the autumn of 1816, A. then being in his eigth year. This removal was partly on account of slavery; but chiefly on account of the difficulty in land titles in Ky.[1]

A grandfather killed by Indians, a father wandering in search of work, failing in his efforts to establish himself as an independent farmer in the hostile atmosphere of a slave society because he lacked sure land titles: this is the picture that Lincoln drew of his Kentucky origins.

He did not like to talk about this period and doubted that it held any significance, but the period draws our interest for many reasons.[2] If it is true that childhood years play an important role in the formation of the personality, then without doubt the images, conversations, and events, both large and small, that marked young Abraham's life between 1809 and 1816 deserve our attention. For this reason, evoking the landscape of Kentucky, the traditions about the Lincoln family, and the recollections of contemporaries can give us a better understanding of the atmosphere of a childhood that Lincoln summed up by borrowing a line from Gray's elegy: "The short and simple annals of the poor."[3]

These facts and images would have little value if they did not help to illustrate a chapter in the development of American civilization: the moment when the Virginians pushed back the Cherokees and the struggle for the possession of the soil moved West. Dividing the spoils of this newly conquered land pitted whites against whites, and the burning issues of the day dealt with land laws, the sale of public lands, and the status of squatters. But the land of Kentucky was not merely the stakes in a battle between individuals or even between classes. Two social systems were in competition: one based on slavery, the other on "free labor," that is, wage-earning and private enterprise.

By a happy coincidence, the autobiography of Abraham Lincoln from the very beginning brings up three issues that dominate the history of the American West and later of the nation itself: the Indian question, the distribution of land, and slavery—three questions for which only the Lincoln administration provided overall answers.

Chance may have arranged things well, but the reason might also be that Kentucky is admirably suited for this kind of conjunction. A border state in the double sense of *border* and of *frontier*, it would long maintain the quality of indecision, of ambiguity, associated with the first word. The Cumberland Gap could lead a pioneer either to Mobile or Chicago. New York served as a lock, bringing immigrants level with America. In the Kentucky passage, they had a choice between two Americas. Two Kentuckians, born a year apart, had their destinies profoundly marked by the choice made by their parents: Abraham Lincoln would head to Indiana, Jefferson Davis to Mississippi.

A DARK AND BLOODY GROUND

As Lincoln reminds us, his native land of Kentucky, too fertile in presidents, was at first soaked by Indian and pioneer blood. In 1809, when Abraham was born, the Indians, although recently pushed to the West, were still remembered vividly. When Abraham's father, Thomas, served in the militia in 1795, one of the main activities of the troops was to defend against Indian raids. That year, Thomas Cooper noted that there "is no part of Kentucky (Lexington perhaps, and a few miles round it excepted) which is perfectly safe from the incursions of the Indians."[4]

Fifteen or twenty years later, the stories that Thomas Lincoln and his brother Mordecai told in the evenings recounted the history of a land conquered by rifles and plows, rum and rails.

When, in the footsteps of Daniel Boone, driven by "that Anglo-Saxon lust of land which seems inseparable from the race,"[5] the pioneers began to appropriate the "dark and bloody ground" of Kentucky, their first priority was to enclose the few acres that they intended to cultivate, thus protecting them from damage by wild or domestic animals. The Virginia or worm-fence, the barrier they built between their cultivated enclosure and the wilderness, became the symbol of civilization, the sign of improvement that irremediably separated individual private property worked by white men from the communitarian spaces where Indians hunted. In contrast to the fence of hastily piled up branches around the common enclosure of the seminomadic Indians, the white man's fence was meant to last. The ambiguous ties that the hunters, trappers, adventurers, and traders had maintained with the "savages," competing with them over territory while also tacitly agreeing to share a common ground (relations for which Boone furnished a model), gave way to a struggle to the death between two mutually exclusive economic and social systems.

The rail fence, those solid beams piled one on top of another as high as a man, which Abraham [Lincoln, Thomas's father] built around 1784–85, constituted an insurmountable barrier between two worlds, both literally and figuratively. It had no door and could be removed only by violence. Symbolically, it was at the moment when Abraham placed the last of the eight rails, the "rider" at the top of the fence, that an Indian lying in ambush killed him with a rifle shot.

Young Thomas, petrified, saw the Indian advance on him. On his chest a silver pendant glimmered: taking it as a target, Mordecai, with a single bullet, avenged his father and saved his brother at the same time.[6]

As they buried their father, the protagonists of this tragedy probably did not see him as a soldier of modern civilization, fallen in the outposts of an expanding American limes, any more than they could have imagined that three-quarters of a century later the biographers of another Abraham would see this bloody episode as the seal of authenticity to be affixed to the person of the pioneer candidate. But the recollection remained forever vivid in Thomas's memory, and especially in the memory of Mordecai, who became one of those "Indian hunters" depicted by Melville in *The Confidence Man*. Lincoln apparently never felt that way, but all of his subsequent relations with Indians were already encapsulated in that confrontation at the border of the field, the symbol of the inevitable conflict between two antagonistic modes of production and ways of life on the same land, although in the case of Lincoln, it was "with malice toward none, and charity for all."

SEARCHING FOR LAND

Most of the first pioneers came to Kentucky, as had the Lincolns, from Virginia, bringing with them the plow and the windmill. Also in their baggage was the old feudal jumble of English customs from which Virginia had not completely freed itself during the American Revolution.

The operation of these outdated laws would set the general course of Thomas Lincoln's life. Indeed, when Abraham Lincoln died intestate in 1784–85, he left an inheritance in land that Louis A. Warren has evaluated at 5,544 acres. Because of primogeniture, which, in the absence of a will, governed real estate in Virginia—and therefore in Kentucky, which then was a part of that state—all of his land went to Mordecai. His personal fortune, to which the other children and the widow would have equal claims, amounted to £68.16s.6d.[7]

This event, painful in itself but made worse by the social and legal system of Virginia, foreshadowed the subsequent problems that led Thomas Lincoln to leave Kentucky in 1816. But before examining the causes of that migration, it is necessary to sketch a picture of the life led by the "wandering laboring boy" Thomas Lincoln, of his efforts to found a home, and of the circumstances and landscapes that formed the setting for Abraham Lincoln's first contact with land and labor.

It was, in fact, the life of a migrant worker that Thomas began to lead. In 1796 and 1797, he was laboring to build a mill for Samuel Haycraft, working side by side with slaves whose master pocketed their pay. In 1798, he visited his Uncle Isaac, who had settled in Tennessee, on the Watauga River. There, Thomas had the opportunity to observe slavery from another point of view because Isaac Lincoln owned several slaves.[8]

Listed on the register of delinquent taxpayers in Washington County in 1803,[9] Thomas appeared in the same year in a more flattering light in Hardin County, as owner of a 238-acre farm on Mill Creek, which he probably rented to his brother-in-law William Brumfield from 1803 to 1809.

How was Thomas Lincoln able to pay the price of £118 in cash, especially in 1803? Even taking into account that he had owned a few acres in Kentucky since 1798, it is difficult to accept Warren's assertion that any twenty-seven-year-old bachelor who was frugal and energetic could save enough money to buy a farm of that size. It is true that skilled labor—Thomas was a cabinetmaker and carpenter—was rare and well paid. But Warren's thesis rests on insufficient evidence to enable one to assert with certainty that Thomas was able to amass such a sum. Based on Haycraft's account book of 1796–97, Warren concludes that Lincoln, while earning 3s. a day, was able to save £118 in five years. That is to set little store by his son's description of Thomas as a migrant worker. Thomas Lincoln doubtless did not find permanent work, and it was only in 1803, as it happens, that he set himself up as a craftsman in Elizabethtown.[10] Furthermore, it is hard to see how the most frugal of sporadic workers could save in five years the value of 750 days of labor, and it is very difficult to explain the listing of Thomas on the register of delinquent taxpayers in Washington County. Finally, it must be added that cash was even rarer than skilled laborers. The account book that Warren cites often mentions payments in whisky or in "rations." Most products had a double price: in kind and in cash.[11] A more likely hypothesis about the source of Thomas's cash is that Mordecai agreed to do something for his younger brother. On the other hand, one can reasonably assume that Thomas's later acquisitions represented the fruit of his own labor.[12]

In 1808, Thomas was a well-established craftsman in Elizabethtown. Married in 1806 to Nancy Hanks, he was the father of a little girl, Sarah, born on February 10, 1807. He owned two lots in Elizabethtown, assessed at $40. It was then that he acquired a three-hundred-acre farm on Nolin Creek for the modest sum of $200 cash; the title, though, was encumbered with a small obligation of £15.12s.4d. ($61.50) owed to a former proprietor. It was not known whether succeeding buyers had discharged the obligation.[13] This good deal, as we will see, would cost Thomas dearly.

On December 12, 1808, Thomas left Elizabethtown to take up residence at Sinking Spring Farm, "just in time to enable Abraham to be born the son of a farmer," which occurred on February 12, 1809.[14]

Thomas Lincoln was disappointed very quickly by his first experience as an independent farmer. The land at Nolin Creek was not fertile, situated as it was on the borders of the barrens described by François-André Michaux. This expanse of sixty thousand square miles was so called because of the lack of water and trees, both of which the pioneers deemed indispensable for agriculture. Grass grew tall, reaching two to three feet in height, and Virginia creeper was abundant. Trees had disappeared because of the Indian custom of burning vegetation in March and April to provide pasture for the buffalo. Water was to be found in great abundance, but under the surface of the soil in the labyrinth of caves and subterranean galleries that make this area of limestone subsoils typical of a karstic region. Sinking Spring Farm owed its name to a geological feature often associated with such landscapes, water spouting up from the soil only to vanish into it immediately.

These characteristics explain the low population in this part of the Pennyrile region where only corn was grown, a decided drawback for subsistence agriculture. Lack of communications and absence of neighbors and of scenery gave the word *barrens* its true meaning.

These features determined Thomas to leave Nolin Creek in 1811 for Knob Creek, a thirty-acre farm that he rented and then purchased in 1813–14. Knob Creek is a deep and rapid stream that flows into Rolling

Fork, a tributary of the Salt River, which runs into the Ohio. Three natural regions converge at that spot: the great pasture lands of the Blue Grass on the east and northeast, the region of the Knobs to the north and northwest, and the Pennyrile and its barrens to the south and west. The great Cumberland plateau, of which the Pennyrile forms the northeastern limits, stops abruptly there at a steep escarpment called Mulder Hill. "Mulder-Hill, a steep and lofty mountain that forms a kind of amphitheater. From its summit, the neighbouring country presents the aspect of an immense valley, covered with forests of an imperceptible extent, whence, as far as the eye can reach, nothing but a gloomy verdant space is seen, formed by the tops of the close-connected trees, and through which not the vestige of a plantation can be discerned."[15]

At the foot of this hill, which at Knob Creek rises to 150 feet, the farm was located. The shaley soil was of good quality and, in addition to corn, also produced clover and alfalfa. The terrain was hilly, "knotty and knobby," and cedars grew on the largest knobs.[16]

First Memories

Young Abraham, except for a few months of school, spent five years wandering with his playmates in the neighboring woods and bathing in the swimming holes of the rivers. And it was on Knob Creek that he began his apprenticeship as an agricultural worker by helping with the planting.[17] His first memories dated from this period and the most striking of them is doubtless the incident he recalled in Washington in 1863 in the company of a Kentuckian:

> I remember that old home very well. Our farm was composed of three fields. It lay in the valley, surrounded by high hills and deep gorges. Sometimes when there came a big rain in the hills the water would come down through the gorges and spread all over the farm. The last thing that I remember of doing there was one Saturday afternoon; the other boys planted the corn in what we called the big field; it contained seven acres—and I dropped the pumpkin seed.... The next Sunday morning there came a big rain in the hills, it did not rain a drop in the valley, but the water coming down through the gorges washed ground, corn, pumpkin seeds and all clear off the field.[18]

This recollection, generally admitted as authentic, and perfectly in conformity with the topography of Knob Creek, testifies to the importance of this image for Lincoln. One can see in it the sign of the omnipotence of fate mocking human efforts. A rustic soul is not inclined to doubt that an unknown and superior force dominates everything that lives down below, for the will of the heavens is clearly manifested in rain and wind, drought and snow. Is it surprising that Calvinist beliefs—and superstitions as well—found a fertile soil and a favorable climate on the frontier?

An Encumbered Land

No matter how rustic the society, fate showed itself not only in the guise of a sometimes hostile nature, but also often in human acts and positive laws, which, though not the products of chance seemed none the less the workings of destiny: "for, in those days, land-titles were rather more uncertain than other human affairs."[19] A bad land title could cost a farmer much more than a bad harvest or bad soil, and Thomas Lincoln experienced on three occasions the truth of Thomas Cooper's observation: "a purchaser in Kentucky buys a law-suit with every plot of unoccupied land he pays for there."[20]

On October 17, 1814, Nancy and Thomas Lincoln sold their property at Mill Creek for £100, £18 less than the price they had paid for it in 1803. Furthermore, the bill of sale authorized the buyer to choose a plot of "200 acres out of the said 238 acres, where he thinks proper." Louis A. Warren first discovered the reason for this surprising clause. An error in the original survey, or a copyist's mistake, had garbled the directions used to identify the plot precisely.[21]

Was it an accident? It almost certainly was, but it was also the often observed result of the old method of *metes and bounds,* which was appropriate to the well defined and confined spaces of feudal England but ineffective for organizing, in a few decades, the distribution of virgin lands to thousands of American pioneers. This surveying process consisted of beginning at a given point of departure and describing a perimeter made up of a broken line whose segments were defined, as to their direction, by reference to the cardinal points of the compass. Their length was defined by both a measurement made by the surveyor and by natural or artificial markers (trees, posts, rocks). The key phrase in the survey was found at the end of the description: "thence South 31 degrees West twenty poles to the starting point." Following the itinerary thus traced, the farmer surveying his field or the officer from the Land Office should finish a complete circuit of the property and return back to the beginning.

The error in the survey, and consequently in the land title to Mill Creek, lay in the fact that the directions did not bring one back to the beginning: "the survey would not close." Whether the error existed in the original survey or was the fault of the clerk who recopied incorrectly one of the directions, it meant that, at the time of the sale, thirty-eight acres (and £18) were lost for Thomas: it was the only way of giving a coherent description to the plot of land.[22]

Numerous factors contributed to making this method unreliable: the markers were ephemeral, often not easily distinguishable (in the description of Mill Creek, one finds frequent references to oak or walnut trees); the proliferation of measurements and the necessity of transcribing the complicated surveys increased the risk of error; and, finally, the fact that each survey was carried out individually without reference to others led to anarchy. It was common to find overlapping plots.

To the inherent uncertainty of this system must be added the excessive liberality with which Virginia made grants of land, which became an inexhaustible source of fraud and speculation. Indeed, by 1784, the amount of land sold by Virginia exceeded the real area of Kentucky. The confusion that resulted from this anarchical system was heavy with consequences. As a traveler reported, "I did not stop at the house of one inhabitant who was persuaded of the validity of his own right but what seemed dubious of his neighbour's."[23]

The doubts often turned into suspicions, suspicions into lawsuits, and the courts were not idle. As the French expression says, "Who has land has conflict," and the *picrocholes* [quarrelsome neighbors] of the frontier several times a year doffed their raccoon caps before the powdered wigs of the judges and lawyers.[24] Among the latter was Ninian Edwards, who practiced at Elizabethtown and would soon represent Illinois in the Senate of the United States. A pro-slavery supporter, his vote would be decisive in defeating the Tallmadge Amendment to the Missouri Compromise.[25] Lincoln would become at a later date a regular visitor in the sumptuous Edwards residence in Springfield, and his marriage would make him an in-law of this illustrious family. Practicing in Lexington, Henry Clay, whom Lincoln called in 1858 "my beau ideal of a statesman," was the brightest star in a constellation of lawyer-politicians of lesser renown, the very images of success.[26]

But the legal profession was not the only beneficiary of the disorder organized by Virginia. In the inextricable jungle of inaccurate surveys, of indistinct boundaries, and of ephemeral landmarks, the law of the jungle inevitably prevailed. A lawsuit was long and expensive—especially in equity—and if a rich man could afford to lose several cases (unavoidable accidents under such conditions), the same was not true for a small farmer, who risked his fortune each time.

Two characters towered over the fray and their victims gave them the same name: the loan-shark and the land-shark, the lender and the speculator. If the struggle between small farmers and these two types of predators constituted the essence of the history of Kentucky from 1800 to 1830, it constituted as well the political and social context that enables us to strip the story of the last two misfortunes of Thomas Lincoln in Kentucky of their anecdotal aspect. The harshness of the conflict opposing creditors and debtors would not be obvious until after the crisis of 1819, which, coming on top of the crisis of 1814, made the situation intolerable for debtors. This opposition dominated the political scene in Kentucky in the 1820s, pitting the "Relief" or "New Court Party" on the side of the debtors against the "Old Court Party," calling for repayment in full of debts. Kentucky newspapers, widely distributed in the new states of Indiana and Illinois and avidly read by Abraham Lincoln, became the echo of the debate between Clay, who chose the side of the creditors, and the Jacksonians, who carried the state and the Union in 1828. Lincoln adopted the views of Clay on this precise point in 1841.[27]

The crisis of 1819 did, in fact, accelerate the process of financial consolidation made possible by harsh laws, particularly those regulating mortgage loans. By 1821, as a consequence of forced sales, almost a third of Kentucky had passed into the hands of eastern banks and speculators.[28]

Thomas Lincoln felt the full severity of those laws on September 12, 1816, when Nolin Creek's three hundred acres were put on public sale to satisfy a creditor. The matter dated back to May 1, 1805, when Richard Mather, a large landowner, sold Nolin Creek to a certain David Vance. Vance, however, would not receive full title to the land (a patent) until he had settled an eighteen-month note for £15.12s.4d., payable "in good trade at cash price." On November 2 of the same year, Vance sold the property thus encumbered to Isaac Bush, who resold it under the same conditions to Thomas Lincoln on December 12, 1808. On September 1, 1813, Vance had long since moved to Mississippi when Mather, stating that the bill had not been paid, initiated proceedings that led to the sale of Nolin Creek in 1816 for $87.74, $62.50 of which went to Mather. As for Thomas Lincoln, his only recourse was to take action against Bush, who would have to find Vance.[29]

By the winter of 1813–14, Thomas Lincoln, faced with Mather's refusal to accept a compromise, had given up holding on to Nolin Creek and had purchased Knob Creek. Less than two years later, on September 19, 1815, "Mr. Thomas Lincoln, tenant in possession" received a notice asking him to vacate the premises. Behind the curious and archaic wording used to evict Lincoln—"John Doe complains of Richard Roe in custody of a plea of trespass"—hid three men, named Stout, Sheridan, and Rhodes, who were heirs of the late Thomas Middleton and owners of a land title covering an estate of ten thousand acres, of which Lincoln's modest plot was only a small part.[30]

These personalities introduce us to yet another character: after the unskilled surveyor, the inattentive clerk, and the persistent creditor, we meet the final plague afflicting the Kentucky farmer: the land speculator.[31] Twenty-one speculators claimed more than a quarter of the area of Kentucky by virtue of original sales made by Virginia. When the territory of Kentucky had wanted to form a new state, Virginia consented, after many obstructions, only on the express condition that all land titles delivered by Virginia would be recognized by the new state, which would besides adopt as its own the real estate laws of the Old Dominion. This contract between the two states was heavy with consequences for Kentucky. No matter what precautions were taken by the settlers to acquire sure land titles, at any moment an "owner" might appear with an older title because titles that had been issued often overlapped and, taken together, they represented more land than actually existed. Speculators often waited a long time before putting forward their rights, either because they had acquired them through a long series of transactions and bankruptcies from other speculators or because they were waiting until the settler had sufficiently improved the land before evicting him.[32]

To remedy the more obviously unjust aspects of these practices, and under pressure from the settlers, legislators in Kentucky passed a series of laws, called occupancy laws, which favored the occupant of the soil who possessed even a semblance of a title to their land. The principle that the land belongs to those who work it, which has been traced back in America to 1641, here made its fledgling reappearance. But these first measures would become the inspiration of the occupancy laws of other states, of preemption laws, and ultimately of the Homestead Act.[33] Indeed, it was inconceivable that the most "real" of properties, land, should be contested to such an extent.

Thus, laws favorable to occupiers of the soil had been voted in 1797, 1799, 1809, and 1812, before the heirs to Thomas Middleton's estate chose to test the validity of their title by bringing an action against one of the ten occupiers of the land they claimed. They chose, as it happens, Thomas Lincoln, whose bad luck in being singled out cannot be explained with certainty.[34] It was the straw that broke the camel's back: Lincoln left Kentucky for Indiana before hearing the outcome of the case.

Beveridge, basing his conclusion on the existence of the occupancy laws, on the well-known partiality of juries comprised of residents in cases involving nonresidents, and on the fact that Lincoln had the best specialist lawyer in the region, argued that his "flight" could not be explained without calling into question his honesty. In fact, Beveridge believed, not possessing a valid title, Lincoln was forced to flee. Besides

Beveridge's partiality, a certain number of facts lead to the rejection of these hypotheses. First, Lincoln won his case in 1818. Second, the state of the proceedings in June 1816 augured ill for Thomas's side. Third, the occupancy laws were still insufficient in the eyes of the settlers of 1816. Indeed, from the day of the verdict, any harvest carried out on the land in dispute went to the owner. If the occupants chose to remain on the premises, they were obliged to pay rent before being able to recover from the owner the taxes they had paid in his place. Laws of 1819 and 1820 abolished those very provisions. Therefore, Lincoln ran a substantial risk, and, in fact, in January 1817, forty bushels of corn he had left with a friend for safe-keeping were seized. Finally, speculators were constantly challenging in the courts the laws favoring occupants. The decision of the Supreme Court in *Green vs. Biddle* (1823), which annulled the laws of 1797 and 1812 and reestablished in full force the real estate laws of Virginia on the grounds of the principle of the inviolability of contracts, demonstrated the reality of the threat.[35]

Did young Abraham Lincoln know about these events, did he understand them? Nobody heretofore has ventured to say that he took part in them. Yet, it is a well-established fact that he was one of the few members of the Lincoln family who could read. And support for the idea comes from an interesting account by an English lawyer, George Borrett, who visited Lincoln in October 1864. In the course of the conversation, the president offered some

> shrewd remarks about the legal systems of the [United States and Great Britain] . . . and then he talked of the landed tenures of England, and said we had some "queer things in the legal way" at home, of which he seemed to think "quit rents" as queer as any. And then he told us how "in the State of Kentucky, where he was raised, they used to be troubled with the same mysterious relics of feudalism, and titles got into such an almighty mess with these pettifoggin' incumbrances turnin' up at every fresh tradin' with the land, and no one knowin' how to get rid of 'em" . . . and how he managed to relieve the titles, and made his first step to fame in doing so.[36]

Several interpretations—not mutually exclusive—of this evidence are possible: Borrett might have misunderstood Lincoln. Two anecdotes might have become telescoped in his memory, leading him to date to the Kentucky years a case that Lincoln dealt with later after becoming a lawyer. It is not at all impossible, however, that the young Abraham, who had a precocious intelligence and who would win renown later in this particular field of the law, should have won the admiration of his circle by contributing to clearing up Thomas's real estate problems. The hypothesis becomes more likely if one remembers that the illiterate Thomas was still embroiled in the lawsuit over Knob Creek in 1818. Finally, the period spent in Indiana (1816–30) offered many opportunities, as we shall see, to tackle problems as typically Kentuckian as those we have just examined. Furthermore, because of the destruction of Thomas Lincoln's family papers in a fire, one cannot assert that the lawsuits of which evidence remains were the only ones involving Thomas Lincoln or his second wife (a Kentuckian who did not come to Indiana until 1819).

In any case, it is obvious that Lincoln, in 1864, clearly understood the connection between the situation of land titles in Kentucky and the "mysterious relics of feudalism" of English origin.

The difference between American real estate law, firmly established by the Revolution of 1776, and the real estate system in England, although less radical than the difference that separated the latter from French law after 1789, was nonetheless marked. The notion, still valid in contemporary English law, of a plurality of property rights in the same piece of land, a notion that corresponds to the distinctions in feudal law between *jus eminens* and *jus utile,* was replaced by bourgeois private property exclusive of any other right. The remnants of feudalism, such as the terms *freehold* or *tenure in fee simple* to apply to full property rights seemed therefore to be baseless, and the outdated relics of the medieval laws and procedures became even more mysterious because they were obviously inconsistent with the dominant form of property. The "mystery" will perhaps be cleared up when we examine the conditions under which a particular type of property was used, that held by the master over the slave.

SLAVERY AND FREE LABOR

Lincoln's expression "chiefly on account of the difficulty in land titles in Ky." can be seen then as a perfectly objective analysis of the reasons that motivated the Lincoln family to leave Kentucky. There remains the other, less important reason that Lincoln was careful to distinguish from the first: slavery.

The discussion of it is easier. Thomas Lincoln, a free laborer, carpenter-cabinetmaker by trade, resided in one of the areas of Kentucky where slave labor was most abundant. However, in 1797, he could be found in competition with slaves during the construction of a mill.[37]

Undeniably the shadow of slavery fell on the relations between employer and employee, already difficult for the person who had to hire himself out. Wage-earning in fact remained problematic because workers had not yet obtained mechanics' lien laws that made them the preferred creditors of their employers.

Thus Thomas Lincoln was forced to bring suit against Denton Geoghegan on March 25, 1807, in order to receive payment for a job of hewing logs. Geoghegan, if the testimony gathered by Beveridge is to be believed, was a large landowner, from a good family, a future justice of the peace, a man respected for his honesty. Sentenced to pay the man he had employed, Geoghegan countersued, accusing him of inadequate work, and sought $100 in damages and interest in June of 1808. He did not abandon the case until October of that year.[38]

Under these conditions, the continual and rapid increase in the number of slaves in the region did little to improve the lot of free laborers. Travelers' tales do not include descriptions (either lyrical or horrified as the case may be) such as can be encountered in regard to the social status of wage-earners in Indiana or Illinois. Lincoln would sum it up in 1859 at Indianapolis, repeating the classic theme of the Republicans' campaign: "The mass of white men were injured by the effect of slave labor in the neighborhood of their own labor."[39] But in Thomas Lincoln's time, the slavery question was seen almost exclusively in a moral or religious light, which did not comprehend completely or exactly all the social conflicts but which mirrored them.

Thomas and Nancy Lincoln's religious commitment was the only way they took of expressing their opposition to slavery at that time, at least as far as is now known. In 1816 they joined the Little Mount Baptist Church, a Separate Baptist group that had broken with the South Fork Baptist Church over the issue of slavery.[40]

The moral condemnation of slavery, completely ineffectual as long as it lacked the strength of material interests (as the history of abolitionism clearly demonstrates), constituted nonetheless an essential way for those who rejected the Southern system to differentiate themselves from those who adapted to it. Emigration toward the free lands of the Northwest was linked to this difference of attitude: it was the active and practical version, just as religious separatism was the static and theoretical version. It is interesting to note that the Lincolns became Baptists a few months before their departure, and they did not feel the need to join a church again before 1823.

Lincoln's life-long attitude of inflexible opposition to the *principle* of slavery can doubtless be attributed to this moral influence. The distaste he felt toward the peculiar institution was the main reason he gave for settling in a free state.[41] "This removal was partly on account of slavery;

but chiefly on account of the difficulty in land titles in Ky." This sentence that Lincoln added, after reflection, to his autobiography in 1860 is significant, although Lincoln himself, half-way between his Republican commitment to Free Soil and his signing of the Homestead Act, did not make the connection between the two evils that afflicted the small farmer in Kentucky.

Nonetheless, slavery and the plantation economy certainly prevented agrarian reform like that carried out in New England, which then became the inspiration for the Northwest Ordinances of 1785 and 1787. Only large slave property could get along with the quasi-feudal system inherited from England. Only a middle class of private farmers could have an interest in agrarian reform, which, on American lands innocent of history, took on the guise of a new creation. To be sure, the omnipresent speculators and the concentration of land that followed agrarian reform as monopoly flows from free competition could mask for a moment the contours of this opposition, of this struggle that moreover sometimes turned to the advantage of the free farmers in the slave states. But the incompatibility of the slave plantation and small private property was truly at the center of American history in this period.

During the time the Lincolns lived there, Kentucky saw an expansion of slavery. At the same time, crushed by the real estate system that Virginia had imposed on Kentucky, many farmers were forced to rent land or become sharecroppers, while many others sought free land further west. The settling of the Ohio Valley and of the state of Illinois attested to that, as did Thomas Lincoln's decision to emigrate to Indiana in 1816.

J. L. Scripps, who wrote a campaign biography of Lincoln in 1860, was not far wrong when he wrote, in the flowery style of this genre: "Meanwhile, the worldly condition of the elder Lincoln did not improve. He realized in his daily experience and observation how slavery oppresses the poorer classes, making their poverty and social disrepute a permanent condition through the degradation which it affixes to labor." And he rightly attributed to the Lincolns, piled in their wagons rolling toward Indiana at the end of November 1816, thoughts that many of his readers could have understood and shared: "gladly taking upon themselves all the privations and hardships of a pioneer life, in view of what they had left behind them."[42]

Kentucky's reputation had already spread overseas, and the anonymous French author of the *Voyage au Kentouckey et sur les bords du Genesée en 1820* could justifiably write, after having summed up the inconveniences of the region: "After this true account, which no honest American would deny, I say to citizens about whom I care, to the families of poor and hard-working laborers, to farmers without pecuniary means, beware of going to Kentucky!"[43]

2

LINCOLN AND INDIANA: ROOTS

"Away back in the fall of 1816, when he was in his eighth year, his father brought him over from the neighboring State of Kentucky, and settled in the State of Indiana, and he grew up to his present enormous height on our own good soil of Indiana."[1] These few lines define perfectly the period from 1816 to 1830, which saw the transformation of a seven-year-old child into a grown man. Abraham Lincoln came to maturity under parental supervision and on a land that he had not chosen. Independent of his own will, the malleable material of human clay was molded by fate, nature, family, and his surroundings. At the same time though, an individual emerged who was something other than, and more than the sum of, these influences, who reacted against some of them, who tried to educate himself (in the etymological sense of the term), who developed and developed himself.

This dual process, mixed and contradictory, was real, as the alternation of passive and active verbs in Lincoln's autobiographical fragments will confirm. This alternation indicates clearly that Lincoln assessed his formative years critically. The fragments are surprisingly sincere: what they say, what they suggest, what they are silent about, create a picture that is contradicted by no biographical fact, no contemporary witness. They will form, once again, the framework of our study because they enable us to contemplate this period from the most interesting angle: his experience.

Having sketched the picture of the Lincoln family's social station, we must now talk about experience from three points of view: first, the experience of living in a free state, which constituted in a way the *a contrario* proof of the wisdom of the decision to migrate, the opposite of the experience of living in Kentucky. Moreover, through this experience young Abraham faced problems that we mentioned in regard to Kentucky but that he was then too young to understand. Comparison with the state on the other side of the Ohio was, in fact, an important part of conversations, newspapers, and daily life, particularly so in a community mainly of Kentucky origin. The second experience was that of direct contact with the frontier, the wilderness, untamed nature. The third, which continued for a time in Illinois, confronted Lincoln with agricultural labor and rural life.

THE NORTHWEST ORDINANCE

When they alighted on the Indiana shore at Thompson's Ferry, the Lincolns arrived in another world. Yet the land, admittedly more wooded, was comprised of the same fine and fertile glacial clay soil that covered the Ohio Valley on both banks and could be found around Knob Creek. The climate, humid and with pronounced seasonal differences in temperature, was the same.[2] The difference lay elsewhere. The Land Ordinance of 1785 had organized the survey and public sale of the lands given to the young republic by the states, notably by Virginia. The Northwest Ordinance of 1787 established the Ohio as the frontier between liberty and slavery.

On the Other Side of the Ohio

Here we broach an essential point: as paradoxical as it may seem, it was in Indiana that Lincoln's ideas on slavery were formed, it was in Indiana that he consciously took up the issue. Lincoln's biographers have generally agreed that Lincoln's first contacts with slavery occurred in the context of New Orleans in 1828, when he went there to escort a shipment of agricultural products for James Gentry, or in 1838, when he carried out an identical task for Denton Offutt.

Relying on John Hanks's testimony, Herndon created a legend according to which Lincoln, attending a slave auction and shocked by the sale of a young mulatto woman, was supposed to have cried out, "If ever I have a chance to hit that thing [meaning slavery], I'll hit it hard."[3] This testimony would be more valuable if Lincoln himself had not explicitly pointed out that John Hanks had gone ashore at St. Louis and was therefore completely unable to "remember" events that took place in New Orleans.[4] The idea that Lincoln experienced an emotional shock on this occasion should not be ruled out, of course, because his letter to Joshua F. Speed of August 24, 1855, showed how sensitive to the misfortunes of slaves he could be. Reminding his friend of a steamboat trip between Louisville and St. Louis in 1841, during which they had seen a dozen blacks sold by their master, separated from their families, and sent to the deep South, Lincoln explained: "That sight was a continual torment to me; and I see something like it every time I touch the Ohio, or any other slave-border."[5] The point is not to cast doubt on the sincerity of his sentiment, expressed in a private letter to his intimate friend, a pro-slavery man to boot. But his remarks should be compared to those in a letter to Speed's sister, Mary, dated September 27, 1841, where he recounts the same incident in a very different way:

> Nothing of interest happened during the passage, except the vexatious delays occasioned by the sand bars be thought interesting. By the way, a fine example was presented on board the boat for contemplating the effect of *condition* upon human happiness. A gentleman had purchased twelve negroes in diferent [*sic*] parts of Kentucky and was taking them to a farm in the South. They were chained six and six together. A small iron clevis was around the left wrist of each, and this fastened to the main chain by a shorter one at a convenient distance from, the others; so that the negroes were strung together precisely like so many fish upon a trot-line.

However, these poor creatures, who were being taken toward the pitiless lash far from all those whom they held dear, seemed completely unaware of the horror of their circumstances: they sang, played cards, joked. And Lincoln concluded: "How true it is that 'God tempers the wind to the shorn lamb,' or in other words, that He renders the worst of human conditions tolerable, while He permits the best, to be nothing better than tolerable."[6]

A certain epistolary coyness characteristic of Lincoln's style during this period (particularly in his relations with women); humor, often not very delicate, with which he covered and shielded sentiments that were a lot more so and which constituted one of the enduring traits of his personality; and the egoistical observation of the popular "philosopher" finding the moral of the scene—all these elements prevented the dawning and maturing of the feeling expressed in the 1855 letter.

If the profound emotion that he felt—so profound that he remembered it perfectly almost fifteen years later—could be effectively blunted by the rather uncouth personal characteristics of the Lincoln of the 1830s, it was because it was not supported by any idea or any social need. It merely provided the occasion for a letter that without it would have been absolutely empty, unless "the vexatious delays occasioned by the sand bars be thought interesting."

Between 1841 and 1855 came the Kansas-Nebraska Act with its threat to extend slavery into all the territories of the United States. This event formed the subject of the 1855 letter, a subject that Lincoln broached immediately after having recalled the 1841 episode.

This juxtaposition confirms Herndon's observation that Lincoln, under a cold exterior, concealed a great capacity for love "but the object must first come in the guise of a principle, next it must be right and true—then it was lovely in his sight."[7] Lincoln had first to be convinced of the indisputability of the anti-slavery principle—to the North of the Missouri Compromise line—before his capacity for feeling a profound revulsion toward slavery could find expression. This sensitive man had not the least trace of sentimentality. Feeling appeared always supported and guided by reason, matured and nourished by a will that broadened and deepened it.

We will have occasion to return to this idea from precisely the opposite point of view; it is not insignificant that Lincoln *introduced* this long political letter by evoking a sentiment that Adam Smith would have called moral. But the preceding discussion helps to clarify the state of the problem in 1828 or 1831. Seeing slavery in New Orleans—or elsewhere during his visits to Kentucky in the 1820s—could have no effect on Lincoln other than to keep alive the moral condemnation of slavery, which he inherited from his environment and which, by itself, did not account for many episodes of his political life. On the other hand, the comparison between the status in a free state and in a slave state of whites descended from what he amusingly called the "second families" of Virginia was certainly the determining factor in making him a Free-Soiler, "aroused" in 1854 by the threat of an extension of slavery in the territories.[8]

The fact that slavery was abolished—and, by the way, that it was Lincoln who abolished it—tends to obscure the reality of the debate on the extension of slavery and to substitute for it the question of abolition and abolitionism. Lincoln was not an abolitionist before 1862. The abolition of slavery was never on the agenda before that date. David Potter suggested that the period from 1847 to 1861 was marked by a false debate (over extension) chosen by both Northern and Southern political leaders in order to avoid confronting the true debate (abolition). The result was not to talk about slavery where it existed and to make a huge commotion about it where it did not exist.[9] Northern politicians, for the most part, did not raise the issue of slavery in the South. But—at this stage—what seemed a contradiction, really was not. For Northern leaders slavery was not an issue where it already existed. It posed no problems for them but certainly did for Southern leaders. And the latter were those who raised the issue concretely in the North with the Kansas-Nebraska Act and the decision in *Dred Scott vs. Sandford* precisely where it did not yet exist (or more accurately, as we shall see, where it *no longer* existed). The peculiar institution might well have worried the ruling class in the North for half a century, but it was the prospect of seeing slavery cease to be peculiar in order to become general that set them in motion.

In answer to Douglas's argument—and that of countless historians—that there was no danger of seeing slavery become established in the territories located to the north of the Missouri Compromise line, Lincoln countered tirelessly that soil and climate had nothing to do with it: only the Ordinance of 1787 prevented a minority of slaveholders from imposing their will on the majority of settlers in the Northwest.[10] Slavery was very close to winning, particularly in Indiana, where the general assembly of the territory more than once asked Congress to revoke the anti-slavery provisions of the Ordinance of 1787.[11]

More than was the case in Illinois, the debate on the Indiana constitution focused on problems linked to slavery.[12] Until the adoption of a constitution, the presence of federal authority supported by the Ordinance of 1787 limited the impact of measures passed by the territorial assembly that guaranteed slaveholders the right to import and use their human chattel.[13] The magnitude of the risk discouraged many slaveholders from settling in the Northwest, and those who carried on regardless, in violation of the ordinance, were the most enterprising and the most persistent. The debate on slavery occupied, then, a central place in the Constitutional Convention of Indiana in 1816. Basing the action of the government of the state on an anti-slavery constitution, Article XI, section 7 of the Indiana constitution put an end to the ambiguity of the territorial period, when federal power had been anti-slavery while the territorial authorities had been pro-slavery.[14] But the slaveholders did not give up, and it was on the slogan "No slavery in Indiana" that Jonathan Jennings campaigned for governor in 1819.[15] The slaveholders in Indiana did not go so far as those in Illinois, who organized a campaign to revise the constitution, but the institution remained vigorous all the same.[16] A local census of the population of Vincennes revealed the existence of thirty-three slaves in 1830, and the national census in 1840 still counted three in Indiana, in clear violation of the law.[17]

The great merit of Francis M. Van Natter's work *Lincoln's Boyhood: A Chronicle of His Indiana Years* is to have shown how much slavery could be felt as a threat by the inhabitants of the free state of Indiana, especially by the Lincolns. The frequent incursion of what they called "patter-rollers" hunting fugitive slaves or those thought to be fugitives, the presence in the immediate neighborhood of large numbers of blacks who had received sentences of labor for life, the sale of blacks through advertisements in the newspapers as late as 1820, all this shows how close, porous, and fragile the border was. "The evils of slave-keeping are not confined to the parts of the country where involuntary labour exists, but the neighbourhood is infected," remarked James Flint, who noted that on the *northern* bank of the Ohio, artisans and agricultural laborers were forced to bring water from the well themselves, their wives and daughters thinking such a task "opprobrious" because, on the other side of the river, slaves did it.[18]

No matter how precarious the legal barrier which, much more than did the Ohio, separated Indiana from the slave world, it was nonetheless the only thing that prevented the spread of the peculiar institution. The sizable number of infiltrations that occurred despite its existence suggested the extent of the tidal wave that its disappearance would have brought on.

Once again, geography had nothing to do with it because a portion of Kentucky is located north of Cincinnati and of a good part of Indiana and the southern half of Illinois is on the same parallel as the northern half of Missouri. If the absence of slavery in the free states of the Northwest could be explained other than by the existence of the Ordinance of 1787, "I confess that it is wholly beyond my power to conceive of it," Lincoln said.[19]

The frontier, as we shall see, guaranteed the Lincolns two things: sure land titles and social esteem enjoyed by free manual laborers in a community of free pioneers. Their destiny was henceforth placed under the protection of the Union.

A Land of Freedom and Prosperity

Thomas Lincoln's skills as an artisan enabled him to occupy an honorable social position rapidly. Having participated in the construction of the Little Pigeon Baptist Church, he became a trustee of this congregation.[20] When he left Indiana in 1830, his position was incomparably better than in 1816. In full possession of a hundred acres of land, forty of which were under cultivation, he raised hogs (he sold about a hundred before leaving) and in 1830 his farming operations— deducting the amount consumed by the family and the livestock— produced a surplus of five hundred bushels of corn. These results, which compared favorably to the average in Indiana at the time even though for Thomas farming constituted only a secondary occupation after his work as an artisan, showed how much he benefited from federal land laws.[21]

The Lincolns' Land in Indiana

The year 1816 saw a spectacular increase in the sale of public lands in Indiana, which attested to the flood of immigrants as much as to the enthusiasm of speculators: sales went from 150,000 acres in 1815 to 375,000 in 1816.[22] After the defeat of Tecumseh, treaties ceding Indian territory to the white lust for land proliferated. The territory that Thomas Lincoln came to explore in the autumn of 1816 to find a piece of land to his liking was now rid of the threat of Indians. Less than a year after his arrival in Little Pigeon Creek, on October 15, 1817, he set out with three neighbors for Vincennes and registered his option to 160 acres, which he intended to buy under the Harrison law.[23] This law, which enabled many settlers to buy land on credit between 1800 and 1820, allowed the payment of a twentieth of the purchase price at the time of entering, with a second payment at the end of two months (one-fifth). The settler then had four years to finish paying the remaining three-quarters. Thomas Lincoln made the first two payments punctually in due time, but he ceased all payments thereafter. He was not the only one in that situation: the crisis of 1819 lowered incomes and prices so much that many buyers of federal land were incapable of honoring their obligations. Those who managed to accumulate the necessary sums were not tempted to pay because the price of lands on the open market was collapsing in Indiana, while those in Kentucky fell to a sixth of their value.[24] Why sacrifice particularly scarce cash to buy lands that were depreciating in value?

The settlers consequently worked to obtain from Congress a moratorium that would permit them to keep possession of the land they were farming until they were in a position to acquire full title to it. This moratorium (a law of March 2, 1821) was accompanied by a series of measures permitting the settlers to relinquish part of their original claim. The sums already paid would then all be put toward paying for the remaining land, thus converting the claim into full possession.

These measures, as the Vincennes *Sun* emphasized, would cease to be applicable on July 4, 1827. On April 25, 1827, Thomas Lincoln appeared at the Vincennes Land Office. He relinquished half of his claim on the farm at Little Pigeon Creek (160 acres), giving him a total credit of $80. To that were added $80 that he obtained by relinquishing another claim (this one half paid for) on eighty acres that he had just bought. After this rather complicated operation (in which Beveridge saw the hand of the rich landowner Gentry), Thomas Lincoln received a quarto parchment signed by President John Quincy Adams guaranteeing him full and complete ownership to his farm, whose area was above average for the period and the region and which he increased still further by buying twenty acres from his neighbor David Casebier.[25]

It seems then that Thomas Lincoln was right to leave Kentucky for the "free" lands of Indiana. That opinion was certainly endorsed by his second wife Sarah Bush, the widow Johnston, whom he brought back from Kentucky in 1819, a year after the death of Nancy, as well as by Thomas and Elizabeth Sparrow, who had joined the Lincolns in the autumn of 1817, after being evicted from their farm in Kentucky, and also by most of the Lincolns' neighbors, like them natives of the Blue Grass State.[26]

Free Laborers

Young Abraham Lincoln must certainly have learned from this family experience. He recognized clearly the superiority of federal control over land, while he also valued relations between employers and employees imbued with a democratic spirit and characterized by friendliness. One is reminded of the famous episode reported by Herndon in which Abraham, having damaged a *Life of Washington* that Josiah ("Blue Nose") Crawford had lent him, repaid Crawford by working for him for two or three days without pay. There is more here than a simple anecdote. Crawford often employed Abraham and his sister Sarah. When Abraham had finished his day's work, he would stay to read the few works in his employer's library, to scribble by the side of the fire, or to chat with company. Thomas Lincoln, who had constructed all of Crawford's furniture when he arrived from Kentucky in 1824, likewise would come to chat once a week.[27] This type of work relationship was typical of an extremely mobile rural society, of which America offered a unique example. Returning from Indiana, a traveler noted: "The farmers of Indiana generally arrive in the country very poor, but somehow they get a great deal of property very soon. They all work, and there are not half so many labourers for hire as there are farmers. The former live with their employers, and are their equals, if they are men of good character."[28]

A difference of position in the economic relationship—which, moreover, was seen as temporary and restricted to one's youth—was not accompanied by a social distinction in rank. Children (young men or young women) owed their labor to their father, and if he had none for them—or if the work did not suit them—other fathers would provide employment. When Abraham Lincoln worked as a boatman for James Taylor in 1825, he shared a room with Green Taylor, the son of his employer, four years his junior, with whom he was on familiar terms.

Thus, one day as the tall adolescent refused to stop teasing Green, the latter, exasperated, threw an ear of corn in his face. In 1828, it was with Allen Gentry, two years his senior, that Abraham escorted a load of hogs and corn to New Orleans for Allen's father, James Gentry.[29]

Such work relations were obviously incompatible with great landed property and slavery, a lesson Abraham surely drew from his own experience. However, later on, whenever he invoked his personal history to illustrate the superiority of a free society over the world of slavery from the wage-earner's point of view, he never mentioned the episodes of his life in Indiana. The reason will be readily apparent once we have taken up the other aspects of what one author called "the missing chapter in the life of Abraham Lincoln."[30]

THE ORDEAL OF THE WILDERNESS

When the Lincolns crossed the Ohio at Troy, they took the road leading to Vincennes through the virgin forest. Despite the efforts of local authorities to enlarge this winding and bumpy "road" and make it suitable for vehicles, Thomas often had to use an axe to clear a path for the wagon through the dense thickets of dogwood, hawthorn, paw-paw, persimmon, and through the tangles of brambles, Virginia creeper, and grapevines that threatened to swallow up the path at every step. Under the best circumstances, instead of the usual path marked by blazed trunks, the "road" consisted of a strip twenty yards wide where the big trees had been roughly cut (two or three feet from the ground). In the middle, to a width of four yards, the stumps had been cut low to permit the passage of the wagon axles. Everywhere were ruts, steep paths, and quagmires. When they were four miles from the end of their trip, the Lincolns had to leave the road and clear a passage in the woods, often chopping down large trees embedded in thickets of grapevines and brambles.[31] It has been said that Abraham Lincoln never "passed through a harder experience" than this part of the trip.[32]

At the end of these nightmarish days, in this winter of "Eighteen-Hundred-and-Froze-to-Death," the Lincolns arrived at the spot that Thomas had chosen when he reconnoitered in the fall and that he had marked, according to custom, by piling up branches and blazing the trunks of trees. The 160 acres that Lincoln picked out were well situated: the ground was fairly level, covered with walnut trees and oaks and a dense thicket of hazelnut trees and various bushes. The presence of a spring fifty yards from the future location of the log cabin guaranteed pure water, an essential element in the decision to settle there.

Furthermore, the presence of a salt lick offered the promise of abundant game.[33]

Unlike most Kentuckians and other pioneers from the South, Lincoln did not choose to settle on the chalky hills so abundant in southern Indiana, but rather chose a region whose altitude (420 feet) was considerably less than the average for the state (700 feet) and not far from swamps. In their putrid water, where fevers were born, grew poisonous sumac.[34]

In 1844, campaigning for Henry Clay, Abraham Lincoln was able to see his father's farm again. "That part of the country is, within itself, as unpoetical as any spot of the earth; but still, seeing it and its objects and inhabitants aroused feelings in me which were certainly poetry; though whether my expression of those feelings is poetry is quite another question." Two poems resulted from this pilgrimage to the scenes of his childhood: "My Childhood's Home I See Again" and "The Bear Hunt," the second stanza of which conveys well the memory that impressed the seven-year-old Lincoln:

> When first my father settled here,
> 'Twas then the frontier line:
> The panther's scream, filled night with fear
> And bears preyed on the swine.[35]

Indeed, brown bears were so numerous that until 1820 it was difficult for the pioneers to raise hogs, and tales were told of children devoured by cougars.[36]

After several days (or perhaps weeks) spent in a half-faced camp, Thomas built a log cabin to shelter the family for the rest of the winter.[37] To build both these structures, and later to clear and enclose land, it was necessary to chop down trees, cut bushes, and fight ceaselessly against the lush nature that blocked the horizon and shut in the people. Overnight, Abraham found himself in the middle of the forest with an axe in his hand. He was seven years old.

As he related it himself, his father "settled in an unbroken forest; and the clearing away of surplus wood was the great task a head. A. though very young, was large of his age, and had an axe put into his hands at once; and from that till within his twenty-third year, he was almost constantly handling that most useful instrument—less, of course, in plowing and harvesting seasons."[38] And again: "an axe was put in his hand; and with the trees and logs and grubs he fought until he reached his twentieth year."[39]

The experience was hard and not one that he had chosen. The only benefit he derived from it was an extraordinarily muscular build and skill as a woodsman that he was happy to show off when an opportunity

arose in Washington in 1862.[40] However, there is not a single autobiographical indication showing Lincoln with an axe in his hand between
1832 and 1862, nor even taking a walk in the woods. The impression left
by his autobiographical fragments is rather of a fierce struggle against a
hostile nature forced on a child who fought his way out, in all the
meanings of the term. Lincoln "literally hewed out his path to manhood"
with an axe.[41]

However, nature was not always so grim. Elizabeth Crawford provided for Herndon a list of flowers from the region that Audubon would
not have disowned: "You wish me to tell you the names of some of our
wild woods flowers. There is the wild sweet william, wild pink, lady
slipper, wild roses, butterfly weed, wild honeysuckle, blue flag, yellow
flag, and there is a great many other kinds, that I can't recollect the
names of at this time."[42]

Although Lincoln never showed any taste for flowers, his interest in
strawberries, hazelnuts, walnuts, blackberries, plums, and wild apples
cannot be doubted, and he sufficiently appreciated the spectacular side
of bear hunts to write a poem on the subject.[43] Personally, Abraham did
not like hunting. Having one time—at the age of seven—shot at a wild
turkey with his father's rifle, he was so astonished at having hit his
target that he never repeated the feat. Nonetheless, he willingly joined
his friends in trapping raccoons and turkeys or stealing pheasant eggs.[44]
His great energy found expression in the games that remained for him
the only pleasant memory of that period:

> Near twenty years have passed away
> Since here I bid farewell
> To woods and fields, and scenes of play,
> And playmates loved so well.[45]

But nature showed itself still more cruel: among the many flowers
that brightened the undergrowth was white snakeroot [Eupatorium
urticaefolium], with its chalky white petals. When cows ate it, they
suffered "the trembles" and died in three days. Although the pioneers
might not have known the real cause of the illness, they understood the
symptoms and especially the consequences. Even before the signs of
trembling appeared in the animals, persons who had drunk the milk
from those cows began to experience symptoms of the milk-sick or
milk-sickness: nausea, vomiting, vertigo, stomach aches, severe thirst, a
coated tongue (first white then brown), trembling, rapid and weak
pulse, then apathy, chills, and coma. Death could come within three
days. Some of the ailing lived for two weeks.[46]

Thomas Sparrow, then Betsy Sparrow, then Nancy Lincoln, Abraham's mother, took to their beds and died. The pioneers believed the disease doubtless came from the water drunk by the cattle, contaminated, they thought, by minerals, or perhaps by an unidentified plant, in any case, some "vegetable or mineral productions of the earth."[47]

The earth, source of death, received the dead. Abraham helped his father prepare a coffin which was buried a few steps from the cabin. The burial mound where Nancy rested was opposite the door and was the first thing the Lincolns saw every morning when they left the cabin.[48]

For Lincoln, the earth meant death. Recalling the circumstances that led him to compose "My Childhood's Home I See Again," he wrote, "I went into the neighborhood in that State in which I was raised, where my mother and only sister were buried, and from which I had been absent about fifteen years."[49] The first canto clearly revealed the image of the earth that haunted Lincoln, as he heard his old friends tell the story of those who had disappeared:

> Till every sound appears a knell,
>   And every spot a grave.
> I range the fields with pensive tread,
>   And pace the hollow rooms,
> And feel (companion of the dead)
>   I'm living in the tombs.

There is little need for commentary. The connotation earth/death was for Lincoln neither an accident nor a cliché. It was expressed often, each time that Lincoln succumbed to his fits of melancholy dominated by obsessive fear of death. Lincoln had a physical feeling of intimate fusion with the dead earth. But the grimacing mask of death or of madness—the second theme of "My Childhood's Home I See Again" and the second cancer that ate away at Lincoln—can represent either farce or tragedy. Sending his poem to Andrew Johnston, Lincoln began by discussing the literary "news" as he perceived it and especially a parody of Poe's "The Raven" (he had not yet read "The Raven," which would become one of his favorite poems). He had found the parody, entitled "The Pole-cat," in the Quincy Whig and thought it excellent, particularly liking the passage where Jeremiah "scrubbed and washed, and prayed and fasted." From that comment he moved on without transition to his favorite poem ("Mortality" by William Knox) before introducing "My Childhood's Home."[50]

One should not see here only what a romantic "artist" would have called a "bourgeois" attitude or merely a provincial lawyer's undiscriminating appetite for culture. With Lincoln, "a man of many moods," the laugh and the grimace often went together.[51] Absurdity and farce are potent antidotes to madness and fear of death.

Let us recall a scene that Whitney seems to have borrowed from Shakespeare, and which captures the very soul of Lincoln's mood. It occurred during the 1850s. Henry Clay Whitney and Lincoln, both lawyers and close political and personal friends, were "on the circuit," going from town to town to plead cases in Judge David Davis's itinerant court. The scene was set on a gloomy October evening between Urbana and Danville. The road followed the bed of a dried-up river through a sinister wood, and Lincoln had to walk in front of the cart to guide the coachman through the increasing darkness among the rocks and the mud. His unusual tall silhouette wading through the puddles quickly faded from sight in front of the horses. The coachman had to be guided by ear, because soon, out of the night, rose a grating voice, singing to the tune of an old Methodist hymn: "Mortal man with face of clay / Here tomorrow, gone to-day."[52]

Thus Lincoln had several ways of being "of the earth, earthy."[53] "My Childhood's Home I See Again" ends with a stanza that illustrates the other image learned in Indiana, that of a soil where one can put down roots and that nourishes those who grow there:

> The very spot where grew the bread
>   That formed my bones, I see.
> How strange, old field, on thee to tread,
>   And feel I'm part of thee![54]

THE PLOW AND THE BOOK

"There was absolutely nothing to excite ambition for education. . . . I was raised to farm work, which I continued till I was twenty two."[55] The simple juxtaposition of these two Lincoln sentences suffices to destroy the myth of a happy childhood, harmoniously divided between farm work and spiritual edification. Lincoln suffered all his life from not having received an education and from having been forced to work the land from earliest childhood.[56]

The opposition between child labor and schooling, between that era's primitive agricultural work and a minimum access to culture, form the backdrop to the years spent in Indiana. Lincoln would have been hard-pressed to understand the ecological themes and the praise of on-the-job apprenticeship found in some biographies.

This implacable opposition was demonstrated in several ways. Work and school first of all competed for the child's time, and it is easy to see which won out: if "the agregate [sic] of all his schooling did not amount to one year,"[57] it was because Lincoln, like other children of country people at the time, could only attend classes during two or three months a year. When snow covered everything between December and February, there was no planting, plowing, harvesting, or clearing.[58] Then the children, carrying bundles containing a slate and food, would head for the log school waiting for them at the end of a walk of several miles (Lincoln walked four miles) over snowy paths or through the woods to arrive no later than 7:30 in the morning.

The schoolmaster kept them until six in the evening, with an hour's break at midday and two five-minute recreation periods.[59] Under these conditions, the quality of the education delivered by the pioneers of the three Rs left a lot to be desired. From his experience in "blab schools" where everybody chanted more or less in unison the texts assigned by the teacher, Lincoln retained the habit of reading aloud.[60]

The second aspect of the opposition lay in the rudimentary state of agricultural techniques, which required no scientific or mechanical knowledge. More than anyone else, Beveridge succeeded in conveying the oppressive nature of the "distasteful toil" of field work for Lincoln, the routine that filled the hours of "slow dull weeks."[61] Only wheat, barley, and oats required the traditional noble posture of sowing broadcast as Victor Hugo evoked it.[62] The main crop, corn, was planted by women and children, then men covered the seeds with a hoe. Harvesting was done with a sickle. The farmers who had come from the South used a rudimentary shovel plow made of rough-hewn wood. In all respects they employed less advanced agricultural techniques than the Yankees.[63] The work, although physically challenging, was in no way improving on the intellectual level, and therein lay the source of Lincoln's aversion to agricultural labor. He would not become reconciled to agriculture (if indeed he ever was) until scientific progress and advanced agricultural machines had transformed it. In 1842, he wrote to his best friend Joshua Fry Speed: "As to your farm matter, I have no sympathy with you. *I* have no farm, nor ever expect to have; and, consequently, have not studied the subject enough to be much interested with it."[64]

Seventeen years later, he addressed the Wisconsin State Agricultural Society in terms that surely surprised his audience. After having asserted that he was in no sense a farmer, he extolled intensive agriculture, using to describe it a term with Cromwellian echoes: "thorough cultivation." He praised the steam plow to the skies. These farming methods required education, knowledge of geology, soil chemistry, mechanics, and botany, which were learned in schools and acquired through *books* and which could alone make agriculture interesting.[65]

The context must, of course, be taken into consideration, even though his tone was much less coaxing than many orators would have used on similar occasions. The meaning of the speech remained nonetheless somewhat equivocal: agriculture interested Lincoln to the degree that it was industrialized and therefore called on science. One might smile at the commonplaces expressed by Lincoln on agriculture, presented as a vast arena of development for the most diverse intellectual fields, and one might be tempted to see in his remarks a sacrifice on the altar of the farm vote, to which he had already paid homage many times. It is true that Lincoln did not like agriculture despite the positive elements he discovered in it, but we can be certain that he felt a genuine interest in those elements, independent of their agricultural object. The lawyer and politician John T. Stuart, who was for some time Lincoln's protector and mentor (it was he who opened for him the doors to both a legal and a political career), testified that he "Has made Geology and other sciences a special study."[66] Lincoln's remarkable liking for inventions found expression notably in cases pitting the makers of agricultural machines against each other during the 1850s. The case of McCormick versus Manny became famous, but it was not the only one in which Lincoln had occasion to study in detail the working of these machines. One of his colleagues, Charles S. Zane, was amazed at the ease with which Lincoln explained the complicated mechanisms of the most recent inventions in reapers.[67]

The third element of opposition, which derived from the other two, can be understood only by recalling very briefly Lincoln's reading in Indiana. It is beyond the scope of our work to list the books read at that time, to analyze them, to attempt to estimate their influence on Lincoln's ultimate thoughts. The literature on that subject is abundant.[68] A careful study of summaries of books that we can assume Lincoln read reveals an extraordinary gap between the subjects treated and daily life in Indiana. The tales of *A Thousand and One Nights,* religious hymns, narratives of captivity among the Barbary pirates, *Robinson Crusoe, Pilgrim's Progress,* the speeches of Demosthenes and Pitt, a collection of jests from the English theater of the eighteenth century, such was the intellectual nourishment of a consumer of corn pone and hominy.[69] As for American books, there was nothing after the Revolution, which was itself narrated in the grand style of Ramsay or Weems. On rural life, the only thing that could be found was *The Deserted Village* by Goldsmith, included in the selections of the *Kentucky Preceptor.*[70] The gulf was indeed wide between the world of writing and representation and the world of living reality. To maintain a sustained interest in such works, one must have a great need for escape. Although it is impossible to make a scholar out of Lincoln, it is easy to discern the difference that developed little by little between him and his companions. He knew how to read and write earlier and better than the others. Even if he did not read—except for very rare instances—anything beyond the books contained in the basic library of the literate pioneer (Defoe, Bunyan, and Aesop forming, outside the Bible, the core of the collection), he read and reread them often, copied them, and learned them by heart.[71]

The Quest for Improvement

The opening words of Lincoln's "First Lecture on Discoveries and Inventions," given in 1858, have failed to arouse much interest among historians and biographers. The stylistic imperfections have relegated to obscurity this rather unhappy production of one of the great masters of the English language.

> All creation is a mine, and every man, a miner.
> The whole earth, and all *within* it, *upon* it, and *round about* it, including *himself,* in his physical, moral and intellectual nature, and his susceptabilities, are the infinitely various "leads" from which, man, from the first, was to dig out his destiny.[72]

Yet, these lines disclose something that is essential in Lincoln. His vision of the world and of men's nature that emerges from this text centers on the notion of improvement: "Man is not the only animal who labors; but he is the only one who *improves* his workmanship."[73]

To define man as the improving animal is a philosophical statement with far-reaching implications. The criterion by which one is to judge how far from a brute a human being has progressed is then the extent to which he has been able to alter nature, including his own nature, for the better. And, by this standard, the farmer is not far removed from the beast. In the lecture on inventions, agriculture is the last industry mentioned (after spinning and weaving, metallurgy, and transportation), and it receives special treatment: "when . . . in consequence of the first transgression, *labor* was imposed on the race, as a *penalty*—a *curse*—we find the first born man—the first heir of the curse—was 'a tiller of the ground.' This was the beginning of agriculture; and although, both in point of time, and of importance, it stands at the head of all branches of human industry, it has derived less direct advantage from Discovery and Invention, than almost any other."[74]

Although Lincoln has already mentioned several forms of work in a lecture replete with biblical quotations, he refers to the original curse only in connection with agriculture. For Lincoln, agriculture is thus set apart from the other forms of work as the archetype of the painful, degrading activity imposed on man for his sins. Even the word *work* seems inappropriate, as it refers to the exercise of all of man's capacities—intellectual as well as physical—to improve nature and "dig out his destiny." *Labor* is a more adequate term.

Discoveries and inventions are the means through which man improves his workmanship. But workmanship hardly applies to agriculture. The only improvement Lincoln deems worth mentioning in that realm is "the conception or idea, of substituting other forces in nature, for man's own muscular power. These other forces, as now used, are principally, the *strength* of animals, and the *power* of the wind, of running streams, and of steam."[75]

Rather than any improvement, this enumeration suggests the invention of labor-saving devices.

This train of thought brings him to other uses of animal power, namely as a means of transportation: "The earliest instance of it mentioned, is when 'Abraham rose up early in the morning, and saddled his ass,['] Gen. 22–3 preparatory to sacraficing [*sic*] Isaac as a burnt-offering."[76] Thus, for Lincoln, progress in agriculture would seem to be little more than a substitution of the animal for the human victim of the original curse. There is no motivation for agricultural labor, only a divine command. The "tiller of the ground" is a son, an "heir" cursed by the Father. The victim is chained to the soil forever; laboring for his food is his destiny.

Contrast this with the other vision of the earth evoked by the metaphor of the mine. The "infinitely various leads" suggest that a complete freedom is given to man so that he can pick up the "lead," the opportunity he prefers, somehow regardless of the stern command of the Father. Mother Earth seems to be generous though mysterious, she will open up to reveal the hidden treasures of her bounteous nature to the curious and hard-working sons of Adam. By applying his mind and body to "anything but that dreary round of daily labor and poor pay" that Lincoln hated so much, man could improve his lot instead of living out the cursed life that had been apportioned to him after the Fall.[77] And indeed, much of Lincoln's originality stems from his distaste for farming in a community where most people tilled the land and everybody tried to own some.

Lincoln and His Father

The forced marriage between Lincoln and agricultural work was dissolved as soon as the young man was in a position to do so. At the same time, he broke most of the ties with his father. He continued to visit him occasionally when professional obligations carried him close to his father's home, and he lent or gave him money. But he did not invite his father to his wedding and refused to go to visit him on his deathbed.[78] It is not our intention to study the complex relationship between Abraham and his father. Psychologists can seek the source of the profound opposition of these two men in such things as the death of Nancy and Thomas's remarriage, the intimacy of log cabins, and Thomas's roughness. For purposes of this study it is enough to point out the conflict between the preoccupations of the father and of the son. Lincoln never showed any interest in cabinetmaking, which his father tried to teach him. He was shocked at Thomas's negligence in money matters and legal affairs. He spoke with contempt of a man "litterally without education. He never did more in the way of writing than to bunglingly sign his own name."[79] Thus, the relationship between Abraham and Thomas Lincoln is (partly) accounted for by the contradiction it crystallizes, that between the need for child labor and Lincoln's thirst for education.

Lacking an impartial witness, we must accept the testimony of Sarah Bush Lincoln, who loved her husband and preferred her step-son to her own child: "As a usual thing Mr. Lincoln never made Abe quit reading to do anything if he could avoid it. He would do it himself first."[80]

However eager Thomas was to see his son acquire a good education, he obviously could not do without his services. His farm required only four months of work a year.[81] Because Abraham did not want to learn cabinetmaking, the proletarian Thomas (in the etymological sense of the term) had to make use of his son by renting out his services. It was the same for everybody. There were very few gentlemen farmers in the area. According to Beveridge, Thomas "exacted rigidly" the pay that Abraham earned.[82] All the children on the frontier found themselves in the same situation. But all did not have Abraham's curiosity, intelligence, extraordinary energy, and insatiable ambition. And we see here appearing a few hints of the "ugly duckling" that Edgar Lee Masters, by a stroke of genius, found in Lincoln.[83]

It would be improper to try to generalize from Lincoln's experience. Nonetheless, one is forced to notice that difficult living conditions sometimes prevent the development of affectionate feelings in the bosom of the family. A surviving document helps to illustrate how exceptional Lincoln's attitudes toward his native surroundings were, as well as how profound was the impact those surroundings had on him. The letter was addressed to Abraham Lincoln by one of his relatives, John Talbot Hanks, on July 22, 1860:

Dear unkel

it has ben a bout Ten years sense I saw you laste . . . I have ben up an down in the world bute no I stand purtey fair for rasing in the worlde I hav a good prospect fur making money I received a lettor from fother the other day he desires fur me to cum home he says that he dont expect to live long in the world and wontes me to cum home doe yu think ite wod be aviseble fur me unkel to returne home when now I hav be gun to prosper I love mi olde fother as well as son could love his fother you no unkel that I was raised a poor boy I had no Chance to make mi self while growing up to man hood . . . I have had to work hard for mi living ever sence I was a boy Eight years old and I think now I had beter look out fur mi self.[84]

With Lincoln, the desire to "live his own life" is inseparable from his intention to live a life different from that of the Hanks and the Lincolns.

RURAL AND AGRICULTURAL LIFE: ROOTS AND REACTIONS

When Lincoln arrived in New Salem in 1831, his attitude toward rural life was already largely formed. It was in Indiana that he determined upon the outlines of the place he wanted to occupy in the rural life of the frontier. It was in Indiana that the rustic traits recognizable throughout his life became ingrained. A time of reaction, either positive or negative, and of immersion, it was not yet a time of action.

The various elements of rural life in Indiana can be arranged according to Lincoln's relationship with them: some he rejected; some he compromised with, often by overcoming and controlling them; others finally permeated him and became an integral part of his personality whether he liked it or not.

Town and Country

The first thing Lincoln rejected was the rural settlement as he had known it in the "community" of Little Pigeon Creek. Where three roads met in the middle of the woods, James Gentry, along with John Romine (his associate and relative who joined him about 1827), established a store. The place was soon known as Gentryville, but the designation *town* was not given to the hamlet in official documents until 1854. Along with the church, it was the center of gravity of a rather numerous but quite scattered community: Little Pigeon Creek.[85]

The Lincolns were, in fact, not isolated in the middle of the wilderness. The nearest neighbors, the Casebiers, lived only five hundred yards away; Dennis and Elizabeth Hanks, eight hundred; and the Barretts, eleven hundred.[86] However, it was not a village, properly so called, but only a vague cluster of settlements, a grouping whose total density reached fewer than two inhabitants per square mile. In the immediate neighborhood of the Lincolns and the Gentrys the population was considerably more concentrated. But there was no indication of anything more than the beginning of a small village. It was, from all evidence, a scattered rural settlement.[87] Without going into details, the difficulties brought on by such a situation can be easily envisioned: the paucity of economic and social exchanges, absence of doctors, distance from commercial and cultural channels, inconvenient and inadequate schooling, and lack of hygiene made worse by crowded housing conditions.[88] It is hard to know to what degree and in what order these factors came into play in the process by which Lincoln rejected this way of life. What is certain, is that from 1831 until his death in 1865 Lincoln lived only in towns or cities.

A Primitive and Passionate World

A second element that Lincoln rejected was alcohol, that whisky that bathed the frontier and was used as money, as a means of stockpiling and transporting grain, as both an internal and external medicine, as a reward for a pupil who obtained a good grade, and, of course, as an intoxicating beverage. In this environment, where alcoholism was pervasive, Lincoln did not imbibe. He had no interest in strong drink any more than in tobacco, which was also widely used.[89] This attitude was all the more unusual because Lincoln was not a fanatic in the fight against "dram-drinking." He thought one should avoid relying on the terroristic sermons of temperance preachers, which were often ineffective and almost always produced unwanted side effects.[90]

Lincoln watched with close attention and amused disdain the gesticulations of the hysterical preachers who sometimes appeared at Little Pigeon Creek. Opportunities for entertainment were not frequent, and the show was of high quality. Back home, he would ape the "holy whine" of the Baptists and the "fire and brimstone" diatribes of the Methodists, and he provided an inexhaustible source of giggles for the children of Little Pigeon Creek, who watched him standing on a tree stump and reciting straight through the sermon he had just heard. The religious excitement of the fanatics held no attraction for him—any more than did the violent, open, and crude disdain for religion and its values that coexisted with it on the frontier.[91]

A former sexton of the congregation, Abraham never asked for admission to the Baptist church, nor indeed to any other religious sect. He "read the Bible some, though not as much as said; he sought more congenial books suitable for his age." He "had no particular religion," "never talked about it," but "sometimes attended church."[92] We should not be mistaken about this point: Lincoln, as he himself said, did not reject Christian values. He was, for all that, a chaste and timid adolescent, kind and compassionate, loyal and honest, courageous and patient to cite only a few of the virtues whose incense rises when one reads the testimony of contemporaries. In a society whose main characteristic is directness—that is, the lack of mediation between perception and action—Lincoln was always surprising for his original, unusual, and quaint side: his reaction was never like that of others. He was not among those who would fight at the drop of a hat—to the point that, in general on the frontier, murderers who acted in the heat of the moment or under the force of emotion were acquitted.[93] Likewise, he could not accept the value of a religion founded on immediate emotional experience caused by an eloquence that appealed to the senses and not to reason, and which was ultimately a form of physical violence. His rejection, by abstention or irony, of the religiosity surrounding him opened the way to the development of his rationalism, which was revealed in New Salem. Despising the oratorical savagery of those who thought they were dealing with brutes, Lincoln brought everything before the tribunal of reason and tried to convince his audience more than to impress it. That was the nature of his eloquence, at the bar as well as at the podium, the eloquence of democracy.

He rejected, then, religious bigotry and a sort of vulgarity of feeling, but he did so prudently. He was careful not to break with his environment. Lincoln was sure of his views once his opinion had become crystalized. He was then confident enough to compromise outwardly without altering his deeply felt views. He remained personally immune to pressure and committed to the essential judgment that he had reached independently. Lincoln could, therefore, reach an accommodation with those aspects of frontier life that, while not unknown, remained foreign to him. Such was the case, for example, with the violence of the West, which was present, either potentially or in actuality, at all social contacts, games, weddings, parties, sermons, and trials, not to mention saloon brawls.

Simple Pleasures

In a world where virility and violence were synonymous, an adolescent with delicate feelings, almost sentimental,[94] had no place, unless he was bigger, stronger, faster, and a better fighter than anybody in the neighborhood. Tales—probably true—abound of the Homeric victories won by Lincoln.[95] However, he never appears as a lover of violence but rather as a sensible boy equally likely to play at fighting and to thrash an aggressor. His aggressiveness was shown rather through his caustic wit, which he used against his adversaries or humorously turned against himself. By that means, he kept in touch with the country people of the frontier and fit in.

This boy, a bookworm by the standards of those around him, abstemious and always well-behaved, would have been considered mentally unbalanced if he had not had at the same time a childish side, which he retained throughout his life.[96] He loved hoaxes, games, sports, jokes, adventures, in short, playing hooky as much as going to school. "His own description of his youth was that of a happy joyous boyhood. It was told with mirth and glee and illustrated by pointed anecdotes, often interrupted by his jocund laugh," Leonard Swett said.[97]

Here was a man who played a ball game with his neighbor on the day before his nomination as a candidate for president in 1860, who when he was over forty would sneak away from his legal friends to go to watch a magic lantern show or an electric machine. In a word, he loved everything that Anglo-Saxons call *sport:* pranks, games, and physical exercise. This good-natured and childish side surely must have won him friends in his youth and helped to secure him a place in a society to which he was otherwise so poorly adapted.

But, to return to Masters's image, Lincoln as a young swan could not have paddled about, sometimes by desire and often by necessity, in the duck pond of the frontier without getting even a speck of mud on its feathers. Some aspects of pioneer culture, singularly lacking in nobility, marked this child of the West forever.

Earthiness and Superstition

Lincoln loved earthy stories that had sexual connotations or were definitely obscene. His friends all agreed: "Lincoln had two characteristics: one of purity, and the other, as it were, an insane love in telling dirty and smutty stories." "Almost any man that would tell a very vulgar story has got, in a degree a vulgar mind, but it was not so with him. . . . It was the wit he was after, the pure jewel, and he would pick it up out of the mud or dirt just as readily as he would from a parlor table." He was marked by a countryside both bawdy and puritanical in which young people sang hymns tinged with damnation and "what is called carnel Songs and love songs."[98] Naturally, no collection of his

unrepeatable stories exists, and it is not easy to find authentic documents to support the assertion that he was coarse to that extent and in
that fashion.[99]

Three irrefutable documents do exist, however. The first is an auto-
graph manuscript that strings together a series of spoonerisms ending
with: "[he] rushed into the house, and found the *door* sick abed, and his
wife standing open. But thank goodness she is getting right *hat* and
farty again."[100] Underlining the point is not necessary, Lincoln has
already done it. The second is a letter from one of Lincoln's colleagues
in the House of Representatives of the United States, the Honorable
Moses Hampton, dated March 30, 1849: "Do you remember the story of
the old Virginian stropping his razor on a certain *member* of a young
negro's body which you told us and connected it with my mission to
Brazil?"[101] We are close to Kentucky, and the earthiness of the frontier
reeks of racism. Finally, here are some excerpts from a series of *public*
speeches given by Lincoln to the students of Illinois College and to the
cultivated public of Springfield and ultimately of all of Illinois. Having
noted that the first discovery was Adam's discovery of nudity, Lincoln
recalled the first invention, the fig-leaf apron, then corrected himself:
"the very first invention was a joint operation, Eve having shared with
Adam in the getting up of the apron. And, indeed, judging from the fact
that sewing has come down to our times as 'woman's work' it is very
probable she took the leading part; he, perhaps, doing no more than to
stand by and thread the needle."[102]

A second primitive aspect of pioneer culture that can be found in
Lincoln is superstition. In touch with the immense forest and its mysteries,
deriving more or less valid principles from their experience, farmers
multiplied superstitious prohibitions. Thus they preferred to sow plants
that bore fruit underground at the time of the waning moon, and those
that bore fruit in the open air at the crescent moon. If a farming tool was
brought into the house, a coffin would soon be taken out of it. Nothing
should be started on Fridays. Lincoln admitted it himself, he was
superstitious and, furthermore, credulous. When his son Robert was
gravely ill, he took him to Terre Haute, Indiana, to have him touch a
miraculous stone, "the madstone."[103]

Country Accents

Thus, earthiness and superstition were the two striking traces of a
country childhood that all the urbanity of his wife and some of his
friends and colleagues could not manage to erase. It would be a mistake

to see in them only the superficial defects of a precious stone that needed more polishing. The whole person, with his saffron-colored complexion and the heavy and sure tread of a farmer rooted in the soil, evoked irresistibly the land where he was born.[104]

As soon as Lincoln opened his mouth, there was no mistaking it: his accent smacked of the soil. The dialect of southern Indiana—and that of Illinois, which was very similar—always gave a particular flavor to his speeches. He began his famous speech at Cooper Institute with the words "Mr. Cheermun." Likewise, he would greet his acquaintances in Springfield with a warm "howdy," and the odds were that the first word that came to him on seeing a horse was "creetur."[105] What professional demagogs claimed was mere affectation was instead an authentic rustic simplicity that gave color and solidity to his character.[106]

Finally, it is impossible to conclude this appraisal of the influences of the rural world of Indiana without mentioning a feature of the culture and civilization that dominated Lincoln's thought from that time on: the intense attachment and prickly veneration the pioneers felt toward private property, which they intended to defend staunchly.[107] The land cleared and won with so much effort and the livestock threatened by wild animals had to be protected from theft. The farmers appreciated and admired men of law, judges, lawyers, policemen—to the degree that they were honest—because they defended their property. People have wondered about the appeal of the law for Lincoln, and especially about why a self-taught youth of eighteen would be inspired to read *The Revised Laws of Indiana adopted and enacted by the General Assembly.* Van Natter provided the answer by digging out the testimony of David Turnham, the constable of Little Pigeon Creek, who disclosed that Lincoln had been his deputy for several months.[108]

ESCAPE ROUTES

Lincoln's assessment of his experience in rural Indiana was, on the whole, negative. A prisoner of his family and his position, he could not yet break with his surroundings, but he seized all opportunities to escape the dreary routine of field work. He loved the festivities that accompanied social activities, such as house raisings, corn huskings, weddings and infares, political barbecues, and "kicking parties" where young people trampled laundry on a wooden floor.[109] But these distractions did not manage to quench his thirst for change.

The Mill Road

Several examples of these escapes will illustrate the lack of attachment Lincoln felt for the land. Many stories report the pleasure he took when still quite a small child in going to the mill to carry corn harvested on his father's farm. At first it was to a hand-mill located about seven miles from Little Pigeon Creek. This trait must be placed in context: children in Indiana as a general rule were afraid of going to the mill over bad roads, of riding horseback, of losing corn along the way, and of encountering wild animals.[110] The trip required courage and force of character, which suggests that young Abraham was willing to run some risks and suffer some inconvenience to gain a little freedom. But it also suggests the attraction for Lincoln of a commercial activity of basically urban nature, because it was often around mills that villages grew up. Before their appearance, development in rural areas was slow and tied to subsistence agriculture. As soon as agricultural surplus could be transformed into flour, marketing became necessary.[111] Mills, especially those built along the Ohio, became important stops on the developing routes taken by merchants.

Commerce and Navigation

Lincoln was fascinated by commercial exchanges that brought a new breath of air into the rural community and by the man who embodied them at Little Pigeon Creek, James Gentry. Gentry was the merchant who made profits—normal for the time—of 100 percent by bringing town products to the farmers and who pocketed 20 percent more when he accepted payment in kind, allowing him to play the role of exporter of agricultural products. He was the land speculator who bought Thomas Lincoln's land in 1830. But he was also the subscriber to the Lexington and Louisville newspapers.[112] He made possible Lincoln's trip to New Orleans and his initiation into the mysteries of national politics.

Lincoln's trip down the Mississippi and his job as a ferryman for James Taylor, who also organized the packing and sending of beef, pork, and game toward New Orleans, constituted examples of escapes.[113] Lincoln's horizons expanded and brightened when fashionable gentlemen threw him two half dollars in silver for rowing them out to embark on a steamboat going down the Ohio.[114] However, he had to continue working the land for Taylor, and it weighed on him. He asked a friend of the family to give him a recommendation to apply for a job on the river.[115] It was on "the main street of western transportation" (the Ohio) with all its bustle that he maneuvered his flatboat, and on the "Appian Way" of

America (the Mississippi) that he descended to New Orleans.[116] As communication improved between producers and consumers, human ties developed as well all along the rivers that ended at New Orleans, America's great cosmopolitan city. The variety of this commerce of products and individuals attracted Lincoln as much as the shady aspect of river society.

Life on the river as immortalized by Mark Twain was lively without being hectic. There was time to talk and exchange news. The boatmen sometimes struck languid poses that contrasted with the permanent tension required by field work. What Lincoln liked most about the earth was to stretch out on it peacefully and take the time to read or talk. A modern Antaeus, "he had to touch the earth again to renew his strength,"[117] and his tall body liked lazy postures that were the privilege of those in comfortable social circumstances: "Their legs *only a little* higher than their heads, and segars in their mouths," like the merchants from Princeton, Indiana, whom Thomas Hulme met in 1819.[118]

Escapes came again when he went to town, to Princeton, Rockport, or Vincennes, to hear lawyers plead or to go shopping. These were simple towns, whose few stone houses were lost among the log cabins. The county seat of Perry County, with the glorious name of Rome, had only twenty wooden houses and one stone building, the jail.[119] Yet, people wanted to do great things, to ape the East. The "internal improvement mania" had already taken hold of the Indiana legislators who aspired to criss-cross the state with roads, canals, and, later, railroads. A law of January 17, 1820, pompously declared Little Pigeon Creek and many other similar waterways "navigable streams." All of this captivated Lincoln, who appreciated the efforts of Clay and Adams, whose farewell gift in 1827 was to grant lands to Indiana for the construction of a canal. Lincoln followed the learned discussions on the comparative advantages of water routes and railroads.[120] In either case, the aim was to end the isolation of rural communities and to develop urban centers. But there was a long way from planning to implementation, and it would be quite a while before Indiana could take pride in a town the size of Elizabethtown, Kentucky, with a brick works, a tannery, a distillery, three shops, and a courthouse, which doubtless remained in Lincoln's memory as the biggest town he had seen before New Orleans.[121]

Kentucky's Other Face

Another image of Kentucky appears here, and this time the comparison with Indiana is not in favor of the Hoosier State. An Englishman who traced the pioneer migration route backward observed in 1818: "A

Traveller who has been four or five months in the wildernesses of the
Illinois Territory, or the gloomy forests of Indiana, is delighted with the
fine clearings of the Kentucky farms."[122] Lincoln certainly held that
opinion. He enjoyed crossing the Ohio to converse with his friend and
mentor Judge Samuel W. Pate, whom he had met during a trial brought
against him by other boatmen.[123] The daily coming and going of the
ferry service put Lincoln alternately in touch with the Indiana bank,
full of noisy taverns that appeared and disappeared with the pace of
speculation,[124] and the elegance of the slave plantations owned by Pate
and his friends on the Kentucky shore. On the southern bank, even
when the houses were modest, they were clean, with a cared for garden,
often an ice house, all of which "strongly contrasts with the dirty Ohio
houses, and the Indiana and Illinois pigsties, in which men, women
and children wallow in promiscuous filth. But the Kentuckians have
servants; and whatever may be the future consequences of Slavery, the
present effects are in these respects most agreeable and beneficial."[125]
This description may be exaggerated, but it is correct on two points. In
Kentucky, rich people were more cultured and women more beautiful
than in Indiana or Illinois.[126] The aristocratic aspects of this brilliant
society had not yet been made conspicuous and called into question by
the Jacksonian movement. Indeed, in the year 1825, when Lincoln
began his apprenticeship on the "Belle Rivière" (the Ohio), the already
lively and refined life in Kentucky towns shone even more brightly than
usual. The Marquis de Lafayette, living symbol of the silk-stocking
Revolution, visited Louisville, and in his honor the town erected trium-
phal arches of flowers. Thousands of people crowded into the Grand
Masonic Hall, where a magnificent ball was given. The slaves were
diligent and discreet, the young people noisily amused themselves. In
this throng of cultured planters, lawyers, and businessmen, the sumptuous finery of the Kentucky belles caused a great sensation.[127] This
milieu nurtured Henry Clay, Lincoln's intellectual guide, Mary S. Owens,
whom he courted in 1836 and 1837, and Mary Ann Todd, his future wife.

The Kentucky "belles" did not spoil their hands doing dishes, and
more than one traveler noticed the influence of slavery on the freshness
of their complexion, the elegance of their manners, and the quality of
their French.[128] Henry Clay, in his magnificent house at Ashland
"brimful of negroes,"[129] could play at the role of gentleman-farmer and
hold forth with as much style and knowledge on agricultural experi-
ments carried out on his lands as he could on the virtues of his
American System.[130]

Abraham was closer here to the tales of A Thousand and One Nights
than he was in the log cabin of the Lincoln-Hanks family, where nine
people slept in one room. Indeed, Flint compared the Kentucky beauties

kept under lock and key to the veiled inhabitants of a Turkish harem.[131] Lincoln was always attracted by the charm of a Kentucky life-style, with its receptions, cultivated and witty conversations, dinners "in town," and carriage rides. Mary Todd Lincoln, who saw in him her "tall Kentuckian," shared his enthusiasm, and this common liking was one of the most solid foundations of their marriage and one of its rare successes.[132]

But obviously this attractive world was inaccessible. What hope was there for a young agricultural laborer in the caste society of Kentucky? Later, once his fortune was made, the question could come up again perhaps. Nothing prevented Lincoln from following his friend Speed to Kentucky in the 1840s, of settling in Lexington, for example, with the backing of his father-in-law, the Whig banker and friend of Clay. But Lincoln always refused to pay the price required for life in the South: black slavery and contempt for poor whites. "Kentucky is growing very rich, and the people are becoming very proud," noted Elyas P. Fordham in 1818.[133] As bewitched as Lincoln was by high society, he was not part of it and would do nothing contrary to his principles in order to enter it. He wanted to rise socially without lowering his humanity. He wanted to become a lawyer or a merchant, live well, enjoy some leisure time, but without despising another. His model was the democratic bourgeois of the frontier who surprised Europeans by his ease and manner with common people. Even lawyers, judges, and military men did not look down on common people an Englishman named Bradbury, who traveled through Indiana in 1811, pointed out with amazement.[134] Many revisionist historians of America do not understand this fact about that time and interpret Lincoln's simplicity as a mere cover for his ambition.

Lincoln married the daughter of a banker, raised in the bosom of a Mammy Sally and educated in a French school, but he nevertheless exclaimed one day against the Southern haughtiness of the Todds, saying that although they spelled their name with two ds, God only needed one.[135] Lincoln's democratic spirit was here expressed in a Protestant vision of the equality of men before God in an elementary truth with decisive consequences that states that, no matter what they do, men are still men, neither more nor less.

With the rejection of the Kentucky temptation we come to the end of the Indiana experience by returning to its beginning: the superiority of life in a free state over a slave culture. But the perspective has changed, or, rather, it has widened as the result of a process described here. Facing difficult living conditions, Lincoln wanted to free himself as soon as possible from the physical and moral constraints of life in the country and escape a milieu in which he was out of place. But he could not and did not want to break entirely with it and thus the personal contradictions.

He naturally looked toward Kentucky, an advanced part of civilization on the western frontier. But Kentucky was not a neutral "East" of
refined and urbane civilization. It was profoundly influenced by its
partially Southern character, which accounts for Lincoln's ambiguous
attitude toward it. To break away from the land without disowning
those who worked it, that was the problem that took shape in Indiana
and whose solution would be found only later in Illinois. When his
family decided to leave Indiana, threatened by a fresh wave of milk
sickness, for the Prairie State with its already proverbial fertility, Lincoln,
who had nothing to lose, was ready to follow.[136] By doing so he repeated
Thomas's choice in 1816, but in a richer and more complete form. He
had confirmed, like his father, that life was easier north of the Ohio for
the farmer or the artisan, the employee or the agricultural laborer. But
he had also acquired the certainty that only in a free state could a poor
man escape from his condition, the farmer from his bondage to the soil,
the worker from the hard toil that wore out his body. No sense of
betrayal cast its shadow on this vague hope of social advancement. He
was not bothered by any hints of a bad conscience, because the condition that Lincoln aspired to did not contradict respect for the common
people from which he sprang.

3

THE ASCENT

THE PROMISED LAND

From 1810 until the Civil War, Illinois, the land of men (Illiniwek in Algonquin), was the world's garden, the gathering place of those to whom the earth was to grant its most bountiful gifts. In 1860, hundreds of thousands of people could sympathize with Scripps's description of the "rich, undulating prairies" toward which the Lincolns went as toward a "land of promise."[1]

"Think of Windsor Park, or Strathfieldsaye, or of the parks for all the noblemen and wealthy landholders in Britain to be had here at a dollar and a-quarter an acre."[2] "The villas and castles seem to have been burnt, the enclosures taken down."[3] These were the reflections of travelers who marveled at the natural munificence and the social availability of Illinois, that "boundless English park,"[4] which began as soon as the Wabash was crossed and the unhealthy and gloomy woods of Indiana were left behind and which was interrupted but not ended by the ha-ha of the cliffs above the Mississippi, beyond which spread the Iowa and Missouri prairies.

The Yorkshire farmer crushed by rising rents or the poor white from Virginia or Kentucky driven out by slavery could finally look forward to acquiring property under favorable conditions.[5]

The years from 1829 to 1830, a turning point for the settlement of Illinois, substantially transformed the state. Immigration leaped forward when the traditional arrivals from Kentucky were joined by thousands of pioneers from all the states in the East, from as far away as Massachusetts, including many Virginians.[6] This veritable stampede toward Illinois (confirmed by the statistics that show a doubling of population between 1825 and 1830) was accompanied by a change in the populated areas.[7] Neglecting the unoccupied lands in the South, the pioneers pushed toward the rapidly growing counties in the center of Illinois: Sangamon, Cass, Macon, and Morgan.[8] Their fertile soil was legendary, especially that of Sangamon County, whose attractions were recognized as early as 1820.[9] The presence of the Sangamon River insured the availability of trees that farmers chopped down to make fences and buildings, an essential factor at a time when the prairie was cultivated only in the proximity of woods.[10] The Lincolns headed in that direction, taking part once again in a great social movement whose causes we need to understand.

The Promise of Illinois in 1830: Land and Labor

The 1829 treaty with the Kickapoos and the Potawatomis pushed back the Indian barrier, and whites appropriated broad fertile spaces that covered immense mineral riches, including lead, coal (exploited as early as 1809), and petroleum (as yet unknown). A Land Office was established in Springfield in 1823, and it quickly became the favorite haunt of settlers who benefited from favorable laws at that time.[11]

In fact, pressured by the state legislature, which was eager to see Illinois become rapidly populated, Congress adopted the law of May 29, 1830, which gave a preemptive right (up to a limit of 160 acres) to those who occupied federal lands in Illinois in 1829. In central Illinois, a claim could be established by merely placing four logs on the soil to outline a foundation area. A campaign to try to soften Congress's traditional policy of obtaining substantial income from the sale of federal lands dominated the work of the general assembly of Illinois in 1828 and 1829 and received a great deal of attention in the press. Many future settlers had heard of Illinois's land policy, which aimed at reducing the price of public lands (notably by a system of graduation, or automatic and gradual reduction in the price of lands that had not been sold), treated squatters quite favorably and made little effort to collect land taxes, which were modest anyway and from which buyers of federal land were exempt for five years.[12]

Conditions for workers in the young state were equally designed to encourage settlement by those who had to sell their labor before they could set up in business for themselves. First they would not face the competition of slave labor. In 1824 the inhabitants of Illinois overwhelmingly rejected a proposal for revising the constitution to allow slavery. The results were especially marked in the central counties: 722 to 153 in Sangamon County, 455 to 42 in Morgan County.[13] Little by little, the last traces of slavery inherited from the French disappeared, and contract slave labor at the salt mines of Shawneetown was abolished in 1825. At the same time, a particularly cruel Black Code forbade freed blacks from competing with whites.[14]

Other legal arrangements showed the favorable attitude toward workers held by a legislature in which Jacksonianism would be established for a long time. A law protecting artisans in the event of their employer's bankruptcy (mechanic's lien law) was voted in 1825 and applied as well to arrangements between agricultural workers and landowners. From 1823 on, debtor's prison was reserved for those who had demonstrated an intention to flee, and detention ceased as soon as security was given for them or they took an oath of insolvency.[15]

These were then the promises of Illinois, as they were propagated by rumor and by John Hanks. Would the Prairie State live up to them? The Lincolns surely asked that question as they crossed the Wabash River at Vincennes in February 1830.

ON THE OTHER SIDE OF THE MIRAGE

The old French city, where elegant houses stood next to log cabins, contrasted sharply with the empty spaces that the Lincolns saw on the other side of the "white river," with its pure waters. The immensity of the empty prairie in that early spring offered the traveler only a sad landscape where flattened grasses were plastered to the soil by mud during the daytime and by ice at night.[16] Even in Lawrence County, which the Lincolns crossed first and which was densely populated (more than six inhabitants per square mile), the roads were barely more than paths and soon gave way to unspoiled virgin prairie. While keeping on course by reference to the sun, the pioneers preferred to travel along the rivers and streams that had been pointed out to them or to ply their route from one stand of timber to the next.[17]

In March 1830 the Lincolns finally arrived at the site chosen by John Hanks on a cliff rising above the Sangamon River, a few miles northwest of Decatur. Cutting down trees, enclosing, clearing, planting, and building a log cabin were the familiar tasks to which the Lincolns applied themselves. When autumn came, fevers (a sort of malaria) struck the newcomers, as was often the case in Illinois, and they were quite feeble as winter came on, that winter of 1830–31 known in the annals of Illinois as the "winter of the deep snow." With weakened resistance and very low spirits—the fevers had convinced them to leave the county—the Lincolns saw the first flakes of snow fall on Christmas Day 1830. A blizzard, then rain that immediately froze on the surface of the snow to form a crust on which a man or a wolf could walk (but not horses, deer, and cattle), temperatures below zero for weeks, and, without stopping, snow that reached a depth of four feet in places and almost covered the shocks of corn made this famous winter of the deep snow unforgettable. Lincoln spent it holed up with his family in their isolated cabin, contemplating his future and, like all Illinoisans, subsisting on the recently harvested corn crop. The survivors called themselves "snowbirds."[18]

Spring finally arrived, and Abraham Lincoln, John Hanks, and John D. Johnston left Macon County for Beardstown to meet a man named Denton Offutt, who had hired them for $12 a month to take a cargo of hogs and corn to New Orleans. Because the roads were even more flooded than usual that spring, the three men went down the Sangamon by canoe as far as Springfield, where they met Offutt. He had been unable to obtain a boat for the trip, so the first task of the employees was to chop down trees "on Congress land" to build one. Then, going down the Sangamon, the raft became stranded on the dam at New Salem, a village located between Springfield and Beardstown. Despite the ingenious efforts displayed by Lincoln, the boat had difficulty getting over the obstacle, and Offutt took the opportunity to reconnoiter the surroundings. With his flair for commercial ventures, he quickly noticed the possibilities for development at New Salem, which were tied to the prospects offered by steam navigation on the Sangamon, much discussed at that time. He took a lease on James Rutledge's saw mill and grain mill (supplied by hydraulic power from the dam) and decided to open a store. Having taken a liking to young Lincoln, he promised to employ him as a clerk on his return from New Orleans. And, indeed, in July 1831, Abraham Lincoln "stopped indefinitely, and, for the first time, as it were, by himself at New-Salem."[19]

The Break

Before studying in detail the period of Lincoln's life that began in 1831 and that would see this son of a farmer become a lawyer and a politician, it is necessary to appreciate the significance of the 1831 decision. At the moment when John Hanks had returned to his wife in Decatur, when John D. Johnston rejoined the Lincolns, and when the Hanks family (which had headed back in the direction of Indiana) settled in Coles County, Illinois, Lincoln by contrast installed himself in Offutt's store "indefinitely."[20]

The ties between Thomas Lincoln, who died on his land in Coles County in 1851, and Dennis Hanks, John D. Johnston, and their families, who remained at his side to the end, were based on land, their great joy and their great concern, the great business of their lives. Squatters between 1831 and 1834 at Buck Grove, they settled in the spring of 1834 at Pleasant Grove. Hanks and Johnston, lazy and not very talented, lived in the shadow of Thomas Lincoln, who succeeded, after many setbacks and with the help of his son, in putting together a property of eighty acres. Purchases, sales, exchanges, lawsuits, mortgages taken out to pay debts contracted after risky commercial ventures, such was the narrow life of unambitious small-scale farmers. After Thomas's death, the atmosphere was tainted by quarrels over inheritance, and John D. Johnston tried to dispossess his mother.[21] In short, a life with no horizon beyond corn, bound like serfs to the soil, in a county that was rather backward demographically and where agricultural performance was mediocre.[22]

For Lincoln, breaking with the land and separating from his family were one and the same movement by which he tore himself away from a confined life, far from the major commercial and cultural currents. It is not surprising to see him follow once again the way of the river, first toward New Orleans, then along the Sangamon, on the banks of which he spent thirty years of his life: at New Salem from 1831 to 1837, then at Springfield from 1837 to 1861. At a time when roads were a precarious means of transportation, eight years before the first train covered the twenty-five miles from Meredosia to Jacksonville, stopping frequently because of the "snake-heads" that protruded from the track, rivers were the principal means of circulation, the axis around which the economic life of the region was organized.[23] Ways of improving the navigability of water routes to make them accessible to steamboats and of tying together the water network by digging canals were questions debated in taverns as well as in the legislature or in Congress, a debate Lincoln had already joined in 1831 at Decatur.[24]

Another advantage of the water route was that it required no effort. By setting oneself adrift, one could watch the eternally immobile earth pass before one's eyes. This route of adventure and destiny dumped its travelers like flotsam here and there as soon as the land rose up and could take them quite far, all the way to the banks of the Potomac. Lincoln described himself as "a piece of floating driftwood" washed up on the New Salem dam, and in July 1864 in Washington, he confided to a Canadian visitor his amazement at how far he had come: "Yes, to think of it, it is very strange that I, a boy brought up in the woods, . . . should be drifted into the very apex of this great event."[25] Yet one must follow the current of progress, and that is undoubtedly what Lincoln did by deciding to settle, for the first time in his life, in a town.

TOWN AND COUNTRY

New Salem, a town? When Lincoln arrived there, it was only a hamlet with a dozen log houses perched on a cliff above the Sangamon. However, if the river became navigable, New Salem was in a good position in relation to Beardstown and Springfield, and the prospects for development were excellent. As William E. Barton told his compatriots, "we who live in America must learn to estimate cities otherwise than by their size."[26]

In its moment of glory in 1832, New Salem boasted two dozen buildings, including a mill, a sawmill, a post office, two or three bars, three or four stores, an inn or tavern (where travelers could spend the night), a blacksmith, a wheelwright-joiner, a cooper, a cobbler, a tanner, a hatter, and two doctors. The log houses, built with rough-hewn trunks, incorporating a brick chimney and glass windows (thanks to a Springfield glazier), sat alongside the most modest cabins.[27] At a time when Springfield numbered only five hundred inhabitants and Chicago only about a hundred, New Salem indisputably deserved the name of town, especially if considered from the viewpoint of its relations with the countryside.

"A hundred feet above the general level of the surrounding country," New Salem dominated in every sense the landscape of forests "diversified by alternate stretches of hills and level lands, with streams between each struggling to reach the river," which flowed on its bed of chalk, sand, and clay.[28] First of all, there was economic domination by the merchants, which we will examine in detail. But there was also intellectual domination expressed by such institutions as the post office, the newspaper depository, and the New Salem Debating Society, in which Presbyterians and free-thinkers debated each other and where Lincoln would shine. It dominated as well by the social superiority of a truly cosmopolitan town where Yankee and Virginian mixed, where the bachelor isolated from his family did not stick out, while the surrounding countryside was entirely populated by a small group of intermarried families originally from Kentucky and Tennessee—the Clarys, Armstrongs, and Greenes.[29]

The economic foundation of this superiority rested in the commercial position of New Salem much more than in its productive capacity. Naturally, it was to New Salem that the farmer brought wool to be carded and leather to be tanned. But most transactions used New Salem only as a route that linked the Illinois countryside with the towns of the East and the South via the Sangamon, the Illinois, then the Ohio and the Mississippi. The rich soil around New Salem brought forth abundant harvests of corn and wheat for St. Louis, New Orleans, New York, Philadelphia, and even Boston. Its silty, predominantly alluvial soils formed a narrow band bordering the Sangamon with its woods of walnut and oak trees, then came the well drained and strongly chalky soil left by glaciers in the vast prairie, where corn was beginning to replace the tall native grasses.[30]

Reciprocally, it was not New Salem, but Lowell or even Liverpool that spun the cotton fabric worn by the young girls when they went dancing. It was New York that furnished the articles that the newspapers that were read in New Salem reproduced, most often verbatim.[31]

It is easy to see that the merchant, the intermediary, was the principal character in the town. For a bushel of corn, he sold the farmer a yard of calico or two pounds of coffee; for five bushels, a pair of shoes; for twenty bushels, a plow and two pewter milk churns. Always ready to extend credit throughout the year, he recorded in his books what everybody purchased; then, at harvest time, accounts were settled up. And often a farmer would discover that, after deducting his purchases, he had made only a few dollars from the harvest that was handed over to the merchant, now transformed into a shipper. What should he do with the money? The merchant, in another metamorphosis as a banker, paid interest, and, using deposits to grant new advances, made loans.[32]

Because of his central role, the merchant enjoyed indisputable social prestige, but he often acquired as well a reputation as a rogue, miser, or social climber. For example, the itinerant merchant based in St. Louis who sold on credit without specifying the due date. For example, the principal merchant in New Salem, Samuel Hill, remembered by posterity as greedy and sly. For example, Denton Offutt, a colorful character for whom New Salem was no more than a step on an ultimately unfinished and unsuccessful conquest of the West.[33]

Lord Charnwood, whose insight can rarely be faulted, nonetheless errs in his perspective when he writes: "from the point of view of most educated men and women in the eastern States or in Europe, many of the associates and competitors of his early manhood, to whom he had to look up as his superiors in knowledge, would certainly have seemed crude people with a narrow horizon."[34] For, just as New Salem was a bridge to the East, likewise Offutt indicated the way to a different world than that of Illinois farmers. Did not even he conceive of New Salem as the port of embarkation toward civilization?

In February 1832, the steamer *Talisman,* Captain Vincent A. Bogue commanding, came up the Sangamon as far as Springfield. For the sum of $40, Lincoln (with the aid of Rowan Herndon) escorted this ship, now unloaded of its cargo of merchandise "direct from the East" as far as

Beardstown. He thus became one of the creators of a venture that produced a "boom" the whole length of the Sangamon. Bogue promised to transport merchandise from St. Louis to Springfield for half the price charged by those who carried it by land, and the smallest village was preparing to divide land along the river into town lots. Symbolically, to his work as a pilot Lincoln added that of land clearer, chopping down the branches that impeded the progress of the steamer toward the confluence of the Sangamon and the Illinois.[35]

Once again in New Salem, Lincoln capitalized on the river experience and his growing popularity by declaring his candidacy for the Illinois state legislature. His platform—issued as a profession of faith distributed to the people—was in fact to spend the public monies of the state of Illinois on a project of public works based especially on improving the navigability of the Sangamon. This program would be more economical than the more ambitious and preferable one of building a railroad from Jacksonville to Springfield. Indeed, the portion upstream from Beardstown, about thirty meandering miles, was the principal obstacle to navigation because drifting timber jammed up there and obstructed the river.

Lincoln proposed creating another and more direct channel for the Sangamon, across the prairie, which was often flooded anyway: "This route is upon prairie land the whole distance;—so that it appears to me, by removing the turf, a sufficient width and damming up the old channel, the whole river in a short time would wash its way through, thereby curtailing the distance, and increasing the velocity of the current very considerably."[36]

Lincoln had obviously observed carefully the topographical characteristics of this part of Illinois, and this point is important because the same arguments found here in favor of water routes turn up later in the case of railroads: the flatness and evenness of Illinois's soil was suited admirably to the construction of railroad tracks. And indeed, "no state or territory in North America can boast of superior facilities of internal navigation" than the Prairie State, and it had no rivals either in the building of railroads.[37]

It is striking that Lincoln's first political involvement was associated with the vast enterprise of the beginnings of American commercial agriculture that would dominate a large part of the social and political problems of his career in Illinois. But at the very moment when Abraham Lincoln made his first steps on the political scene, two events disrupted his electoral campaign. Offutt disappeared, leaving behind only debts (some of which Lincoln was forced to pay), and the Indian chief Black Hawk entered Illinois. When the governor called for volunteers, Lincoln, unemployed and without a family, joined up and was "elated" to be on campaign.[38]

A MILITARY INTERLUDE:
LINCOLN AND THE INDIANS

Lincoln's eagerness to throw himself into this adventure is reminiscent of his love of escape. But another and new factor was also at work here, a sort of collective enthusiasm that took hold of a large portion of the young people, especially in New Salem. The semihoodlums from Clary's Grove "who pretended to be 'regulators' " signed up en masse in the militia called up by Governor Reynolds on April 14.[39] For them, as for Lincoln, who earned a position of honor in their ranks by virtue of his strength and cheerful disposition, the campaign offered a chance to quit farm work. For these landless young people, it was an unexpected opportunity. But for self-employed farmers with families to feed, it was a calamity. They refused to join, and the governor had to draft men who preferred planting corn to chasing Indians.[40]

War supporters knew that most soldiers and most pacifists would be recruited from among the farmers. They therefore spared no opportunity in touching the right chord, landed property. The rallying cry of the local press was that the Indians refused to stop " 'making corn on their old grounds.' These Indians must be taught to respect their treaties."[41]

It was indeed a violation of the 1804 treaty (reaffirmed in 1816) for Black Hawk and a band of several hundred Sauks and Foxes, men, women, and children, to come back across the Mississippi to plant corn on their old land at the mouth of the Rock River. They had been forced to leave it the previous year both by provocations on the part of the settlers and by a small expedition of volunteers and regular soldiers of the United States under the command of General Edmund P. Gaines. After a difficult winter in Iowa, in hostile territory, Black Hawk's undernourished followers were in no mood to abide by the provisions of the June 27, 1804 treaty signed at St. Louis by the "spokesmen" (without mandate) of their nation. The treaty ceded an immense territory to the federal government in exchange for a nominal sum. For the fifty million acres located between the Mississippi, the Wisconsin, the Fox and the Illinois rivers, the "spokesmen" received $2,234.50 in kind, and the government promised to pay in addition an annuity of $1,000.[42]

But could a treaty really deprive a people of their right to exist? Could land, the collective property of a nation whose mythic roots stretched back to the beginning of time, be alienated by a few individuals? For Black Hawk such a notion was absurd, inconceivable. Recalling his confirmation of the 1804 treaty in 1816, he said: "I touched the goose quill to the treaty, not knowing, however, that, by that act, I consented to give away my village. . . . What do we know of the manners, the laws and the customs of the white people? They might buy our bodies for dissection, and we would touch the goose quill to confirm it and not know what we were doing. . . . There is no place like that where the bones of our forefathers lie to go to when in grief."[43]

They could not give up eight hundred acres planted in corn, the rest in bluegrass for the horses, any more than the bodies of their ancestors, the very soul of the tribe, could be reduced to a market value, no matter what the terms, always in such cases based on fraud. And they could not give up the living bodies of the men, their individual and collective survival, which was threatened by the private appropriation of the land.

Under these conditions, the behavior of the squatters who had arrived since 1823 was a genuine provocation. The whites "turned stock into the Indian corn fields, erected fences, beat squaws who climbed over them, plowed up Indian graves, and finally in 1827 [and again in 1830], when the natives were away on a hunting trip, set fire to the vacant lodges." They took out preemption rights for most of the village and petitioned the authorities to protect their property rights.[44]

All of these provocations and even the winter spent cold and hungry at the mouth of the Des Moines River had not managed to destroy the Indians' composure. Peacefully they took the road leading to the village they were forced to abandon the previous year without even bringing in the harvest. Before them, the countryside was in turmoil. The fear of the red men was fed by memories and rumors, by false news spread by settlers and Potawatomis. Everywhere armed bands of militiamen criss-crossed the countryside, making "war upon the pigs and chickens," drinking and yelling, "a hard-looking set of men, unkempt and unshaved, wearing shirts of dark calico, and sometimes calico capotes."[45]

Among them were Abraham Lincoln and all the young men of New Salem. Lincoln owed his election as captain of his militia company to his popularity and his talents as a storyteller, a fighter, and an umpire. A promising success! This election—the first of his long career—gave him immense pleasure, surpassed by nothing before 1860.[46]

He enjoyed for the first time the power of leading people who loved him, simple men like himself, but who had chosen him to direct them. Soon he confirmed the truth of the saying "I am their leader, therefore I have to follow them." For an entire day, Lincoln had to wear a wooden sword as punishment after his men had given free rein to their love of drink and fighting. Like a modern Xenophon, he led his band of adventurers along paths marked by blazed trees and along makeshift roads through an uninhabited country, roads trampled by crowds of Indian hunters until they became "as dusty as the highways of New York Island." Then, after a month of this happy life, the company was disbanded when they arrived at the edge of the water, at the mouth of the Fox River, on May 27, 1832.[47]

Lincoln immediately signed up again as a simple soldier in the scout company of Elijah Iles, one of the biggest landowners and cattle raisers in the Springfield region.[48] This time things were more serious. It was no longer simply mobilization, but war. A troop of 341 volunteer militiamen under the command of Isaiah Stillman massacred three negotiators sent by Black Hawk, then at Dixon's Ferry attacked a group of thirty or forty Indians who had sent the negotiators. The three hundred men were put to rout ("Stillman's Run") and fled across Illinois, spreading rumors of Indian atrocities. Hostilities had begun. They ended on August 2 with the massacre at Bad Axe. Only 150 Indians (out of the thousand who followed Black Hawk) escaped the crossfire of U.S. army troops and Mississippi gunboats.[49]

But for Lincoln, the war was only a vague echo in the distance, the brutal sight of bodies being interred, a succession of uncomfortable bivouacs warmed by camaraderie: coffee ground at the bottom of a tin cup with the handle of a hatchet, bread cooked on the end of a ramrod, eating utensils of elm bark, patient searches in the tall grass of Gratiot's Grove for victims of an ambush, and a sole omnipresent enemy, mosquitoes.[50]

Lincoln had no land to defend or to lose, no vengeance to take on the Indians. Thus he came to the defense of an old Indian, a former agent for Harrison, whom the militiamen wanted to manhandle despite his possessing a safe-conduct because the cruelty of these brutes was equaled only by their cowardice in battle. Did Lincoln, then, serve only for his pay? No, because, without his knowledge, he had just earned most of his landed fortune. In the 1850s, he came to benefit from the generosity that Congress showed toward veterans by issuing land warrants. On the other hand, he quite consciously made friends and acquaintances, such as Stuart, a lawyer who opened new horizons for him and helped him in his career, and Captain Maltby, whom he would much later name Indian agent in California, where the government's "protected Indians" furnished cheap agricultural labor.[51]

Lincoln's second encounter with the Indian question was marked by the same inevitability as the first, the one that saw the death of his eponymous grandfather on the Kentucky frontier. The tide of civilization engulfed Indian land to divide it up and sell it and would not stop, thanks in part to Lincoln, until it reached the shores of the Pacific.

LEAVING THE LAND: A NEW RELATIONSHIP

"Lincoln, as we have seen already, was not enamored of the life of a common laborer. . . . He preferred to clerk, to go to war, to enter politics, —any thing but that dreary round of daily toil and poor pay."[52]

Anything, but what? Lincoln envisioned and tried several solutions for escaping the soil, which threatened him again since Offutt's departure. Lawyer? His meeting with Stuart gave him the idea, but he would need a better education. Blacksmith? He considered it.[53] Admittedly, the ideal, the ideal for someone who wanted to rise in the world, would be to make a fortune by embarking on some commercial enterprise, some safe speculation that would permit him to put a big stack of dollars between himself and work. That was, after all, the very justification for free enterprise, one of the three recognized ways of making a name for oneself. "For many poor boys have lived to make a mark on history, but as a rule they have entered early on a life either of learning or of adventure or of large business."[54]

How can one launch a large business if one is penniless? It requires credit, boldness, and luck. Whatever credit he possessed derived in part from his considerable personal qualities. Besides, the people of New Salem admired the electoral campaign of the "humble Abraham Lincoln," who ran a Jacksonian campaign on Clay's principles, helped along by the strong-arm tactics of the Clary's Grove boys. They gave him 277 votes out of 284. Lincoln was hardly known outside New Salem, and that cost him the victory. But he was the hero of New Salem, and the miracle occurred. In a few days, in association with William F. Berry, he was able to buy a store on credit and then a stock of merchandise that another storekeeper being terrorized by the Clary's Grove hoodlums was willing to relinquish for a small sum.[55]

Overnight he found himself an established merchant, newspaper agent, keeper of the last salon for conversation, similar to that storekeeper from Pekin, Illinois, whom Patrick Shirreff found in 1833 "stretched at full length with his back on the counter, and his feet touching the roof," and who answered "dryly without altering his position" the questions asked by the Scottish traveler who wanted to buy some shoe laces.[56]

Berry drank, Lincoln read: "Of course they did nothing but get deeper and deeper in debt."[57] Soon they were forced to sell out. With Berry's death, Lincoln found himself burdened with debts and spent many years paying back what he called the "national debt" down to the last penny. One must not imagine an American César Birotteau, who suffers and dies for his honesty, for in this country, "The public is very indulgent on this point, because it considers a failure what it really is nineteen times out of twenty, a misfortune and not a fraud. The bankrupt is looked upon as a wounded soldier, who is to be treated with sympathy, and not with contempt."[58]

This sympathy was expressed several times. Named postmaster at New Salem, Lincoln continued to play a key role in the community despite his financial situation. He received—and read—the newspapers, read their mail to the illiterates, was generous with the public's money by franking his friends' letters. The salary for this job was, however, quite low, and Lincoln was forced to take the road back to the fields to work the land, to husk corn, to split rails. He naturally was pleased when John Calhoun, the county surveyor, offered him a job as his assistant. Modestly, Lincoln explained that "He accepted, procured a compass and chain, studied Flint, and Gibson a little, and went at it. This procured bread, and kept soul and body together."[59]

As was true for the postmaster's job, Lincoln owed this promotion to his small store of scholarship. But he had to work very hard this time to learn the principles of plane geometry and trigonometry, as well as arithmetic, logarithms, decimal fractions, and finding square roots, all essential to surveying and measuring surfaces.

However, this science had nothing ethereal about it, and if Lincoln read Gibson "a little," he surely did not miss the first sentences of the preface: "The word geometry imports no more than to measure the earth, or to measure land." The origins can be found, moreover, in Egypt, where the landed proprietors were compelled to find a system to distinguish the "limits of their respective grounds" when the Nile floods erased the landmarks and boundary markers.[60] It was an uncanny analogy to the prairie of Sangamon County, always flooded in the springtime but also an irresistible appeal to reason, the mother of justice against the iniquitous disorder of the landed tenure of the South. On these grounds it surely held an attraction for Lincoln, whose family had suffered from that plague. According to Scripture, Moses brought back geometry from Pharaonic Egypt, a tribute of vice to virtue. What new Moses would bring the law of geometry to the south of Cairo, that town in the southernmost tip of Illinois, popularly called "Egypt"?

The logical rigor of Lincoln's thought owes a great deal to mathematics, which he began to learn because of surveying and which he continued to study into the 1850s, mastering Euclid's propositions while on the "circuit."[61] The notion of boundaries or barriers, of separation between categories, was a major element in a rigorous and often rigid thinking, and it went together perfectly with a lawyerly mode of thinking to produce the kind of reasoning that Lincoln held on the Mexican War, the Kansas-Nebraska Act, or even the terms of the Emancipation Proclamation.

There were, however, more immediate and more down-to-earth consequences of Lincoln's new relationship to the countryside surrounding New Salem. He had to leave his urban sedentary position to go on-site. He thus became acquainted with the whole county and became a character as well known as a Calhoun or a Cartwright. Armed at first, so the story goes, with only vine shoots then later with a chain, Abraham Lincoln surveyed the prairie with his grasshopper legs. New and more intimate, more cordial, relations developed between Lincoln and farmers. For example, he surveyed eighty acres located six miles north of New Salem for Russell Godbey and received from him as payment two buckskins that Hannah Armstrong sewed into trousers. Lincoln lent his horse to a man named Chandler so that he could get ahead of a wicked speculator and beat him to the purchase of a neighboring piece of land.[62]

Despite the illustrious example of Washington, he would be an honest surveyor, content to collect his $3 a day and not venturing to speculate, although his position—along with that of receiver of the Land Office—was the best vantage point for making good deals. His friends paid tribute to his honesty when his horse and surveying instruments were seized to pay his debts: a farmer, James Short, bought them back for him.[63] Lincoln would remember for a long time this difficult period, and his attitude toward debtors would be marked by it. Why deprive the worker of the means of repaying his debt?

Lincoln was a good surveyor. Of course, one cannot completely believe Herndon's story that Lincoln's measuring was so precise that he rediscovered an old buried boundary marker. But the results remain. Lincoln surveyed three roads, three school sections, a dozen farm properties measuring from four to 160 acres, and five towns: Petersburg, New Boston, Albany, Huron, and Bath. In 1858 in the course of his election campaign he would remind the inhabitants of Bath of his work there.[64]

In his subsequent career, especially when he became a lawyer, his knowledge of this field would be invaluable. For example, out of the eight pages of a bill in chancery written by Lincoln, Logan, Stuart, and Baker in 1837, only six and a half lines are in Lincoln's hand, those describing the parcel in dispute. Although he might have made some errors, his reputation was sufficiently established that in 1859 he was asked to give an opinion on the exact meaning of the law of February 11,

1805 concerning the legal procedure for dividing sections into quarters.[65] These beginnings of specialization are, as we shall see, of great interest in the study of Lincoln's career as a lawyer.

Postmaster, surveyor, was Lincoln satisfied? No, he aspired to something else. Politics attracted him, the lofty politics that was the subject of the newspapers Lincoln spent hours reading when he was at the post office: the *Sangamo Journal* from Springfield, the Louisville *Journal,* the St. Louis *Republican,* the Cincinnati *Gazette.*[66] Real Life was in Washington, or at least in Vandalia, the capital of Illinois. The speeches of Clay, Webster, Adams, and Calhoun took up most of the space in the papers, and no room remained for local life. One paper informed its readers of the weather conditions during the winter of the deep snow only because it had to offer excuses for not having appeared for a month.[67] It was easier to find in the newspapers "an account of the hop yield in Silesia than of the wheat crop in Illinois."[68] Access to the outside world interested a young man who had read Paine and Volney and associated with Freemasons. And then, as he confessed to Herndon one evening in Washington in January 1862, there was "the voracious desire of office—this struggle to live without toil—work and labor . . . from which I am not free myself."[69]

What place was there in this scheme for the inhabitants of New Salem who "believed in him as a man of their own blood, their own spiritual accent?"[70] They elected him, and he served them to the best of his ability before being imperceptibly drawn up toward so-called superior spheres. In 1834, Lincoln was elected to the Illinois general assembly as one of the representatives from Sangamon County. He had found a way out of his dilemma, a way that only the American frontier offered at that time, where population grew rapidly, more quickly than the number of "talents." In three years, Lincoln had become a person of some consequence. In three more years, he would leave New Salem— which was dying—for Springfield, the new capital. More than a chapter in Lincoln's life was closing. It was the end of an era.

4

THE RISE AND FALL OF A PROVINCIAL POLITICIAN, 1834-42

To understand the events occurring in the 1830s and 1840s and the role Lincoln played in them, it is important to review quickly the situation in Illinois relative to the distribution of land, the world of work, and more generally the economy of the state around 1835, just before the tremendous wave of public works and agricultural development that began in 1836.[1]

To begin with, the population was growing steadily: 157,000 in 1830, 270,000 in 1835, 476,000 in 1840. Sangamon and Morgan counties each had nearly twenty thousand inhabitants. Similarly, the sale of public lands was climbing, reaching an average of 260,000 acres a year for the six years between 1829 and 1834, as opposed to an average of 65,000 for the six preceding years (1823-28).[2]

In the hope of attracting new settlers, Illinois did not tax land occupied by squatters nor public lands during the first five years after their purchase. On the other hand, land taxes were extremely heavy for nonresident speculators (eight times higher than in Kentucky, for example). In 1832, this levy constituted 93 percent of the state's income.[3] Land speculators had been particularly drawn to the Illinois Military Tract, an immense and rich expanse of prairie between the Illinois and the Mississippi rivers that Congress allocated for those who fought against England during the War of 1812. It generously dispensed "Military Bounty Warrants" or "Land Warrants," in other words, land reserved for veterans, on condition that they registered or located a claim for it. Usually, the veterans did not take advantage of this opportunity and sold their rights at very low prices to speculators, who were thus able to acquire large quantities of fertile land for a few cents.

However, after 1832, speculation by nonresidents began to decline, and in 1836 only 10 percent of Illinois's revenue came from taxing nonresidents. One cause for this decline was that speculators had found a way around the tax law by transferring land to residents—this was, after all, the aim of the measure. Furthermore, many of them went bankrupt back in the East. In the winter of 1833–34, the contraction of credit caused by the struggle between Jackson and the Bank of the United States had affected the stockmarket, and many speculators were hurt.

The squatters' situation was difficult, because when commercial agriculture began to make its appearance farmers were forced into debt. But squatters could not mortgage their land, because they did not own it. In order to buy materials or seeds or to consider buying their farms, they had to resort to the local sharks, who, by an ingenious maneuver, evaded the law on usury (which imposed a legal maximum of 12 percent interest). The squatter sold his preemption claim to the loan shark, who bought the land and then sold it back to the squatter for a higher price on credit (12 percent). By this means, the real cost of the money could reach as much as 28 percent.[4]

Understanding the realities of land purchase in Illinois can help to clarify one of Lincoln's statements that has long puzzled biographers. In the last part of his "Communication to the People of Sangamo County" of 1832, the young candidate for the legislature considered a current question, "the practice of loaning money at exorbitant rates of interest." After denouncing the evils of usury as a tax on the great mass of the people to the benefit of a few rich men, Lincoln declared himself in favor of a law limiting the legally applicable interest rate and concluded: "In cases of extreme necessity there could always be means found to cheat the law, while in all other cases it would have its intended effect."[5]

It would be impossible to mention here the multiplicity of glosses on this question, inspired by attempts to reconcile this episode with the image of the exemplary lawyer, defender of justice and right, with "Honest Abe," who became legendary by returning to a client a few cents in change that he had inadvertently kept while he was minding store in New Salem. No one has previously connected this statement to the fundamental question for a farmer: how to get money to purchase his land. To avoid losing the land he occupied, a squatter might be forced to pay usurious rates to borrow money to acquire the land from the government rather than see it sold at public auction to the highest bidder.

Faced with the greediness of speculators and the difficulty of obtaining credit, groups of squatters in the north of the state organized "claims associations" to defend the settlers' right of preemption and to prevent, by force if necessary, speculators from acquiring their lands at auction sales. Local juries recognized a right of self-defense for the squatter who knocked down and threw out of the office the buyer of the piece of land that he was cultivating.[6]

But we would be lacking in discernment to see in the agricultural population of Illinois only two categories, the squatter who became (or failed to become) a small (or middling) proprietor and the large speculator. An entire category of people of modest means with a small amount of capital arrived by wagon. Some came alone, like those that Dickens encountered in the middle of the "rank unseemly growth" animated by "the perpetual chorus of frogs": "Here and there, and frequently too, we encountered a solitary broken-down waggon, full of some new settler's goods . . . deep in the mire; the axle-tree broken; a wheel lying idly by its side; the man gone miles away, to look for assistance; the woman seated among their wandering household goods with a baby at her breast, a picture of forlorn, dejected patience."[7]

Others, more prudent, chose to arrive in groups, like that caravan of fifty-two New Englanders that reached Sangamon County in 1833.[8] Some of these new arrivals brought more sumptuous baggage, and some men had as their only luggage a bill of exchange. For, as Stephen A. Douglas wrote home to his family back in the East when he reached Illinois in 1833, the "Garden of the World" was a paradise for those who arrived with capital. One could make four times as much there by investing money judiciously as by working to increase it in New York.[9] Thus, by speculating, working the land, trading and lending money, renting out and leasing land, quite a middle class began to develop in Illinois.

Little by little, the northern part of the state became populated, and the prairie was plowed. The first elements appeared of the movement that would tip Illinois's orientation toward the north and the east. The upper Mississippi Valley experienced an enormous growth, and, except for the small error of timing, merely later than he had foreseen, Calvin Colton in 1832 prophesied correctly the future of the region and of Lincoln himself: "In twenty years, the bulk of the nation will be there; in half a century, the *nation* will be there."[10] The first signs of industrialization could already be discerned. Steam was replacing hydraulic power in some mills and sawmills. Vandalia boasted a steam-powered sawmill.[11]

Development remained extremely unequal, however. The first rats that immigrated from the East Coast encountered the last cougars in the southwestern part of the state. Cholera, which left India in 1817, reached the Mississippi in October 1832, while the lack of penitentiaries meant criminals were being punished in the Asian manner by the whip. Thus in Carrollton in that year, a horse thief publicly received thirty lashes with a rawhide, a crop of twisted untanned leather that raised blisters on the skin. While free Negroes were still being kidnapped and Illinois's congressional delegation was voting for the "gag rule," which forbade discussion of petitions calling for the abolition of slavery, the first abolition societies were being organized in the north and the east of the state in 1835.[12]

Thus, more than ever, the frontier in the years 1834–36 was changing, open to powerful and diverse influences. There was room for an impoverished and ambitious young man in a political class which, as we will see, was also in full ferment.

THE FARMER AND THE POLITICIAN

politicians; a set of men who have interests aside from the interests of the people, and who, to say the most of them, are, taken as a mass, at least one long step removed from honest men. I say this with the greater freedom because, being a politician myself, none can regard it as personal.[13]

Obviously, the beginnings of a political career disrupted a man's relationships with his neighbors who were farmers and changed his way of envisioning political issues such as land law and apportionment. In this sense, as we shall see, the politician had interests different from, and sometimes in opposition to, those of his fellow citizens. However, a majority of the representatives in the Illinois legislature identified closely with the views and preoccupations of the farmers who elected them, for they were themselves farmers on either a small or a large scale.[14] Indeed, American farmers—and they are not the only ones— have always tended to seek models and leaders among the richest members of their group. The phenomenon was especially marked in the United States inasmuch as no nobility existed and therefore the separation between small and large landowners could be viewed as temporary. Thus, among the Whig, Democratic, and Republican leaders could be found large landowners who enjoyed the admiring and respectful confidence of men of modest means. In the same way, the cattle kings and estate holders at the end of the century managed to control the direction taken by the Granger and populist movements in rural areas, preventing their joining with the labor movement.

Understanding these ties is indispensable for dealing with Lincoln's early political career for two reasons. Because of his distance from the preoccupations and interests—but not the realities—of the agricultural world, Lincoln tended more and more to demonstrate in his political actions the interests peculiar to a politician. For the same reason, and more important, he would find elsewhere the interests—both financial and intellectual—that would motivate his political commitment. This double orientation expressed itself in the choice made in 1836–37 of a specific profession that we will study in detail separately, that of a lawyer.

However, Lincoln's transformation did not begin in 1834. He campaigned then on his reputation as an honest man and jolly fellow. Both Whigs and Democrats voted for him. He earned votes by mowing wheat faster than his electors, and the number of hands he shook amounted to more than the number of words that he spoke. He continued to draw up abstracts as a surveyor until 1836, and he remained postmaster at New Salem until 1835. He still did favors for his neighbors, writing letters to straighten out their real estate affairs, for example. Above all, he still lived in New Salem, where he enjoyed the presence of numerous friends and was noted for his kindness.[15]

The Beginnings of a Career: From Jackson to Clay

Arriving in Vandalia, the capital of the state, with $200 that he had borrowed so that he could make a good impression, Lincoln had a nice suit made so that he could show himself worthy of the position that everybody agreed was the peak of ambition for the average Illinoisan. He looked more like a farmer in his Sunday clothes, and his "very countrified" bearing might lead one to believe that he was as much a farmer turned representative as he was a representative of the farmers' interest.[16]

When he took his place in the capitol at Vandalia, amid the rubble that fell from the ceiling when someone spoke too loudly, in the middle of cigar smoke and jets of saliva from the tobacco-chewers, he discovered a "turbulent political arena." The Democratic and Whig parties were in complete upheaval. The Whigs were barely organized, whereas the Democrats were divided between opponents and supporters of Van Buren. Lincoln himself, although on the whole a Whig, voted for Democrats several times.[17] Before all other concerns, the legislators were the relentless defenders of private interests: "Almost everything there was done from personal motives. Special legislation for the benefit of friends occupied members, and diverted their attention from such measures as were for the general benefit."[18] To recall the opinion of a former representative, Peter Cartwright: "But I say, without any desire to speak evil of the rulers of the people, I found a great deal of corruption in our legislature; and I found that almost every measure had to be carried by a corrupt bargain and sale; which should cause every honest man to blush for his country!"[19]

Lobbies, local interests, and political adventurers reigned supreme. Everybody revered Jackson in one way or another. Clay, still "Harry of the West," enjoyed a huge popularity. What was the difference between the two parties? The poorly organized Whigs favored the Bank of the United States, advocated a high protective tariff to promote industry, and called for distribution to the states of revenue raised by the sale of public lands to finance internal improvements. The divided Democrats regrouped behind the federal administration and opposed those projects. They espoused free trade, proposed guaranteeing the rights of squatters through preemption, and wanted to abolish the national bank, whose power served the manufacturing East, threatened the South, and disrupted the nation itself.

Lincoln, guided by John T. Stuart, gradually lined up with the Illinois Whigs. At first the party was comprised of varied tendencies, and its sociological contours before the years 1836–37 are difficult to draw precisely. At first, until 1834, it recruited among anti-Jacksonians in the southern part of the state. But during the same period, it also served as the framework in which Yankee anti-slavery advocates from the northern part of the state (who would dominate the party after 1832) were becoming organized. It remained nonetheless a rather loose collection of Van Buren opponents, and the boundaries were so poorly drawn that elections to some important posts (governors and congressmen, for example) produced extremely contradictory results, with some persons voting for candidates of both parties at the same election. Three factors came to characterize the core of the Whig party, which became consolidated during the 1840s following the example of the Democratic party reorganized by Douglas: (1) the predominance of sectional interests (the north, support for the Illinois and Michigan Canal); (2) rejection of slavery extension and its moral condemnation; and (3) the connections of the leaders of the Whig party and of the Illinois state bank to eastern capitalists and financiers.[20]

Lincoln's development from 1834 to 1837, when he emerged as a Whig leader, exactly paralleled his changing attitude toward his constituency. In the first phase, from 1834 to 1836, Lincoln demonstrated all the characteristics of a representative of farmers in the Jacksonian mold, with only a few exceptions.

During his first term, his legislative activity reflected interests and problems typical of the rural area he represented. He voted for a bonus for killing wolves and in favor of organizing agricultural societies; he drafted proposed legislation concerning abandoned animals and cattle branding; and he played an active role in road construction and defended the private interests of his constituents.[21]

On several occasions he took a clear stand in favor of issues typical of the Jacksonian movement. He voted for measures that favored the interests of squatters and of people of modest means in towns and in the countryside: He voted against taxing federal lands during the five years following their sale (December 6, 1834); he voted for extending the right of preemption and lowering the price of public lands (January 1835); he offered an amendment to the 1829 law on insolvent debtors that would accelerate the procedure by which they could seek relief (December 1835);[22] and he voted against the "Little Bull Law" (an important vote because had he adopted the opposite standpoint the odds are that his political career would have ended then). Eager to protect their purebred cattle from the libertine incursions of native bulls (animals that were thinner and smaller than anywhere else in the United States), rich cattle breeders who were beginning to lay the bases of their dominance in Illinois persuaded the legislature to pass a law stating that "no bull over one year old shall be permitted to run at large out of enclosure." The fines imposed on offenders were paid to the owners of the "three best bulls, the three best cows, and the three best heifers" in the county.[23] The law therefore forced small farmers owning only a few head of ordinary cattle to subsidize the big cattlemen, either by paying them fines or by being responsible for the construction of fences—necessarily rather vast—to graze their sole bull so that the "best cows" of the breeders might wander with impunity in the neighboring prairie and, if need be, in the neighboring cornfield. As for the stockbreeders, they had in any case isolated their reproducing males to guarantee the selection of pure breeds.

Modest farmers reacted violently to this unfair law, and the political landscape of the 1836–38 legislature was completely changed by the elimination in the 1836 elections of almost all the legislators who had voted for this law. Lincoln's position on this point was even more interesting because the changing of legislative personnel in 1836 would allow him to play a prominent role. It is, on the other hand, quite suggestive in light of the ties that would soon bind Lincoln to the cattle kings.

Under these conditions, how did Lincoln's Whiggism manifest itself during his first term? In what ways did he demonstrate concern for questions other than those favoring the interests of the agricultural district he represented? The two questions are related.

As early as the first session (January 10, 1835), at the moment that he was voting for the preemption proposal, Lincoln offered a resolution favoring distribution of federal lands (on the model of Clay's). This idea should be compared to the proposal made by Governor Ninian Edwards of Illinois during his farewell message of December 7, 1830, which had provoked a lively reaction. He had declared that all public lands were by law the property of the states in which they were located.[24]

At the same time, Lincoln voted in favor of incorporating the Bank of the State of Illinois at Springfield, a basically Whig concern tied to eastern financiers and land speculators. An amendment he presented in the next session (December 22, 1835) to obligate the bank to present an annual report on the state of its finances and on "all lands then owned by the same, and the amount for which such lands have been taken" did not pass. Subsequent events proved that such a requirement would have been totally inadequate to verify that the bank was operating legally, or to untangle the web of land speculations that it organized to such an extent that it earned the nickname of "the Octopus" well before another Illinoisan, Frank Norris, told the story of the pillage of agriculture by the other modern hydra, the railroad.[25]

Finally, he took a position in favor of the Illinois and Michigan Canal, which would enable Chicago to surpass St. Louis as the port of embarkation for Illinois agricultural produce.[26]

These last two points were indicative of the great storm that would shake the West in the following years and give a new stamp to Lincoln's politics: the internal improvement mania and its consequence, the most unbridled land speculation. When Lincoln presented, in the name of the committee on public accounts and expenditures, a proposed budget of $90,000 for the year 1836, and when he campaigned by stressing his contributions to balancing the state's finances, few people could have suspected that he would play a prominent role in the mania that would take Illinois to bankruptcy and put it in debt for $15 million.[27]

At the time Lincoln resumed campaigning in 1836, he had been receiving a good salary as a representative for two years, rounded out by surveying and postal earnings. He had been paid in cash, a commodity that would soon be rare (except among government officials) because of the crisis that struck in 1837 and hit Ilinois, then in the midst of an immense program of public works, especially hard.[28]

The Internal Improvements Scheme

The idea of furnishing Illinois with a network of railroads and canals derived from the necessity of developing commercial agriculture to insure a return on the capital that was now being invested in the state's agriculture. Moreover, it corresponded with the desire of eastern and European industrialists to create a market for their production of rolling stock, rails, and bridges; with the appetite of financiers from New York, Boston, and London that could be satisfied only by putting into motion large masses of capital; and, finally, with the desire of land speculators to increase gains on land they owned and create new possibilities for themselves.

The idea can be best understood in a larger framework of a speculative and inflationist period on the national level, which affected all levels of propertied classes no matter how paltry their possessions. In Illinois, the idea of criss-crossing the state with canals and railroads was greeted with enthusiasm by the great majority of farmers, who easily imagined the growth in earnings that would result from increased prices when their harvest was sold in urban markets. The farmers and their representatives had already been contemplating this grandiose scheme. Then, in 1836, a general climate of euphoria, an envisioned liquidation of the state's public debt, and pressure from eastern interests all contributed to create conditions for its fulfillment.

Lincoln conducted a very different campaign in 1836 than in 1834. He no longer merely shook hands and harvested wheat, but rather went from farm to farm, from hamlet to hamlet, unrolling the magical panorama of the railroad future, and everywhere the good news was greeted enthusiastically, whether preached by Whigs or Democrats. The Whigs, however, were the most fervent, and led by Lincoln they carried Sangamon County resoundingly. In 1832 Sangamon had elected three Democrats (among whom was Cartwright) and one Whig (Stuart); in 1834, two Whigs (Lincoln and Stuart, who came in second and fourth) and two Democrats. Population growth and Lincoln's hard work meant that in 1836 seven Whigs (with Lincoln obtaining the highest number of votes) now monopolized the representation in the lower house. If to these were added the two Whig senators from the county, one got the "Long Nine" of the Sangamon delegation, so named for their tallness, with Lincoln towering over them from his height of six feet four inches.[29]

Lincoln had defined his program clearly during the campaign. He favored the distribution of federal lands to the states in which they were located in order "to dig canals and construct rail roads, without borrowing money and paying interest on it."[30] Land distribution appeared to be merely a means of developing internal improvements, and we shall see that the desire to reach that goal would take precedence over all other considerations.

At the beginning of the 1836–37 session (which would be followed by a special session in July 1837 and a regular session in 1838–39, all of these constituting his second term), Lincoln faced four problems: the program of internal improvements, the situation of the Bank of the State of Illinois at Springfield, the possible transfer of the capital from Vandalia to Springfield (which he favored), and the division of Sangamon County.

The first question, that of internal improvements, must be considered from several points of view: facts and dates as well as his attitude. Historians and biographers have long repeated the opinions of the Democratic governor and historian Thomas Ford, of Robert L. Wilson (one of the Long Nine), and of W. L. D. Ewing (representative of Effingham County and of Fayette County, where Vandalia was located). They believed that the Sangamon delegation, under Lincoln's leadership, had bargained their support for all the internal improvement schemes put forward by various counties in exchange for the representatives of those counties supporting their sole aim: the transfer of the capital from Vandalia to Springfield. The effect of such an argument later was to free Lincoln from the responsibility of having supported internal improvements *as such,* therefore concealing the reality of his economic doctrine by presenting him as a man of the West, astutely practicing parliamentary log-rolling.

But the work of John H. Krenkel showed that the Long Nine did not play a specific role, as a group, in the adoption of internal improvements projects. In fact, as Paul Simon demonstrated, their bargaining remained within the limits of parliamentary tradition, the nine from Sangamon did not always vote as a block, and Lincoln could not therefore have orchestrated their action. As a matter of fact, opponents of internal improvements tended more than others to vote in favor of Springfield. This can be easily understood, given the fact that the plan for internal improvements in southern Illinois was completely artificial and intended only to get the southerners' support for the Illinois and Michigan Canal. Moving the capital from Vandalia to Springfield, on the other hand, was to the advantage of the northern part of the state. There were northerners who did not agree with the deal that appropriated money for southern internal improvements. They, of course, voted for the transfer of the capital to Springfield. The real bargaining, then, concerned southern support for the canal in exchange for the north's support for internal improvements in the south. The question of transferring the capital was still open.[31]

Under these circumstances, Lincoln's attitude of unswerving support for internal improvements demonstrated his attachment to the canal. Elements of Whig economic doctrine, such as state debt opening the way to land distribution, strengthening of the bank, and growth of federal intervention and influence ("consolidation") can perhaps also be seen in his stand.

His vision at this time was explained most clearly by Lincoln himself when he confided to his friend Speed that his goal was to become "the DeWitt Clinton of Illinois."[32] The plan for the Illinois and Michigan Canal and for its structure was, moreover, inspired by the desire to create something as grand and wonderful as the Erie Canal, and the enterprise would have doubtless proved equally successful had Illinois not gotten into difficulties by "adding to the Michigan canal other enterprises completely beyond its capacities."[33]

The second problem Lincoln confronted concerned the State Bank at Springfield, which had already begun to furnish ample credit for all sorts of speculations. It is impossible to enter into the details of the complex financial operations that the Springfield bank, continuing the practices of its predecessors, undertook. Ties among political cliques, local interests, and use of state funds created an interlocking network, the pattern of which was ultimately fashioned by large eastern financiers. In the face of still rather vague attacks launched by Democrats, Lincoln defended without difficulty the interests of the state bank by preventing a possible inquiry. Indeed, most of the work of defense was done in May 1837, when Governor Joseph Duncan (a Whig) permitted the bank to suspend payment in specie.[34]

An imputation of embezzlement gave Lincoln the opportunity to demonstrate his attachment to this Whig institution, this ersatz Bank of the United States for the Prairie State. The arguments that he presented were quite demagogic. Why should the legislature be concerned with swindles that certain "capitalists" (Whigs in this case, but Lincoln did not mention it) perpetrated against other capitalists (Democrats in this case)? Those who considered themselves wronged and "whose money is a burden to them" were free to "pay the costs of a suit." Legislative interference would promote a "mobocratic spirit" and would serve only the interests of politicians. Indeed, Lincoln argued, public interest was not at stake because this institution provided bank credit, which had benefited farmers by leading to a doubling of agricultural prices, while artisans and workers also benefited by receiving wages in "a sound circulating medium."[35]

Faced with the congenital distrust for banks felt by ordinary people in both town and country, which Jacksonianism was able to use and redirect, Lincoln presented an argument equally convincing for these same people of easy money and sound money. This subject will be considered again in its relation to land speculation; for the moment the point to be noted is the continuity of Lincoln's attitude in this area.

Lincoln's third objective was to secure the transfer of the capital to Springfield. In 1819 Vandalia had been chosen provisional capital for the years from 1820 to 1840. That decision now either had to be made permanent or annulled. After all sorts of incidents, Springfield won out over its rivals. It was an immense success for Lincoln because Springfield, the county seat of Sangamon County and a Whig bastion, was also the site of the state bank and of Stuart's law office, which Lincoln was about to join. From now on, Lincoln's life and career centered on this town in the heart of the richest agricultural county in Illinois. However, it should be noted that a referendum in 1834 showed an overwhelming majority in the New Salem district favored the transfer to Springfield (250 out of 256). Without knowing it, the inhabitants of the village were thus preparing the break between themselves and their hero, which was completed by the division of Sangamon County, the fourth question that Lincoln had to settle.[36]

Several factors coalesced to render inevitable the division of Sangamon County. First, the growth and the spread of population made it more and more difficult for distant farmers, increasingly being brought out of their isolation by commercial development, to reach the county seat at Springfield. At the same time, "town promoters," land speculators who specialized in town lots, were exerting pressure for division so that their creation could become the seat of a new county. Lincoln's aim was to bring about a subtle balance between the desires and pretensions of both sides but above all to preserve as long as possible the unity of the Whig county (which he managed to do from December 1836 until February 1839) and to bring about a final division that was as favorable as possible for his party.

His interests as a politician did, in fact, win out over the interest of farmers and those of speculators although he was forced into compromise. Proof of this was the fierce battle of amendments, petitions, and maneuvers that put him in opposition to Douglas, who was playing the same game on behalf of the Democrats. Lincoln was justified in responding to a friend, angered by the law on division that he got passed in February 1839, that he had not sold out to land speculators John Taylor (a Petersburg promoter), John Wright, and George W. Turley (Mt. Pulaski promoters). He had only compromised. After long explanations, he concluded that he ought not to be blamed "for being unable to accomplish impossibilities."[37]

Lincoln was particularly satisfied with the accomplishments of the 1836–37 sessions. He thus participated in the general euphoria of these wild years when speculation was raging.

The Boom Years of Speculation

A wild wind was blowing on Illinois: "The year 1836 will long be remembered. Speculation was then in its zenith; its unregulated spirit filled every bosom, possessed every class in the community, controlled every avenue to business, monopolized every species of influence, absorbed the whole public attention; and, for a while, subjected to its control all that was valuable, all that was desirable here on earth."[38]

All, and particularly, the land. The prospect of internal improvements was used to increase the value of private land and to attract toward Illinois thousands of settlers lured by the prospect of buying federal land at $1.25 an acre, although they might end up buying from speculators after being disappointed to find that the best land had already been taken. Advertising brochures disguised as guides for emigrants from the East painted in glowing colors the riches of Illinois: "No state in the Union possesses such facilities for intercommunication by canals and railways, at so cheap a rate, and which can be so equally distributed to its population." Nothing better for agriculture or commerce could be found in all the west than the "delightful region" of the Illinois Military Tract, where land could be bought for $1.25 an acre.[39]

This panegyric is even spicier—except for the hundreds of suckers who believed it—considering that at that date not one inch of rail had been laid in Illinois and that lands around Quincy (center of the Illinois Military Tract), monopolized by speculators, would soon be selling for $10 an acre.[40] The author of the guide owned 124,000 acres.[41]

Lincoln himself was infected by the speculative fever, and his first real estate transactions dated from this period. His income had increased because the legislators had granted themselves a raise of 33 percent for the 1836 and 1837 sessions. Lincoln received $510 from that source while also beginning to record some modest earnings as a lawyer. His financial situation nonetheless remained poor, and the only luxury he permitted himself consisted in a few speculative transactions.

His first speculation focused on the region around Huron (in the present-day Menard County) and was tied to the proposed digging of the Beardstown Canal in the Sangamon Valley. Several episodes of Lincoln's life came together on this occasion. The canal was actually a variation of the plan that he put forward in his "Communication" of 1832. In addition, he had already obtained a certain number of lots in Huron in payment for surveying work (all traces of which have been lost). Finally, he was the reporter of the bill to authorize the building of the canal, which passed in the 1835–36 session. On March 16, 1836, once the bill had been passed, Lincoln bought forty-seven acres of land near Huron for the sum of $58.75, more than one-third of his salary as legislator for that session ($162). Unfortunately for him, the canal met the fate of many projects of the time, not a single shovelful of dirt was dug.

In May 1837, when this result became obvious, Lincoln sold half of the parcel for $30. He would sell the other half only in 1848, for a profit of $20. Without counting the 1837 transaction (which, considering transfer costs, taxes, and opportunity cost, came out even), the profit on the sums invested from 1837 to 1848 was less than 5 percent gross, 4 percent net, which falls exactly within the average (3–6 percent) for "tracts acquired just before depression set in and held for many years while settlers filtered slowly in and tax bills mounted." Unfortunately, it is impossible to ascertain whether Lincoln succeeded in renting his lands, but the decision to sell in 1848, at the moment when land taxes were being raised again, leads one to think that he had not. During this entire period, until around 1870, the return on a mortgage loan in the region was never less than 10 percent, and we will see that Lincoln, richer and more mature, would prefer this surer form for exploiting the riches of land and labor.[42]

The second speculation was more fortunate. Lincoln used another third of his salary ($50) to buy two town lots in Springfield on March 24, 1836. In February 1837, he succeeded in effecting the transfer of the state capital to that town. On April 2, 1837 (five days after his arrival in Springfield), he sold one of the lots for $75, an appreciation of 200 percent in one year.[43]

Thus Lincoln speculated like a politician, only on "sure things" and not counting on any event unless he instigated it. Lincoln demonstrated at that time great self-restraint despite his ferocious appetite for land (for tidy land, convertible into cash, and not for soil to be cultivated). This appetite led him to establish a contract with his client in the legal and political affair of *Anderson vs. Adams* stipulating that, in the event of success, lawyer's fees would be paid in kind by the transfer of a town lot in Springfield that was in contention in the case.[44]

This first series of real estate purchases ended in 1838 with the acquisition of two lots in Springfield (for $300), which would not be sold until the 1850s (in 1850 and 1853 for a total of $500). These purchases could more accurately be termed investments rather than speculations.[45]

THE 1837 CRASH AND ITS CONSEQUENCES

The collapse of land speculation in the West was an integral part of the Panic of 1837, which had features characteristic of all commercial crises including a slump in all merchandise, decreases in salaries and prices, and bankruptcies leading to further bankruptcies. Land speculation had, moreover, constituted one of the principal factors in this crisis.

In Illinois, the panic showed peculiar characteristics, and the history of its unfolding and the attempts to promote recovery were tied up with Lincoln's political activity between 1838 and 1842. The positions he adopted gradually brought about a complete divorce between the young legislator and the rural areas that he represented.

For the Illinois farmer, the crisis was translated first into a drop in agricultural prices. Their index (1825 equals 100) fell from 137.7 in 1836, to 134.6 in 1839, to 113.8 in 1840, to 79.4 in 1843. At that date, and for the first time since 1825, the index of agricultural prices fell below the general price index (80.3).[46]

Nevertheless, immigration continued, and the state had 476,000 inhabitants in 1840. The question of transferring a part of the tax burden to these new arrivals was taken up in the 1840s because Illinois was handicapped by the internal improvements plan imprudently adopted in 1837, which drained essential resources from a population in financial straits. Only in 1847–48, with the end of the tax exemption granted to buyers of public lands and the creation of a permanent poll tax, was the problem finally resolved. In 1838, the issue was formulated in the following way: Democrats favored an increase in taxes, Whigs favored federal involvement through a system of distribution of public lands. Lincoln's attitude in this period must be considered from two angles: his position toward distribution, which is part of a general philosophy of the use of the public domain, and his position on tax policy.

The Evolution of Lincoln's Thought on the Use of the Public Domain

We have seen that until 1836, Lincoln combined Jacksonian positions (preemption, for example) and western Whig positions (distribution) tied to what was then only the prospect of an internal improvements system. Faced with the debt problem ($600,000 of interest a year to be paid out of an annual revenue of $200,000), he adopted a much less ambiguous attitude and moved deliberately in the direction indicated by Clay.

As the reporter for the Committee on Finance in January 1839, he proposed a variation on the theme of distribution. The federal government would be asked to sell to Illinois all the public lands found there at a price of 25 cents an acre. Illinois, by reselling the lands at $1.25 an acre (the official price), could thus finance its debt as well as the debt entered into by this purchase. It would then be possible to solve the disastrous situation created by the internal improvements plan. The proposal was certainly just, for did not the program of public works, financed by the state of Illinois, increase the value of the public lands within the state? Archibald Williams, his lieutenant, the Whig from Quincy in Adams County, responded that it was merely a plan to enrich the state, which objection did not prevent its passage in the house and then in the senate with the support of the Democrats.[47]

The plan Lincoln presented deviated sufficiently from the Clay line to interest the Democrats because it was not directly linked to the tariff (the decrease in revenue for the federal government was not as sudden nor as severe as in the plan for distribution pure and simple because the lands were to be sold to the states), and it did not call into question New York's commercial politics nor Southern free-trade sentiment. This was, however, what made the plan unacceptable to the East. Lincoln was here joining John C. Calhoun, who had presented a similar proposal in the Senate, and he also asked Stuart to transmit the resolutions of the Illinois general assembly to the senator from South Carolina.[48] Neither Lincoln nor Calhoun (at that time a "nationalist") had in mind the situation of small American farmers or of eastern workers who believed land should belong first of all to those who worked it.

Lincoln henceforth was completely committed to the idea that public lands should serve exclusively to finance industrial and commercial development through the intermediary of public works. He made no further efforts to conciliate the interests of squatters, workers, and urban artisans who wanted cheap land or, if possible, free land with those of public works entrepreneurs, railroad companies, and large merchants (who wanted to appropriate the product of the sale of the lands in the form of contracts for equipment and commercial profits) or with those of large financial creditors of the states and the federal government (who did not want to watch placidly as the goods of their debtors were dissipated).

That is the explanation for the position Lincoln took in favor of high prices for public lands in the very midst of his speech in the house on his distribution plan. He observed how much low land prices encouraged speculation, alluding to the Military Tract. What conclusion would he draw? Had he decided to thwart the practice of grants of land titles to veterans? He was one of the warmest supporters of it. Was he going to introduce a homestead proposal as his colleague Dawson did—in vain—during Lincoln's absence on December 31, 1836? He remained reticent on that question until 1862.

He no longer favored graduation, the gradual lowering of the price of land after it was first put up for sale. Had he changed his mind on preemption? The question did not come up, but in the debates and votes in Congress after 1836, distribution and preemption were always totally opposed to each other. In 1838 he joined with the house majority in voting against a bill authorizing squatters to register preemption rights, even for improvements under $100, before a justice of the peace (more likely to be influenced than the people at the Land Office).[49]

His growing estrangement from the preoccupations of the lower classes of town and country was nowhere more in evidence—thanks to Douglas—than in his defense of the Springfield bank, now accused of speculating in pork, land, lead, and its own stock. Douglas, a land speculator corrupt to the marrow, who unscrupulously used his administrative positions (register of the Springfield Land Office) and his political ones (of which there were many) to make his fortune, reveled in every opportunity to denounce Lincoln for protecting with all his might the "Octopus."[50] After having managed to prevent any inquiry into the bank for a long time, Lincoln succeeded in having himself appointed to head the committee that was finally given that responsibility, and he delivered the report, pointing out several traditional misappropriations of funds by the state bank (purchase of stock with money on deposit), answering in a more or less convincing fashion the issues about pork and lead, and concluding: "The undersigned have not been able to asscertain [sic] that the bank has dealt or speculated in lands further than was absolutely necessary for the erection of her Banking houses."[51]

The people of Illinois knew that the governors of the bank (whom Lincoln called "the most respectable men in the State") included John Tillson, Jr., Winthrop Gilman, and others, all of whom made mortgage loans, seized, sold, and bought.[52] The small landowner threatened with seizure, the squatter who sold his clothes to keep his rights of preemption from falling into the hands of speculators, had trouble recognizing one of their own kind in Lincoln, now that the great dream of 1836 was translated into an increase in taxes, which Lincoln would play a leading role in bringing about.[53]

Lincoln and the Land Tax, 1838–40

If the Whigs were in general less ready than the Democrats to vote for increases (they pretended to count on distribution), Lincoln occupied too important a position (as an influential member of the Committee on Finance) to adopt a demagogic attitude.

Until 1839, the greatest part of revenues came from various sources (for example, rent of salt mines and taxation of nonresidents). Residents paid only a county tax, equivalent to five-thousandths of the declared value of their land, and at the end of five years a state tax of two-thousandths on the same base. This declared value depended on the location of the property and on the good will of the sheriff. It amounted to $2 an acre for the best lands and $1.50 for the others. Thus, a small family farm of a viable size (eighty acres) and of mediocre quality was subject to an annual tax of 84 cents. To that must be added a poll tax of three days of labor a year (estimated at 75 cents in 1839), imposed on white males from eighteen to sixty years old, payable in cash or in kind, and exceptional surtaxes that tended to become permanent under various forms but that did not exceed two-thirds of county taxes.

Just as they could not guarantee sure profits to themselves, land speculators were incapable of furnishing regular income to the state because it was precisely speculators who were most affected by the crisis. Between 1834 and 1836, many lands in the Military Tract had already been sold at tax sales, when speculators were unable to pay their taxes, and the phenomenon continued when the slump in land took hold.

Thus in 1839, even before the impact of interest due because of the public works plan and even before the financial collapse of the state, Illinois's revenue needed to be increased. The 1839 tax law would increase the product of the land tax by substituting for the old system of classes a real evaluation of the taxable property carried out by an assessor. The income from the land tax went from $90,000 between 1836 and 1838 to $125,000 between 1838 and 1840.[54]

Lincoln voted for this revenue law and explained it in a letter of March 1839. He asserted that this new way of calculating the tax base, because it took account of the real value of property, fell on the "wealthy few" rather than on the "many poor." We will soon see how accurate that was.[55]

It was already difficult to get a tax increase accepted, especially among people who "seemed to think there was something ignoble about paying taxes" and who, each according to his means, did all in their power to put their practice in line with their opinions. But it took a certain recklessness to inflict visits by tax assessors upon bold pioneers,

who had easy access to feathers, tar, and rails, in a free country and in
the nineteenth century to boot. The reactions against the assessors were
energetic. Would the legislators suffer the same fate? On April 13, 1830,
just after the session, Lincoln and his four Sangamon County friends,
who had voted for the offending text (two Whigs and two Democrats),
organized a public meeting to give information and justify their actions.[56]

Frontier society, thanks to the democracy of its institutions, could
absorb that first tax shock without too much damage. Richer men
bribed and pleaded, poorer ones coaxed and threatened. The sheriffs
clung to their jobs and tried to make everybody happy. But when the
financial collapse of 1840 occurred, the great constitutional principle of
equality in taxation was considered fully applicable. If at first rich
people were made to pay, now, to avoid strangling them completely, it
was necessary to make poor people pay. And having once determined to
make the poor pay, few scruples remained about exempting the rich.

The 1840–42 Bankruptcy and Its Consequences

The combination of the 1837 crisis and the immense costs of the
internal improvements system put Illinois in an untenable financial
position at the beginning of the 1840–41 session. The 6 percent bonds
that it issued for a total of $15 million fell to 48 percent of their face
value at the beginning of 1841, while Indiana 5 percent bonds, hardly
more brilliant, stood at 53 percent, and Ohio's 6 percent bonds were at
90 percent. The state bank had not made any payments since the spring
of 1840. Governor Thomas Carlin spent the summer trying to calm the
creditors in the City of London by sending representatives of his administration to England, and he sent pathetic letters, such as the one on
June 25, 1840, begging his agent to do his utmost to pay the interest due
in London on July 1![57]

Therefore, Lincoln, reelected with difficulty in 1840 (the last of the
five Whigs of the county), faced a genuine disaster at the opening of the
session. He had known since December 1838 that "his own course was
identified with the system." And he added, "We had gone too far to
recede, even if we were disposed to do so."[58] During the previous session,
he had again proposed that the state issue provisional certificates, or
scrip, to be used to pay for the work on the canal. Moreover, the task of
untangling the financial and real estate imbroglio that this caused
would fall in part to him in 1853, when he was appointed one of two
commissioners to investigate claims arising. He again implored the
representatives to work "to save something to the State, from the general
wreck."[59]

On February 26, 1841, he again proposed to issue $3 million in bonds to finish the canal, attracting a particularly harsh comment from a Democratic colleague, who transposed into "sucker" language a cutting remark that Jefferson, in his day, had hurled at Hamilton.

> We were already prostrated by debt, and that gentleman thought it would be for the interest of the State to go still deeper. . . . it reminded him of an anecdote, which he would relate. A drunkard in Arkansas took so much of the *cretur*, that he lost his reason and remained for some time in a state of insensibility. His wife tried every experiment to cure him; but it was of no avail, until a neighbor came to the house and recommended some *brandy toddy*. The insensible man rose at the word *toddy*, and said "that is the stuff."[60]

Thanks to Lincoln and his friends, the Michigan canal would be finished in 1848. It is today the only evidence of the 1837 plan. Already made obsolete by the railroad at the moment of its inauguration, it was nonetheless the determining factor in the replacement of St. Louis by Chicago as the port of embarkation for grain from the upper Mississippi Valley.

But Illinois in 1840–41 had to borrow to cover its expenses in the much shorter run. The interests on the debt had to be paid, and Lincoln proposed issuing new bonds (Illinois interest bonds), intended for paying the interest on the old ones (state bonds). The payment of the interest on the new bonds, and the eventual reimbursement of the principal (in 1865), would be accomplished thanks to a special allocation of new income for a fund called the Illinois Interest Fund, which would receive the revenue from the land tax on newly taxable lands (those that were exempt before 1840, for example, public lands sold in 1836). The overall tax burden would remain seventy-thousandths, but it would be apportioned differently: the state would receive thirty-thousandths instead of twenty, and the counties forty-thousandths instead of fifty. The budgetary effort was translated then into a decrease of public expenses and not by an increase in tax pressure. Thus the 1837 plan ended, when all was said and done, paradoxically, in a decline in the quality of public services.[61]

The prudence of this proposition can be understood when the general outcry raised by the reform of the tax base several months before is recalled. Any increase of the tax rates would have made the effects of that increase of the tax base by about one-third even more deeply felt. At the same time, the growth in county revenues that resulted could temporarily alleviate the financial difficulties resulting from the proposed transfer of resources.

After some debate, Lincoln reported a new bill on December 7, and this time it was impossible to cheat. The land tax was increased by one-thousandth, to be especially allocated to the Interest Fund. To combat the tendency of the sheriffs and their assessors to condone and to be lenient, the evaluation of taxable lands could not fall below $4 an acre.[62]

Such a plan for financial recovery showed that Lincoln's borrowing fervor was equaled only by his determination to repay debts in full. The idea of a repudiation made him shudder. He declared himself ready, irrespective of any tax solution, to vote "for the naked proposition, simply to pay the interest due."[63] In that way, at least, he would have been "the DeWitt Clinton of Illinois."

His finance law was finally adopted with only a few modifications (the floor on evaluations was set at $3 an acre). To return to the example of the small farm of eighty acres, it was now subject to a tax of $1.92 a year, or double the amount of 1839. In the decade between 1840 and 1850, the tax burden was increased continuously, and the state's credit definitely restored by the provision in the constitution (revised in 1848) of a land tax of two-thousandths, intended to pay off the debt, and a poll tax that especially targeted those of moderate means. It is impossible to guess the attitude Lincoln would have taken had he sat in the Illinois general assembly from 1842 to 1848, or in the 1848 convention. But we know that he declared he was "pleased" with the convention's decisions, in particular on the poll tax.[64] Michel Chevalier's praise was perhaps directed at Lincoln more than at anybody else: "To judge, indeed, by the votes of the legislature during the session which opened in the last days of 1840, the people of Illinois are enduring the consequences of their faults with resolution. Nothing has been neglected to insure that the debt is paid. Taxes have been increased by fifty percent."[65]

Nothing had been neglected, and yet they forgot to raise the tax paid by lawyers and legislators until the issue was put on the agenda in February 1841. Lincoln managed to arrange for lawyers to pay professional taxes only in the counties where they resided and nowhere else. One of his colleagues reduced their tax to $10. When one representative proposed imposing a $5 tax on legislators, Lincoln suggested "that there was a rule preventing them from voting in cases in which they were interested, and it appeared to him they were interested in this case (a laugh)."[66] No longer to be found here are the scruples that actuated Lincoln when he presented the law on finances "with great diffidence" because he "felt his share of the responsibility devolving upon us in the present crisis."[67]

LINCOLN, SQUATTERS, AND THE
"KINGS OF THE PRAIRIE"

When one has decided to make poor people pay and to exempt oneself, it is easy to be accused of serving the rich. Lincoln had already become famous by defending the right of the state bank to continue its operations after it had violated its charter and suspended specie payment. He had even been forced (while trying to prevent—in vain—a quorum that would put an end to this situation) to jump out of the window of the capitol in Springfield along with two Whig colleagues. There was something symbolic in this jump, which remained for Lincoln one of the bitterest memories of his life. This unorthodox exit from the Illinois house of representatives foreshadowed another one by the front door. The Sangamon Whigs did not want Lincoln to be their candidate in 1842. Another symbol was that Lincoln's two accomplices in this little adventure were Joe Gillespie, a lawyer, and Asahel Gridley, a land speculator. Lincoln would spend much more time with these two categories of men than with ordinary people during the 1840s, and he had already formed real ties with them in 1839–40.[68] Some of the positions taken by Lincoln cannot be explained except in relation to these ties, in particular those with land speculators. Such is the case, for example, of the monetary policy that he defended at this time.

Although Lincoln supported a rigorous tax policy, he also advocated a lax monetary policy founded on abundant credit. Such a point of view could not help but appeal to the inhabitants of the West, where liquid assets were always lacking because of its deficit trade balance with the East and because of the inroads made on the money supply by the purchase of public lands. This was the sense of a passage from his speech on the subtreasury in December 1839, in which he warned that a sudden contraction in the amount of money in circulation would result from forcing the subtreasury to keep the public money in its coffers. He added:

> The Land Offices in those States and Territories, as all know, form the great gulf by which all, or nearly all, the money in them, is swallowed up. When the quantity of money shall be reduced, and consequently every thing under individual control brought down in proportion, the price of those lands, being fixed by law, will remain as now. Of necessity, it will follow that the *produce* or *labor* that *now* raises money sufficient to purchase 80 acres, will *then* raise but sufficient to purchase 40. . . . Knowing, as I well do, the difficulty that poor people *now* encounter in procuring homes, I hesitate not to say, that when the price of the public lands shall

be doubled or trebled . . . it will be little less than impossible for them to procure those homes at all.[69]

The strength of this argument was undeniable. It corresponded to the realities of the fears of small farmers, to their desire to have cheap money to buy land. The close connection between the money question and the future of rural areas would find expression later in the green-back movement, which firmly supported the proliferation of the bills with green backs issued from 1862 on to cover the costs of the Civil War.

The characteristic feature of this move was that it united the interests of all landowners, whatever the size of their property, and those farmers who aspired to become landowners. Inflation was to the advantage of big speculators as well as of small farmers and squatters. And to the extent that the advantages that resulted were directly in proportion to the quantity of money at one's disposal, it benefited speculators infinitely more. Moreover, to put a brake on speculation, a circular had been issued in 1836 requiring purchasers of public lands to pay in specie. Whigs had opposed this measure and had denounced it as one of the causes of the Panic of 1837, although it had merely triggered it.

The logic of this position could not but benefit those with large quantities of paper money. This became clear in 1842, when collapsing prices made the situation of small farmers very difficult. In a series of "Letters from the Lost Townships" signed by a certain "Rebecca," Lincoln, Mary Todd, and several Whig friends violently criticized Governor Carlin's decision, published under the signature of State Auditor James Shields, to refuse taxpayers the right of paying their taxes with bills of the Bank of the State of Illinois at Springfield, bankrupt since February 1842, and whose notes were circulating at only half their face value.[70]

Lincoln no longer put forward the 1839 arguments on the purchase of federal lands. The preemption law of 1841 had, in fact, considerably satisfied those who wanted to acquire land without having the means of doing so. Rebecca stuck to ad hominem attacks (which earned Lincoln a duel with Shields) against officials paid in gold who wanted to bleed poor people to satisfy their own love of lucre. The position was completely demagogic. Lincoln was not asking for a reduction in the tax rate—which he had himself contributed in raising more than anybody else—or a moratorium to take account of the situation, but rather he proposed giving large, landed proprietors the possibility of fulfilling their tax obligations with worthless bills, thus aggravating the state's deficit. Such a measure, once more, could only go against small farmers, who always ended up bearing the brunt of the thousand and one ploys used by speculators to avoid paying their taxes.[71]

The Letters from the Lost Townships are extremely revealing of Lincoln's attitude toward the countryside in 1842. Attracted by the wealth and the brilliance of the clique gravitating around Mary Todd, he condoned the aristocratic pride of these Southerners who deeply scorned the Illinois rustics.[72] Anti-Irish racism, shameless demagoguery, and mocking imitation of the local speech were combined to make this series of anonymous letters a veritable manifesto against country people under cover of a denunciation of Jacksonianism.

Lincoln here inscribed himself in the long and still-living American tradition that used the mask of a rural man to deceive rustic minds more easily. How many letters in the American press—from the eighteenth century on—were modestly signed "Farmer" and actually presented the views of a lawyer, a speculator, or a politician? Wearing a mask usually means being up to no good, and Lincoln knew it. He began his speech to the Wisconsin State Agricultural Society in 1859 by declaring that he was not a farmer. The Letters from the Lost Townships are the sole example of this attitude on Lincoln's part.

Naturally, such attacks against Jacksonianism were possible only to the degree that the Democratic leaders were themselves on a social level closer to that of the Whig bankers than of the Jacksonian squatters. Shields was an easy target, as was a Democrat named Taylor, whom Lincoln interrupted one day in the middle of a diatribe against the Whig aristocracy by unbuttoning Taylor's coat to reveal a ruffled shirt, gold watch chains, and jewels. He then had an easy opportunity of recalling the modesty of his own origins, of which he made much at that time, as if they constituted a lifetime guarantee of his democratic spirit.[73]

After 1842, however, the humble Abraham Lincoln was no longer a big success in Sangamon County, where he could not obtain the necessary votes in his favor at the convention that met to name the delegates who were to participate in choosing the Whig candidate for Congress. Writing to Martin S. Morris, the delegate from Menard County to the district convention that was to make the decision, Lincoln expressed his pleasure that his old friends from New Salem (now located in the recently created Menard County) had not forgotten him and had declared in his favor. He added, "It would astonish if not amuse, the older citizens of your County who twelve years ago knew me a strange[r], friendless, uneducated, penniless boy, working on a flat boat—at ten dollars per month to learn that I have been put down here as the candidate of pride, wealth, and arristocratic [sic] family distinction."[74]

The assessment of Lincoln's political activity during the years of speculation and bankruptcy no doubt had a lot to do with the failures of his hopes in 1840 and 1844. It was not until 1846 that he managed to obtain the support of the Whigs of his district for a new elective office: representative to the Congress of the United States. Because of his particularly visible position at the head of the defenders of the Bank of the State of Illinois at Springfield, he could be convincingly attacked as a "Whig aristocrat" who increasingly kept his distance from common people, associating with bankers, lawyers, politicians, large landowners, and speculators.

An inventory of Lincoln's relationships among large landowners and speculators from 1840 on can highlight the most important of these. Indeed, it was during the campaign for Whig General Benjamin Harrison, the most demagogic campaign in the history of the frontier, for which Lincoln was the principal organizer in Illinois, that he became connected with the "kings of the prairie." The "hard cider and log cabin" campaign, which tried to present Harrison as a penniless pioneer of Spartan habits, grouped behind Lincoln most of the "kings" of Illinois: kings of cattle or corn, the architects of the "Little Bull Law," and opponents of preemption.

In the Harrison campaign were found old Whigs, such as Elijah Iles, Lincoln's captain during the war, a Clay supporter, and four-term state senator. This son of a sheriff, related to Davy Crockett on his mother's side, owned one-quarter of a section in Springfield, where he ran the American House, the biggest hotel in the state. Lincoln had worked for him as a surveyor and often had dealings with him as a lawyer.[75]

Another of Lincoln's old acquaintances was Levi Davis, a lawyer, Whig politician, and land speculator, whom Lincoln recommended to Governor Duncan for the post of auditor in 1835. A cousin of the lawyer and future large land speculator David Davis, he was always willing to help Lincoln obtain information on the financial status of a piece of land and its owner or to assist in a matter concerning the transfer of the capital to Springfield.[76] By 1834, Lincoln was also a close friend of Jesse Wilson Fell's, another large land speculator.[77]

The campaign committee included (besides Speed, Edward Baker, and Anson G. Henry) another close friend of Lincoln's, Richard F. Barrett, a doctor and land speculator, who had acquired 45,600 acres of land in Illinois during the 1830s by means of a settlers' bank he directed. In 1836, he bought in addition thirty thousand acres in Indiana. As fund commissioner since February 1, 1840, he was managing Illinois's debt, and he was also one of those who masterminded Springfield's rise.[78]

The Whigs of Sangamon County named James Nicholas Brown of Island Grove as one of five candidates they presented in the elections of 1840, and Brown was elected along with Lincoln to the Illinois house of representatives. Brown was one of the cattle kings of Sangamon County, where he owned 2,250 acres. A native of Kentucky, he arrived in Illinois in 1834, where he would soon become known as a pioneer in the improvement of cattle breeding, by importing short-horn cattle from England. Representing Sangamon County in the years 1840–44, 1846–48, and 1852–54, he was an important figure whose friendship Lincoln always cultivated.[79]

Another Whig elected in 1840, in McLean County, was Isaac Funk, the cattle king of Funk's Grove, which he had founded in 1824 and would become during the 1850s one of those model and very profitable farms popularly called "bonanza farms." Attracted, no doubt, by the democratic character of the Harrison campaign, two members of the family of cattle king Leonard K. Scroggin (from Mt. Pulaski in Logan County) deserted Van Buren for the party of "hard cider and log cabins."[80]

After Harrison's victory it was time to divide the spoils, which fell to the Whigs for the first time. Jobs controlled by the executive branch, from embassies to post offices, had to be handed out to political friends— and preferably to personal friends. Consulted by Stuart, Lincoln was forced to overcome his repugnance for the spoils system instituted by Jackson: "This affair of appointment to office is very annoying—more so to you than to me, doubtless. I am, as you know, opposed to removals to make places for our friends. Bearing this in mind, I express my preference in a few cases." There followed a list on which the name of Dr. Benjamin Franklin Edwards figured prominently. He had bought 19,800 acres of land in Illinois during the 1830s.[81]

CONCLUSION

Thus, his legislative career, which ended with defeat, had introduced Lincoln to the world of the bourgeoisie, of bankers, and of speculators. Inspired by a perhaps excessive enthusiasm, often lacking in prudence in his personal behavior as well as in his management of public affairs, he appeared even further removed from the world of common people from which he had come. His ambition, that "little engine that knew no rest," carried him further than he probably wanted.[82] His marriage to the aristocratic Mary Todd was an important factor in this evolution.

It would, however, be incorrect to see in this experience only negative features. During these years, Lincoln once more demonstrated his interest in the economic development of the West on the model of the industrialized East, with its corollary of liberal intellectual growth in opposition to the fundamentalism of the inhabitants of the region. In their way, the large landowners with their injustices, the banks with their corruption, the public works entrepreneurs with their swindles, represented more than mere material progress over the world of the pioneers with calloused hands and narrow horizons. Furthermore, the haste with which farmers approved the colossal get-rich schemes of 1837 appears to indicate a certain community of interest—for the dollar— among those whose interests were in conflict, which forces us to consider the moral character of the stakes more calmly than did the Jacksonians and the neo-Jacksonians.

The attraction felt by the Northwest for the manufacturing East and its values went hand in hand with the economic development that Lincoln championed tirelessly. Can the decisive role of the upper Mississippi Valley in the "Second American Revolution" be imagined without the actions of Lincoln and his peers? Is it credible that "frontier democracy" could have spread in the region if the economic influence of the South had perpetuated itself and been accompanied by its social and political influence? It is time to follow Lincoln's example and take more notice of what might be termed "the significance of the Northeast in frontier history."

5

THE YEARS OF MATURATION

On March 1, 1837, Abraham Lincoln took the oath for admission to the Illinois bar. This was the beginning of a solid, though not brilliant, career, somewhat eclipsed by his political activities. On March 7, 1849, Lincoln, who was not reelected to Congress, was admitted to practice before the Supreme Court of the United States, thus closing the first part of his professional life on a successful note. Indeed, the period from 1837 to 1849 displays a great degree of unity. It was a time of apprenticeship because Lincoln was for a long time merely the associate of more experienced and more famous lawyers. The first was John Todd Stuart (March 1837–May 1841), an Illinois congressman, followed by Stephen Trigg Logan, an astute jurist and land speculator (May 1841–December 1844), before Lincoln became head of the law office of Lincoln and Herndon (December 1844–April 1865). Furthermore, until the 1850s, Lincoln held only a modest position in legal circles, and the cases he tried were much less important than those in the later period when economic and social changes and his own professional, personal, and political position brought him qualitatively different cases.

Lincoln's successful entry into a profession known for its social prestige was the decisive factor in his break with New Salem and rural life. After having hesitated between the professions of blacksmith and lawyer, he finally turned toward the latter. Themis won out over Vulcan in what one author has amusingly called the case of "Blacksmith vs. Blackstone."[1] This final choice of intellectual labor over manual labor, even in the most highly developed form of that time, corresponded to both a social advancement and a geographical rupture. Lincoln left New Salem for Springfield on April 15, 1837, six weeks after becoming a member of the bar and three years after his election to the Illinois general assembly.[2]

POLITICAL, INTELLECTUAL, AND SOCIAL AMBITIONS

Lincoln became a lawyer only because it provided a way for him to pursue a political career, which was his real passion. To his ambitious mind, the prestige and financial gains obtained in the law courts were merely the means to a higher goal. From 1837 to 1849, he pursued the two occupations simultaneously, one reinforcing the other. The successful—and quite prevalent—symbiosis between these two professions can be explained by the relationships that were formed, the hybrid nature of numerous politico-judicial affairs, and a rise in social status. Half of the legislature was made up of farmers but one-fourth consisted of lawyers. And among the "Long Nine" the proportion was inverted: five lawyers, three farmers, and one inn-keeper.[3] Professional success increased the politicians' influence, and the prestige of elective office brought them new business as another lawyer-politician, Stephen A. Douglas, commented at the time.[4] In 1849, when Lincoln had the impression that he had definitely failed at politics, he devoted himself almost exclusively to the law. Only his election to the presidency brought his legal career to an end.

Because of numerous examples of overlap, completely separating the two activities is difficult. Thus Lincoln tried to persuade the legislature to pass bills permitting his clients to sell land owned jointly with minors and to be divorced. In a case of fraud he defended before the courts, as well as before public opinion, the Widow Anderson against General Adams, who was, in fact, one of his political adversaries.[5] Finally, Stuart provided Lincoln with opportunities for the joint practice of the professions of lawyer and of politician, and the leisure and security afforded by his work as a representative allowed him to study law.

Stretched out at the foot of an oak tree, shifting position from time to time to remain in the shade and attracting incredulous comments from New Salem farmers, Lincoln was initiated into the mysteries of the law. With the pride of the self-taught man, he wrote in 1855 to a young man who had asked advice on how to become a lawyer, "I did not read with any one. . . . I read at New-Salem, which never had three hundred people living in it. The *books,* and your *capacity* for understanding them, are just the same in all places."[6]

Which books? At first, he read only the laws of Illinois, especially several basic manuals containing legal forms that could be copied out with proper names inserted. Again his ability to write was important, and Lincoln naturally began to help his neighbors by drawing up for them various documents, IOUs, bills of sale, and mortgages.[7]

Then he embarked on reading technical works, such as *Chitty's Pleadings* and *Greenleaf's Evidence* (which later appeared on a short list he drew up for law students who asked him for advice), and finally Blackstone. At a time when there was no formal examination for admission to the bar, when a lawyer who mentioned the *New York Law Reports* would be regarded as an inhabitant of another planet, this meager baggage was sufficient for a man who "reads the books for himself without an instructer [*sic*]."[8]

Almost a century after their appearance, Blackstone's *Commentaries* remained the best work dealing with the general principles of modern Anglo-Saxon law, basing an entire edifice of civil, constitutional, and criminal law on natural right as expressed by English common law. Lincoln, confronted daily with civil matters concerning land, the major form of wealth of the time, certainly recognized the contemporary relevance of the ideas expounded by Blackstone, which must have seemed an echo of Gibson's treatise on surveying. Because land, Blackstone wrote, is the principal form of wealth, real estate questions are the most frequent. In this area as in all of civil law, the legal maxim is "Render to each man his due." Landed property must therefore by founded on rights, and Blackstone devoted a short passage to that subject before describing the different aspects of property law and the hazards of its practice: the property right in land follows from possession. Blackstone did not take sides in the dispute between Grotius and Pufendorf on one side, who held that the first occupier received the tacit consent of all humanity, and Locke on the other, who founded property on the minimum physical labor that the occupier must expend to possess the soil. According to the pragmatic Blackstone, who followed Titius and Barbeyrac in misinterpreting Locke, it is "a dispute that savours too much of nice and scholastic refinement."[9]

It was certainly not due to a quibbling mind that a pragmatic nineteenth-century American was forced to reflect on the theoretical question of the foundation of bourgeois property rights, which went back, through Locke, to the English Revolution. For, indeed, without tackling the theory, how could the rules of preemption rights, about which Lincoln would become a specialist, be understood, because they dealt precisely with evaluating the improvements that human labor had made to the land, the very basis of the right of property? We will see again, in Lincoln's social and economic thought, this close link between property and labor. It affected his vision of social progress, of relations between classes, and his attitude toward slavery.

Yet once property was founded on reason, it was important to defend it. That was the role of justice and men of law, who were responsible for interpreting and enforcing customs and laws. Although Lincoln was more likely to invoke written laws than precepts drawn from the Common Law, the peculiar character of civil juries in the West constantly forced him to emphasize the "general principles" of natural rights and equity.[10] All the witnesses agreed on his eloquence in front of juries. Now, such a success cannot be explained only by oratorical skill. It rested on the clarity with which Lincoln expressed in specific cases the common fund of sentiments and opinions that he shared with those who made up the juries, first among them being devotion to property.

His entry into the world of lawyers put Lincoln into a very different position socially and economically from the one he had occupied before. Tocqueville described this world marvellously, noting that "American aristocracy . . . occupies the judicial bench and the bar." It constituted "a sort of privileged body in the scale of intellect," men who, having studied law, "derive from this occupation certain habits of order, a taste for formalities, and a kind of instinctive regard for the regular connection of ideas, which naturally render them very hostile to the revolutionary spirit and the unreflecting passions of the multitude."[11]

Many authors, latching onto this aspect of the judicial function, have made it the key to their interpretation of Lincoln.[12] But Tocqueville conceived the question in an infinitely more wide-ranging and more subtle fashion, for he observed the lawyer in his relations with ordinary people, and his general definition conjures up Lincoln's particular position better than many of the biographies. "Lawyers belong to the people by birth and interest, and to the aristocracy by habit and taste; they may be looked upon as the connecting link between the two great classes of society. The profession of the law is the only aristocratic element that can be amalgamated without violence with the natural elements of democracy and be advantageously and permanently combined with them."

Lincoln's eloquence before juries demonstrated the depth of the bonds that attached him to ordinary people, and he learned by that means to understand them even better, to try out on them the strength of arguments based on "underlying principles" that he would use in his political speeches. For "the only enlightened class whom the people do not mistrust" "exercises its conservative influence upon the minds of men; and the most abundant source of its authority is the institution of the civil jury."[13]

Lawyers and Country People

Indeed, the "excellent gravity" with which Lord Coke wished to embellish the magistracy in a democratic country that spurned robes and wigs was not necessary, for "the pioneers were not peasants who had to be impressed by ceremonials and awed into a respect for authority."[14] The first courts in Illinois were closer to those of Indiana than to Judge Pate's courtroom in Kentucky. When the log cabin in which Judge Reynolds held court on the "circuit" consisted of only one room, the judge sat down on the bed while the jury went out to deliberate in the nearby woods.[15] The social superiority of this magistrate would be expressed only later, when he was elected governor of the state.

Bowling Green's court, which Lincoln attended, was presided over by the large, ruddy man, semiliterate, drunk and rowdy when he felt like it, who "sat" half lying down in his armchair, his feet on the table, the apparently customary symbol of an above-average social status. They smoked, they spat, they chewed, they joked, and Themis tended to behave like the respectful guest of Ceres and Diana if we are to believe a lawyer who rode the first circuit (Greene, Sangamon, Peoria, Fulton, Schuyler, Adams, Pike, and Calhoun counties) in 1827: "On this circuit we found but little business in any of the counties—parties, jurymen, and witnesses were reported in all the counties after Peoria, as being absent bee and deer hunting—a business that was then profitable, as well as necessary to the sustenance of families during the winter."[16]

Several years later, customs began to change; judges were no longer found dressed in buckskin, and Lincoln himself had to learn to dress in a more refined manner than was his custom and to polish his manners. One of his first clients, outraged to see that Stuart had sent Lincoln to represent the law office, sent him back with loud protests, declaring later that the young lawyer looked like a "country rustic on his visit to the circus."[17]

A lawyer by then enjoyed a social status superior to that of an ordinary small farmer, a status founded on easier material circumstances. John McAuley Palmer, who became one of the most important political figures in Illinois, joined the bar after having peddled watches from town to town. He noted that, at that time, lawyers' modest earnings were quite respectable, considering the low cost of public lands ($1.25 an acre) or even of average quality farms ($5 an acre). The difference was even sharper in the years from 1840 to 1848 because the real estate market collapsed along with most prices, which allowed lawyers to invest their revenues advantageously so that they declined less abruptly than those of farmers.[18]

Lincoln and Stuart generally charged reasonable fees to most of their clients, who were ordinary country people. In contrast to Logan, who received $1,200 as the lawyer for the state bank in 1840, they did not profit from the manna that flowed from the development of the banking system nor from the numerous litigations engendered by the implementation of the internal improvements scheme to which the state of Illinois was a party. However, their incomes were substantial, and Lincoln, who was fortunate to have taken the place in Stuart's office of an excellent lawyer, Henry E. Dummer, quickly became comfortable economically.[19]

The crisis of 1837 and its consequences, felt in Illinois from 1839 on, at first meant an increase in lawyers' revenues because of the growing number of bankruptcies and suits for debt. The contrast between their position and that of small farmers, which had always been precarious, was striking. Thus, on October 8, 1836, Thomas Lincoln (along with J. D. Johnston and J. Hall) was sentenced to pay $138.67 for the rental of a sawmill on which he could not make a profit. Prisoner of the mortgages that he had made, he was forced to sell his farm, Muddy Point (the forty acres sold for $140, for a profit $65 over the 1834 purchase price). Then, after a series of family exchanges and rearrangements, he was the owner of 160 acres (Goosenest Prairie Farm) in December 1840. But the crisis became firmly entrenched, taxes increased, and agricultural prices continued to fall. And it was Abraham who came to his father's rescue on October 25, 1841 by buying from him for $200 a parcel of forty acres (which Thomas had bought for $50 ten months earlier), by leaving it for his father's use, and by agreeing to sell it to John D. Johnston at the death of Thomas and Sarah. Despite this help, Thomas had to mortgage half of the eighty acres that he still owned to pay overdue school taxes of $50 on March 13, 1842.[20]

Lincoln's income continued to rise after 1842, and when he worked with William Herndon from 1845 to 1857, he never received a fee lower than $3, and that for simply drawing a power of attorney. However, because of the same crisis, revenues remained uncertain, and a lawyer might have to sue for payment from clients who were in difficulties (which Lincoln did six times during this period) or be forced to accept payment in kind because of the lack of cash: a coat for Stuart, several days of lodging at a hotel for Lincoln, "twenty dollars in good fire wood about four feet in length, at the selling price when delivered," or a subscription to the *Illinois Republican*.[21]

THE CIRCUIT AND RURAL LIFE

Lincoln and Stuart could not restrict their practice to Springfield even though their office was among the most important in the city from the very beginning, trying sixty cases before the Sangamon circuit court in July 1837, more than any other firm. They had to seek business elsewhere on the circuit to be able to live comfortably from their profession. Two sorts of lawyers could be identified: those who owned land and worked it or had it worked by farmers or laborers, and those who lived exclusively from their fees. Only the latter "rode the circuit" regularly. Lincoln obviously fit into the second category. Once again, his lack of interest in land would determine his life for twenty years, twenty years spent on the eighth circuit, the "mud circuit," into which he waded twice a year until 1859. In 1840, this circuit consisted of nine counties, among them Sangamon (14,716 inhabitants), Tazewell (7,222), McLean (6,565), Menard (4,431), DeWitt (3,247), Macon (3,039), and Christian (1,878), then reached a high of fifteen counties in 1845.[22]

Until 1849, the circuit of Judge Samuel H. Treat, an influential Democrat, was made on horseback. The roads were barely visible, and the group would ride sometimes for miles without seeing the merest shadow of a dwelling or a cultivated field, across the flooded prairie, to arrive at an isolated village with only two or three cases. The "court houses" were often no more than modest buildings—often in imitation of ancient Greek style—consisting of only one room furnished simply with the judge's platform, his chair, and his desk, a table for the clerk, and another (sometimes) for the lawyers. In other places, a log house was the site of the court, and the public as well as the lawyers sat on benches of rough-hewn wood. But the court house was always the most imposing building in the village.[23]

Lincoln soon felt at ease among the small group of lawyers who rode the circuit. Because of his height he was sent by his colleagues to reconnoiter the river fords, which reveals a great deal about the state of the roads at the time. On their arrival, the legal fraternity were besieged by parties to the cases, who chose one or another of them according to the nature of the case and the reputation of the lawyers, and Lincoln held his own. This was important because the speeches were not meant to result only in victory in the case. They were occasions for demonstrating many diverse talents such as humor, intelligence, presence of mind, and quick-wittedness in front of an audience of regulars who looked upon trials as the equivalent of sporting events and rooted for their favorite champions—among them, Lincoln. The social problems of the frontier came before the judge wearing the mask of tragedy or of comedy, and the rural population never missed a chance to attend the entertainment, this rare moment of excitement that broke the monotony of field work.[24]

Before the railroad, the telegraph, or the daily newspaper, the court was also the only channel by which news arrived in the country, and its sessions were the ideal moment for organizing political debates.[25] The election of 1846 proves that in the political sphere, the lawyer's only serious competitor was the preacher. Along with the influential large landowner who was in league with everyone in town, they monopolized the political representation of rural communities.

In the first half of Lincoln's professional career, the bulk of the cases he dealt with were determined by the rural character of the region in which he practiced. "The courts consumed as much time deciding who had committed an assault or a trespass on a neighbor's ground, as it spent in the solution of questions arising on contracts," and lawyers "the greatest as well as the least had to join the general scramble for practice." What types of cases were these? They dealt with land, first of all, such as violation of property and title disputes, and the thousand and one forms of trespass, contested sales, or swindles. Next came theft, theft of animals, horses, hogs, and the fraudulent sale of moribund donkeys. Cases of immorality were complicated by a multitude of suits for slander, which saw Lincoln defending the honor of a free-thinking school teacher and establishing a jurisprudence for corruption of minors. There were also crimes of violence, rapes and frequent murders in a community where lynch law often prevailed and temporary insanity might lead religious fanatics to carry out human sacrifices.[26]

A list exists of Lincoln's cases in Coles County from 1840 to 1857. Because of the backward character of that region we can infer that this sample was representative of Lincoln's activity in the years from 1837 to 1849. Among the twenty-three cases were found two property disputes, two thefts, two suits for damages and interest, four complaints for slander, five suits for debt, one paternity suit, one attempted murder, one murder, one aggression, one corruption of a minor, and one recovery of a fugitive slave (the Matson case, which we will consider later).[27]

LAWYER OR REALTOR?

Suits for debt constituted the bulk of lawyers' activity, and the depression at the beginning of the 1840s caused a spectacular growth in cases of this type. The seriousness of the crisis led authorities to soften bankruptcy proceedings and during the year when the new bankruptcy law was in effect (March 1842 to March 1843) lawyers were flooded with requests. Very quickly a fee scale arose, although during the preceding period Lincoln had remarked, "I can not say there is any custom on the subject," and the minimum cost became established at $20, of which $5.75 were filing costs. Although the Logan and Lincoln law office had taken the precaution of having declaration of bankruptcy forms printed up for the use of clients, it had difficulty handling all the cases it received.[28]

Many lands changed hands by sale after a mortgage foreclosure or after a seizure for nonpayment of taxes. Lincoln was asked by his friend Speed, now in Kentucky, to follow a large number of land transactions. Indeed, Speed, either in his own name or (secretly) for his clients, was the successful bidder for many properties in the Springfield region.

As Lincoln had commented in 1838 during a debate in the Illinois house about a law concerning mortgage foreclosures, "few appeared at the sale of property, and the judgment creditor usually bids it in at half its value." That was precisely what occurred for Speed, who thus acquired lands whose value, taking into consideration the "improvements" that the debtor had made, "must be worth much more than the debt; but whether any body will redeem it in these hard times, I can not say."[29]

Ironically, Lincoln organized the transfer of one repossessed property, with Speed serving only as figurehead, to a creditor named Peter Van Bergen, who was none other than the man who had had Lincoln's horse and surveying instruments seized in 1834.[30] The Supreme Court of the United States, having declared unconstitutional an Illinois law establishing a moratorium on payment of personal debts (a law Lincoln, as a representative, had opposed), Logan and Lincoln wrote to a client that they were "a little encouraged to make some further attempts to make some collections." In the name of the law office, Lincoln answered this client, who had asked them to negotiate the sale of a piece of land that he had acquired through a foreclosure sale: "As to the real estate, we can not attend to it, as agents, & we therefore recommend that you give the charge of it, to Mr. Isaac S. Britton, a trust-worthy man, & one whom the Lord made on purpose for such bussiness [sic]."[31]

This is an important point for although Logan speculated in land on his own account, Logan and Lincoln did not cross over the boundary that separated the attorney from the real estate agent. Doubtless Lincoln believed that he was not "made on purpose for such business." Did his distaste for this lucrative profession stem from the disappointment he experienced in his speculations in 1836 and 1837? Did it reflect the fear of having to take an interest in managing a farm at a time when he confided to Speed his complete lack of interest in that type of activity?[32]

Whatever the case, by doing so Lincoln followed a route different from that of many of his lawyer friends. Thus, for example, in 1844, the very year in which Lincoln referred his clients to Mr. Britton, the lawyer David Davis, who became one of his closest friends, laid the foundations of his real estate empire. His clients not wishing to be burdened with 1,900 acres of land that they had just obtained from a debtor, Davis and his associate bought the land on credit for the modest sum of $1,700. The next year, having increased their acquisitions of land sold at auction for nonpayment of taxes, Davis and Colton owned 2,730 acres of prairie in McLean County.[33]

At the same time, Lincoln did not line up with those lawyers who became the agents of rapacious speculators who scoured the archives of the local land office or the General Land Office in Washington to discover errors in land titles that allowed them to begin lawsuits. Lincoln certainly had these men in mind when he jotted down his advice to young lawyers: "Who can be more nearly a fiend than he who habitually overhauls the register of deeds in search of defects in titles, whereon to stir up strife, and put money in his pocket?"[34]

Indeed, at that time speculators employed dozens of lawyers in Washington to discover original land titles offered by the government to veterans. The Supreme Court had recently ruled that the original titles ("patent titles") were worth more than "tax titles," which the government delivered to those who paid the back taxes on property sold for nonpayment of land taxes. Finding a veteran who still owned his title allowed the speculator who bought it to start a lawsuit by which the occupier, possessing only a tax title, would have to abandon the land and his "improvements." In this way, the measures that had been taken by the Illinois legislature in 1835 and 1839 to set a statute of limitations of seven years during which land titles could be contested were now annulled, and large estates that had been divided by speculators' bankruptcies were reconstituted to the profit of other eastern giants.[35]

Thus, by refusing to speculate for himself or to transform himself into a real estate agent, by despising unscrupulous lawyers who called into question, for purely formal irregularities, a right of property legally and legitimately acquired, Lincoln now drew close to the world of farmers just as earlier he had distanced himself from it by upholding causes as unpopular as internal improvements after 1839, tax increases, or defense of the privileges of the bank. Outside of Springfield and its social whirl, Lincoln was a man of simple habits, who felt at home in Menard County in 1846, and who would go to drink a bowl of buttermilk at an old friend's home. He had "an easy and approachable bearing toward all classes."[36]

Once the mists of the 1836–37 intoxication had dissipated, Lincoln managed his patrimony as a prudent head of the family, as was appropriate because he had become a father in 1843. Receiving, doubtless in lieu of a fee, one-quarter of a town lot in Springfield in 1842, he got rid of it in 1844 when he acquired his house at the corner of 8th and Jackson streets.[37] His existence, however, was not limited to his professional and family lives. Released from the burden of elective responsibility, Lincoln remained a political activist who pursued that interest under new circumstances.

THE RUSTICATED POLITICIAN

When a politician is kept out of power, the issues of the platform and the party's commitments take on for him a considerable importance. Freed from the daily pressure of making decisions, which often renders the official party line unrecognizable, he is, at the same time, deprived of the maneuvering room in regard to that same party that his position as the people's elected representative gives him. No longer having to answer individual and local questions, he can devote a great deal of attention to general problems and national politics.

Lincoln's thoughts, then, were steered in two directions: on the practical level toward the preparation of an internal Whig electoral campaign that lasted four years (1842–46) and resulted in his nomination for election to the U.S. House of Representatives, and on the theoretical level toward the study of the details of Whig doctrine, which he defended during national electoral campaigns, pursuing on Clay's behalf in 1844 the ideas begun in 1840 during the campaign for Harrison. Elected to Congress, he committed most of the results of his work to several pages of closely written text.

The Tariff and Agriculture

Throughout the period, Lincoln specialized in defending the protectionist theory preached by the Federalist Whig school, with its prophets such as Mathew and Henry Carey, Alexander Hamilton, Calvin Colton, and Horace Greeley, whose works he consulted, with Herndon helping him to look up the sources.[38] By so doing, he reflected the interests of northeastern industrial capitalism in its international competition against Great Britain and its national competition against the free-trade of the South and the large maritime interests, especially those from New York.

This position presents, from the point of view of our study, a dual interest. On the one hand, it demonstrates once again Lincoln's general economic orientation, his support for the industrial development of the United States. At this time, the "American System" (protectionism) was in opposition to the "British system" (free trade) under geographic, social, and political conditions that considerably favored American workers over their European, especially their English, brothers. Because the American labor market was unbalanced by the existence of a vast and relatively cheap territory that attracted laborers from towns, the general level of wages was much higher there than in England, where the combination of an early industrial revolution with an archaic social and political system provoked a massive rural exodus that lowered the price of labor. In that way an identity of interests was created between American industrialists and workers that enabled Lincoln to give a democratic substance to his nationalism.[39]

On the other hand, and this is the most important element in the way Lincoln was forced to approach the problem, he faced the difficult task of trying to prove to farmers, as the Democratic papers expressed it maliciously, "that the high pressure tariff made every thing they bought cheaper."[40] Industrial development continued, in fact, to put town and country in opposition, and the tariff question was not a minor example of that. In the course of his campaigns, Lincoln tried numerous arguments. He explained first that high tariffs were levied only on fine silks, jewels, and other luxurious objects that the farmer—at least one who fit the Jacksonian model—had no interest in. He maintained next—after having conceded that it was indeed the consumer who in the end paid the total of the tariff duties[41]—that the weight of taxes so raised fell equally on the consumer, the middleman, and the producer, and perhaps even only on the last two categories.[42]

Finally, with a certain audacity on the part of the author of the tax reforms of 1839–40, he evoked the specter of direct taxes, the only solution, according to him, that would make possible avoiding a higher tariff: "by the direct tax system, the land must be literally covered with assessors and collectors, going forth like swarms of Egyptian locusts, devouring every blade of grass and other green thing."[43] The effect of this quotation from Exodus on the Bible-reading farmers of Sangamon County is not known, but it was designed to scare them.

Of all the Illinois Whigs, Lincoln was the only one (or almost the only one) who dealt with the issue of the tariff in electoral meetings in 1840.[44] Once again, he demonstrated his political courage by going against the general opinion of rural Illinois. In 1843–44 he perhaps took advantage of the rise in agricultural prices, particularly of wool, in comparison to the general index of prices. The rise, which coincided with the adoption of a Whig tariff in 1842, increasing duties by an average of 34.4 percent, made it possible to describe the short-term advantages of protectionism for the farmer.[45] This concern will be found again later in Lincoln's efforts in Congress to obtain protection for American hemp.

Basically, Lincoln's theoretical position, which placed him in "the avant-garde of American tariff economics," was identical to that of Henry Carey's. He refused to see any contradiction at all, even temporary, between agricultural and industrial interests, or between classes of landed property owners, capitalists, and workers. Although the particular conditions of development in the United States, as Marx pointed out, make it possible for one to treat the issues for awhile without taking into account contradictions between these classes, it is a great deal more difficult to demonstrate "the harmony of interests" between town and country. Indeed, although no organized workers' movement existed to make the voice of this particular class heard independently from the industrial bourgeoisie, the Democratic party did offer a framework in which farmers, particularly those from the West, could, under the leadership of the slave South and of the great commercial interests of the Middle Atlantic states, express their interest, distinct from those of northeastern industrial capitalism.[46]

This is the root cause for the practical impossibility of ignoring the contradiction between town and country. The antagonism between capital and labor, on the contrary, remained hidden by the conspicuous weakness of the labor movement, linked to the fluidity of the world of workers and to the alternation of periods of very rapid economic growth and of crises that were destructive to the union movement. There again, the Democratic party succeeded in becoming the political representative of labor in numerous cases, but labor's energies were directed toward demands (the fight against the bank, for example) that did not put possessors of the means of production and wage earners into opposition.[47] Whigs did the same thing by developing the American System of collaboration between industrialists and workers in the fight for protection of American industry. Both parties likewise took into account the aspirations of workers to leave the factory for the farm—for that was the real driving force of the homestead movement—through the intermediaries of wings of their parties that favored reforming laws on public lands, the Horace Greeley wing for the Whigs and the Martin Van Buren wing for the Democrats. The only political faction willing to allow the expression of antagonism between the interests of capital and of labor in the industrial world did so without the least risk: the "fire-eaters" of the slave South had no influence among the working masses, who were at least perfectly conscious of the fact that the defenders of black slavery could not really oppose "white slavery," the term then widely used to describe working conditions in the Northeast.

It is not surprising, therefore, to find that when Lincoln came to consider the relationship between town and country in a long manuscript drafted after his election to Congress, he did not think about the relationship between capital and labor.[48] At the moment he entered into the councils of the nation, Lincoln took stock of the protectionist campaign that the Illinois Whigs had waged in 1844, from which, by his own reckoning, they had emerged "gloriously whipped," and appealed to theory to establish the harmony of agricultural and industrial interests, seriously challenged by the "Walker tariff" of 1846, which lowered the average custom duty to less than 25 percent.[49] This decision by the Polk administration seriously threatened Northern interests, and Lincoln, who detected in it the risk of economic catastrophe, reflected the anxiety of many politicians who saw the South increasing its domination over the Democratic party.[50] The break between David Wilmot (D.-Penn.) and the Democratic administration dated perhaps from this decision. It certainly caused the alienation of Illinoisan John Wentworth, who represented Chicago in the House of Representatives.[51]

Lincoln therefore thought it more and more urgent to convince western farmers that their interests were no different from those of Pennsylvania or Massachusetts industrialists. In the long-winded draft (embellished with a prosopopoeia of Vulcan and agriculture, in the style of Carey), stuffed with very concrete examples that did more to help Lincoln clarify his own thoughts than to enlighten the reader, can be found the essentials of the Lincoln credo. After a theoretical preamble basing value on the quantity of work incorporated in the product (the theory generally in fashion, devised by Wayland), Lincoln proceeded to study how the price of commodities—expressed in terms of a day's wages—varied whether subjected to a protective tariff or not and to study the consequences of these variations on the evolution of agricultural markets.

We will leave to economists the discussion of the theoretical premises of the analysis—which appear completely erroneous inasmuch as although Lincoln assumed variations in the price of labor he completely overlooked any notion of labor productivity. Instead, we will consider the two arguments to which this reflection boils down: on the one hand, protectionism does away with the socially negative cost of the transportation of goods from one continent to another and thus suppresses an expenditure of "useless labour" and makes possible a direct and therefore economical exchange between the manufacturer and the farmer "whose lands are adjoining."[52] The entire society would benefit from this streamlining.On the other hand, the creation of a stable internal market for agricultural products is a positive element that directly favors farmers.

Of these two arguments, the second is the more interesting. Indeed, the suppression of middlemen can be considered only by simultaneously studying the evolution of labor productivity and by also contemplating the role of "useless labour" in providing a market for agriculture. On the second point it is obvious that Lincoln's thesis might seduce midwestern farmers eager to enlarge the American market. Industrial growth is certainly essential for the development of commercial agriculture. But the reduction of the tariff (in the Walker tariff and a further reduction in 1857) did not put a brake on the expansion of American industry during the 1850s, at least not so as to cause agriculture to suffer. Ironically, the decisive impetus to the development of the Midwest was given by wheat and flour exports of the 1850s, which began to increase rapidly in the very year that Lincoln composed his notes (see table 1). Because the protection afforded to English farmers by the Corn Laws was abolished in 1846, wheat and flour exports (measured by value) tripled to $6 million in 1847, and their growth accelerated thanks to the Crimean War. Thus, the increase of 72 percent in the production of wheat during the 1850s appears to refute Lincoln's protectionist theses.[53] But what about the growth of American agriculture from 1862 to 1934, a period when customs duties, on the average, were never lower than 40 percent (except during the brief period from 1913 to 1922)?

Table 1. Value of Exports of Wheat and Flour (in millions of dollars)

1830	6	1851	11.5	1856	44	1861	63
1840	12	1852	14.5	1857	48	1865	47
1846	2	1853	19	1858	28	1870	68
1847	6	1854	40	1859	17	1874	131
1850	8	1855	12	1860	19	1880	226

The connections between town and country cannot be reduced to gross production statistics. The ratio between the urban population and the rural population, which began to increase at that time, foreshadowed the extraordinary rural exodus of the years from 1880 to 1935, which corresponded to the arrival of the United States into the first rank of industrial powers. The 1850s would also witness the growth of social tensions linked to the anarchical development of industry and agriculture. But the exuberance of expansion, especially in the West, would drown these contradictions under the wave of progress. Lincoln's vision would become truly relevant as a comprehensive conception of the connections between town and country when railroads had opened the prairie to the influences of industrial America, sealing the doom of agrarian Jeffersonianism.

The Distribution of Public Lands

The same desire of linking the destiny of the West to that of the industrial Northeast can be easily seen in Lincoln's defense of Clay's policy on the question of public lands: distribution.

During the 1840s, the position of various classes and sections developed as follows. The working class favored homestead legislation, or, as a last resort, preemption laws. The "old states" of the East, where there were no longer any public lands, favored maintaining the status quo (selling at $1.25 an acre) unless they could obtain something in return. The states of the West favored either distribution of public lands (or the product of their sales) to the states in which they were located as an encouragement to public works or preemption, which allowed farmers to round out their holdings. The compromise law of 1841 satisfied no one. It linked distribution and preemption so as to provide the strict minimum indispensable for the western states, but Clay failed in his effort to get the support of the East by linking distribution and the tariff. On the contrary, distribution would come to an end each time the tariff rose above 20 percent. It became impossible to do what Clay had hoped: to empty the federal treasury by distributing the product of the sale of public lands so as to make the increase of customs duties inevitable. Instead, distribution ceased in 1842 as the tariff climbed.

After 1841, all attempts inspired by Clay to revive the distribution movement by cementing an alliance between western and northeastern Whigs came up against a coalition of the Democratic party and southern Whigs, of whom President John Tyler was the most eminent representative. The South in general had no interest at all in distribution and likewise feared preemption, which contributed to the development of the free states of the Northwest and their rapid population growth. The situation was at a standstill during that decade and slowly brought about a rift in the Democratic party exemplified by the defections first of Van Buren and then of Thomas Hart Benton, who left a party that had become more the party of Calhoun than that of Jackson.[54] The question of the territorial expansion of the two kinds of American economies, industrial capitalism and agrarian slavery, was thus already

apparent just beneath the surface in a debate obscured by the multiplicity of private interests at stake. In the issues of Mexico, Cuba, and
Oregon, and in the development of the crisis in the 1850s, the problem
would be stated in different terms.

For the time being, westerners had to be satisfied with what the law
of 1841 granted them: 10 percent of the value of the sales of public
lands. Lincoln took that position in the debate over Illinois's accepting
the federal gift, while Democrats, led by Governor Thomas Ford, wanted
to refuse the proceeds of distribution in the hopes of getting more. In the
crisis situation that Illinois was in, what other source of revenue was
there for the indebted state? Had the Democrats, who were promising
the moon (graduation, preemption), ever managed to unite to pass a law
favorable to the West? Was it really conceivable that the "old states" of
the East would be willing to be more generous to Illinois? "The wonder
is, that they ever permitted one to pass so favorable as Mr. Clay's." No
reason existed for expecting an improvement in the situation, especially
since the number of "old states" increased as settlement took place, and
therefore "new states" with public lands would never be in the majority.[55]

G. S. Boritt has pointed out that Lincoln presented such measures as
graduation and cession as positive and concluded that Lincoln only
adopted Clay's Whig policies under duress, as the least he could do and
still remain a Whig.[56] However, since his principal preoccupations
were paying Illinois's debt and securing a plan of transportation development in the state, his attitude summed up the entire logic of his
evolution since 1836. The defensive appearance of his argument reflects
less his profound convictions than the very nature of the document he
was writing, a circular intended to enable Whig activists to participate
in the campaign by responding to Democratic criticism. Likewise, the
fact that he generally refrained from vigorously criticizing preemption
and graduation does not mean that he was not hostile to those aspects of
the Democratic program. Lincoln, as was his custom, simply refrained
from attacking head-on opinions that he knew to be popular unless he
was forced to do so by an absolute necessity of protecting essential
interests.

In this case, the essential for him since 1836 had been financing the
plan of internal improvements. From that point of view, although he
might be ready to sacrifice certain dogmas of Whig orthodoxy (there
being, furthermore, several positions within the party on the question
of public lands), he had no reason to adopt the position of a Benton. He
might go so far as to join Calhoun in his plan of ceding public lands to
the states in which they were located—abandoning the Whig federalist
vision for the states' rightism of the senator from South Carolina. But,

taken as a whole, his positions belie the hypothesis that after 1836 he accepted the idea that the state might alienate the public domain without, in one way or another, guaranteeing the financing of internal improvements in Illinois. That was the connecting thread of his ideas throughout his entire career, from his 1835 plan all the way to putting the Pacific railroad in place. Thus, as was always the case with Lincoln, real life came from the city by train; the only emotions that the land could elicit had the gloomy odor of an obsession with death that united Lincoln's favorite poets in a romantic communion throughout the ages.

POETICAL DIVERSIONS

The 1840s are the most important years for contemplating the nurturing effect of poetry on Lincoln. It was then that he composed poetry and that he corresponded with other poetry lovers. We have already examined his poem "My Childhood's Home I See Again." His writing is testimony to the transformation that Lincoln went through on his professional and political peregrinations, in the quiet of his office in Springfield (where there was an "office copy" of Burns), or in Mary's company in society drawing rooms. The distance that developed between him and the land gave rise to a painful nostalgia that was not a longing for Arcadia but rather the haunting evocation of a thought that can be summed up by the expression of divine malediction. After having cursed the soil and condemned man to eat his bread by the sweat of his brow, did not God add: "Dust thou art and unto dust shalt thou return"?

　　Which were Lincoln's favorite poems at this time? Burns, first of all, whom he knew almost by heart. He admired his satiric and democratic verve ("A Man's a Man for a' That," "Tam o' Shanter"), but he was especially touched by the nostalgia of "The Cotter's Saturday Night"; the plaintive tone of "Annie Laurie," "Mary of Argyle," and "Auld Robin Gray"; and the morbid sadness of "Highland Mary," "Bonnie Doon," and "Flow Gently, Sweet Afton." His romanticism attracted him to Scotland, the Mecca of the somber Gothic, and his favorite poem was "Mortality" by William Knox, whose fourteen lines tirelessly pull the living to remember those dead whose earthly journey they are retracing before joining them underground. This poem sums up in one line Lincoln's feeling about agriculture. It draws irresistibly the image of the dead who haunt us, the living, "That work on the turf that lies on their brow." With the death of his son Eddie in 1850 at four years of age, Lincoln would have yet another reason for liking "Mortality."

Lincoln was particularly devoted to Shakespeare, and certain passages captivated him to the point that he recited them often to his friends: the fratricidal king's soliloquy in *Hamlet* and Macbeth's after the murder of Duncan. In *Macbeth* again, probably his favorite play, he liked the speech on fleeting time, which leads to "dusty death," and especially that of Richard II—"Let's talk of graves, of worms, and epitaphs"—in which the deposed king no longer possesses anything but his death "And that small model of the barren earth which serves as paste and cover to our bones."

Lincoln loved Byron and Longfellow, poets of liberty, but he was fascinated by Poe, "The Haunted House" by Thomas Hood (whose humor he likewise admired), and "The Last Leaf" by Oliver Wendell Holmes.[57] And yet, in the next decade, Lincoln's path would cross that of Whitman's in the national reconciliation of the Machine and the Garden, accomplished by one and celebrated by the other. Melancholic periods alternated with moments of enthusiasm during which the earth seemed no longer simply acceptable but also almost lovable.

Did the nostalgic and morbid romanticism that fascinated Lincoln constitute the obverse of the spirit of economic, social, intellectual, and moral progress that inspired him? At the beginning of the new decade, the "attainments" of the 1840s were measured not only in terms of social status (middle class), but also in terms of mode of thinking (lawyerly) and political skill (partisan). These were the forms of a mechanistically progressive mind still incapable of grasping the antagonistic nature of the contradictions in the development of the United States. At that point, Lincoln had not yet considered the importance of the question of slavery from the point of view of national unity and of the progress of civilization. For his logical mind, one plus one equaled two: North plus South equalled the Union. All that was needed was to add elements of progress one by one in order to advance on the road to a better future: more roads, railways, and schools. His sole interest in public lands was to further this economic and social growth throughout the entire the American West, which was not envisioned as an open space, as the field of battle between two modes of production.

THE QUESTION OF SLAVERY

Several years would pass before Lincoln developed a new conception of slavery. Before 1848, Lincoln was an anti-slavery Whig on moral grounds and an anti-abolitionist on legal grounds. The key to his position—which remained valid for the heart of the slavery question at least as late as

1860[58]—was expressed in a "Protest" cosigned with Daniel Stone on March 3, 1837 and published in the journal of the Illinois house of representatives. In answer to a motion violently condemning abolitionism and concluding that Congress could not suppress slavery in the District of Columbia "without a manifest breach of good faith," Lincoln and Stone asserted that abolitionist doctrines were blameworthy only to the extent that they tended to aggravate the evils of slavery ("founded on both injustice and bad policy") rather than to cure them, and that Congress had the constitutional right of abolishing slavery in the District of Columbia but ought not do so unless the inhabitants of the District requested it.[59] This protest was different in tone and direction from those of the most extreme anti-abolitionist speeches, but it resulted in no practical consequences. Opposition expressed in this way was symbolic in all senses of the term. By deploring the "foul blot"[60] upon the federal capital and the presence of a slave market in the showplace of democratic America for all the world to see, Clay, Lincoln, and others were proclaiming themselves the representatives of a system other than that of the peculiar institution. They agreed in thinking liberal capitalism more suited to the American genius than a society founded on the whip and the chain.

For Lincoln, slavery was always a moral question, a kind of abstract evil but not yet a political question confronted directly as such. The text that best expresses his opinion on the subject is his speech on temperance of February 1842, whose conclusion is surprising: "And when the victory shall be complete—when there shall be neither a slave nor a drunkard on the earth—how proud the title of the *Land*, which may truly claim to be the birth-place and the cradle of both those revolutions, that shall have ended in that victory."[61] It is striking to notice that the slavery of which Lincoln speaks is in no sense that of blacks but rather the political slavery of colonial America under the British yoke, that he was able to elaborate at length upon the comparison between slavery and the slavery of alcohol, using the technical term *manumission* without saying a word about the situation of black people. Yet this audience was used to hearing fine speeches on the troublesome question. This shows how distant and unimportant the solution to the moral problem of slavery appeared to him. Lincoln's sensitivity was awakened, merely for an instant, in the midst of the oratorical excitement of the debates in the 1848–49 Congress only to become dulled again in the Springfield routine from 1850 to 1853. It was the Kansas-Nebraska Act that would stir Lincoln's patriotic and revolutionary chord, that "Spirit of 1776" that drove the temperance speech of 1842. The threat against the white democratic ideal would make the question of black slavery a "torment" for him. To go from that point to the destruction of that torment was still a long way off because it involved the destruction of $2 billion worth of property.

In the meantime, to use one of Lincoln's favorite expressions regarding that other moral evil, alcoholism, "I'm temperate in this . . . I don't drink," which on the slavery question as well as on the temperance question constituted progress over Clay.[62] Waiting patiently and calmly for the sinner to repent, Lincoln refused—after reflection—to condemn severely those in New England who opposed the application of the fugitive slave law. He denounced the illegal lynching of blacks and abolitionists, such as Elijah P. Lovejoy's in 1837.[63]

All of this remained very abstract for him. Writing in October 1845 to an abolitionist he hoped to win back to the Whig party, he tried to show him that the election of the pro-slavery Clay in 1844 would have prevented the annexation of Texas, which his correspondent linked to the extension of slavery. But for himself, although Lincoln affirmed the abstract principle of no further slavery extension ("we should never knowingly lend ourselves directly or indirectly, to prevent that slavery from dying a natural death—to find new places for it to live in, when it can no longer exist in the old"), he could not understand at all how the annexation of Texas could lead to that result. His opposition to annexation, then, was not linked to an anti-slavery position, and he was not well prepared for the controversy surrounding the Mexican War.[64] Conversely, the refusal of slavery extension did not have any content for him at that time.

Just before his departure for Washington, in October 1847, Lincoln agreed to argue for the plaintiff in *Matson vs. Rutherford,* in which Matson, a Kentucky slaveholder, tried to recover slaves who had fled after he had taken them to Illinois, only for the season, Lincoln would maintain. Studying the contents of the plea is useless. Lincoln and Usher F. Linder (who had led the lynching of Lovejoy in 1837) employed arguments exactly opposite to the ones used in the 1841 case of *Bailey vs. Cromwell* in which Lincoln had argued successfully that there existed in Illinois a presumption of liberty in favor of all residents, no matter what their race. The opposing side, defended by the pro-slavery lawyers Orlando B. Ficklin and Charles H. Constable, neglected to invoke that precedent but won the case nonetheless. Lincoln, embarrassed by the position he was forced to take, had apparently presented a mediocre defense. But nothing had forced him to defend Matson. In any event, a militant or merely committed anti-slavery lawyer would have avoided taking such a case, especially since Lincoln's position as an elected representative made him particularly conspicuous. Had he wanted to wage even the most moderate sort of battle over slavery principles, he would have refused.

But, as Lincoln explained to Seward, he had not gauged the importance of the slavery question until his term in Congress in 1848 and 1849.[65] The appearance of the problem sounded the death knell of the old parties and of the old ideas. All of Lincoln's past experience was reduced to naught by the premises of the threatening crisis, and for a time the development of his thought was at a standstill.

6

WASHINGTON AND
DISARRAY

LINCOLN AND HIS CUSTOM–MADE DISTRICT

Once he had obtained the Whig nomination, Lincoln's election was a mere formality in the Seventh District of Illinois. On August 3, 1846, Lincoln crushed his Democratic opponent, the former Methodist minister Peter Cartwright, by 6,340 votes to 4,829, winning eight out of the eleven counties in the district (Sangamon, Putnam, Marshall, Woodford, Tazewell, Mason, Menard, Cass, Morgan, Scott, and Logan). Cartwright had based his campaign on attacking Lincoln's religious opinions, and Lincoln had had no trouble defending himself.[1]

But doubtless the profound knowledge of the region that Lincoln had acquired while riding the circuit had played a major role in the indisputable personal success represented by such a large victory over Cartwright, far greater than those of his predecessors John J. Hardin and Edward D. Baker. In July 1847, a journalist from the Boston *Courier*, J. H. Buckingham, happened to share a stagecoach between Peoria and Springfield with the newly elected congressman, and he noticed with curiosity Lincoln's behavior. "We were now in the district represented by our Whig Congressman, and he knew, or appeared to know, every body we met, the name of the tenant of every farm-house, and the owner of every plat of ground. Such a shaking of hands—such a howd'ye-do—such a greeting of different kinds, as we saw, was never seen before; it seemed as if he knew every thing, and he had a kind word, a smile and a bow for every body on the road, even to the horses, and the cattle, and the swine."[2]

The young journalist's ironic enthusiasm can be explained, of course, by the tricks of the politician's trade, country version, that Lincoln knew to perfection and that he would demonstrate in Springfield in

1860 to another inexperienced person, the painter Thomas Hicks, who was painting his portrait. While he was sitting for his portrait, Lincoln received the visit of two large young men, obviously arrived from the country, and questioned them skillfully on the condition of the harvest, the health of their family, and so forth until he managed to put a name with their faces.[3] Still, one had to know the people and the business of the region well in order to succeed at this game. Lincoln was able to indicate the owner of every one of the fields that made up the "miles and miles of tall corn" surrounding Springfield because the former surveyor and the meticulous lawyer had used his photographic memory to file away the survey information.[4]

Resoundingly elected and knowing to perfection his district, Lincoln, who left his friend Herndon behind to keep an eye open for problems, held all the cards for realizing a brilliant career in Congress.

An Indelible Stain

Going through Lexington, Kentucky, on his way to Washington, Lincoln heard his hero Henry Clay denounce the Mexican War in particularly violent terms and reaffirm the position of the national Whig party and of those like the "Conscience Whigs" of Massachusetts and Joshua Giddings of Ohio that the war was an "offensive aggression" aimed at acquiring foreign territory.[5] Contrary to the great mass of Illinois Whigs, infected with the war fever that swept through the state—Baker and Hardin fought brilliantly—Lincoln decided to tie his destiny to that of the Washington Whigs, independently of the attitude of his district. Why? Lincoln was ambitious. He foresaw a national career, as is proved by what followed during his congressional career. The economic argument for "internal improvements" as it existed perhaps also played a role in his opposition to annexing new territory. Lincoln had, in fact, just attended the Chicago River and Harbor Convention.[6]

In any case, he obviously saw in the issue an opportunity not to be missed, a morally indisputable question that would allow him to draw attention to himself. On December 13, 1847, he wrote to Herndon, "As you are all so anxious for me to distinguish myself, I have concluded to do so, before long." And on December 22, he presented to the House of Representatives his "spot resolutions." President James K. Polk having stated that Mexican troops began hostilities on American soil, Lincoln asked him eight questions concerning the exact legal status of the "spot" (the word is repeated at the beginning of the first three questions) where the first bloodshed occurred.[7]

Utilizing in this way the technique of questioning witnesses, perfected during his career as a lawyer, Lincoln took a position of strictest legality, a formal position devoid of content.[8] He criticized a legal irregularity and condemned the fact that the war was "unnecessarily and unconstitutionally commenced."[9] The legalistic nature of his position is of interest to us only for its notion of boundaries, of frontiers that separated in some way two distinct properties. There again we encounter his training as a surveyor and a lawyer, which taught him that everything has its proper place. On those grounds, Lincoln felt comfortable. Lincoln would choose exactly the same position against Douglas in 1854: slavery in the South, wage labor and free enterprise in the North, everything in its proper place.

But in 1847–48, Lincoln was incapable of putting together an argument that went beyond the question of facts. There was no economic or social vision, no moral position, nothing of consequence in his condemnation of the war. He said so himself by revealing that he did not see how the annexation of Texas could open the way to slavery. He voted against the proposition to conclude a peace without annexation (but with an indemnity), and he voted war credits, defended the military glory of the Whig generals, and vigorously supported veterans.[10] When all is said and done, his actions merely reflected the timidity with which the Whig party, and the North in general, met the bold adventure led by the Democrats to the advantage of the South, allowing them also to monopolize patriotic fervor for a cause whose philosophy Lincoln summed up by imitating back-country language, "I ain't greedy 'bout land; I only just wants what jines mine."[11] Thus, the spot resolutions took "a form which any lawyer might follow if he were trying a case of claim to adverse possession. . . . The matter of whether the spot was really American or Mexican seemed to Lincoln to be reducible to the question of land title, or matter of ownership of soil."[12]

The untimely character of the questions asked (only a few weeks away from the peace) was not lost on the Whigs, who barely defended Lincoln, nor on the Democrats, who did not bother to respond to the speech he gave in support of his resolutions.[13] If Lincoln had hoped that his attacks would mark Polk forever with the stain of shame—which would reveal his crime to the electors—like the blood of Duncan stuck to Macbeth's hands, he was doubly wrong. His rhetoric was turned against him. The Democrats of Illinois jumped at the chance to nickname the only Whig from the state "Spotty Lincoln."

Basing themselves on Herndon—and the Democratic press—historians long believed that the spot resolution speech had sounded the death knell of Lincoln's popularity in Illinois. In the 1970s, the work of G. S. Boritt and Mark E. Neely, Jr., reestablished the truth.[14] Lincoln's attitude did not shock his electors. Lincoln did not run again in 1848 because of a long-standing agreement among the potential Whig candidates of the Seventh District. And the defeat of the Whig candidate in that previously secure district was due to personality because Stephen T. Logan, Lincoln's friend and designated successor, had little talent for electoral campaigning. However, the predominance of the thesis that Lincoln committed "political suicide" when his spot resolutions collided with the warlike sentiments of his electors has had an important consequence.[15]

Historians and biographers have been so struck by the supposed rift between Lincoln and his district that they have, in general, underestimated the real work accomplished by the representative of the Seventh District for his electors. In particular, no one has noticed his efforts in favor of the hemp growers of the Sangamon.[16] However, Lincoln's interest in such agricultural problems should not be ignored.

Defense of Agricultural Interests

Hemp, traditionally grown in Kentucky, Tennessee, and Ohio, had two uses: sacks used for baling cotton and ropes especially intended for the American navy. The ease with which hemp could be planted and harvested—and the impressive yields that could be obtained without expending great care in cultivation—attracted numerous farmers from Missouri, Illinois, Georgia, and elsewhere. Two elements were indispensable to the success of their enterprise: the presence of competent industrialists ready to invest large sums to carry out the delicate process of macerating the hemp and separating the fibers from the woody part of the plant and the existence of a protected market because production costs for Americans were higher than those of their competitors, in particular the Russians. The Whig tariff of 1842, raising duties on imported hemp to $40 a ton, aroused great hopes. But the cotton-producing South, which was hostile to any rise in the price of materials for baling cotton, managed to get the duties on that article reduced in the Walker tariff of 1846 and again in 1857.

From then on, the future of this crop depended on the other market, supplying the navy. In 1841, Congress had decided to give priority to the purchase of American hemp. In 1843 hemp-buying agencies were created, and in 1845 a special credit of $50,000 was appropriated to enable the navy to buy American. However, naval authorities had trouble finding contracts both quantitatively and qualitatively satisfactory and preferred doing most of their business with Russian producers.[17]

Illinois farmers had been enthusiastic about the prospect of quick profits that hemp seemed to guarantee. The *Prairie Farmer* of July 1846 pointed to an epidemic of "hemp fever" in Sangamon County, a "very contagious and sometimes . . . fatal" disease.[18] Moving from the South because of his dislike of slavery, J. Vincent Brown, a hemp processor, had indeed just arrived in Sangamon County, where he contracted with local farmers who subsequently planted 2,500 acres in hemp. Comparative trials carried out by the navy in 1847 had concluded that this production was of the highest quality. "Hemp fever," born in the 1840s, was not limited to Sangamon County. Encouraged by the booming agricultural press, farmers rushed to try the miracle plant in northern and southern Illinois. The phenomenon continued throughout the 1850s, with the Illinois State Agricultural Society even organizing competitions for the "best half acre of hemp."[19]

The hemp producers of the Sangamon had no need of Lincoln's theoretical arguments on the tariff to be protectionists. This position was a peculiarity of the agricultural zone around Springfield in the 1840s. Those who grew hemp and those who raised sheep for wool favored protectionism. The latter in particular, who had obtained a high tariff on wool imports in 1828 (a compound duty of 4 cents per pound and 40 percent ad valorem), succeeded in consolidating their privileged position in 1846 especially, for the Walker tariff granted them protection equal to that enjoyed by spun and woven wool. Sangamon, with an annual production of 120,000 pounds of wool in 1850, was by far the principal wool-producing county (the second, Fulton, produced forty thousand pounds less).[20] This was doubtless one of the reasons for the Whig domination in this region, their only stronghold in Illinois during the 1840s.

The importance that defending this particular category of farmers had for Lincoln can be easily understood. He had the opportunity of doing so on March 22, 1848, when the House of Representatives received a proposal for a resolution passed two days before by the Senate, authorizing the government to buy water-rotted American hemp at a price not higher than the average of the last five years and on condition that the quality be comparable to the best foreign hemp. This proposition, which had been presented by the Florida Democrat David L. Yulee, a rabid free-trader and chairman of the Committee on Naval Affairs, provoked indignant or amused remarks on the part of protectionist senators from the industrial North. Simon Cameron, Democrat from Pennsylvania and Lincoln's future secretary of war, wondered about the value of a measure intended to promote only the interests of the West while the interests of Pennsylvania coal and iron were systematically slighted. John M. Niles, a Connecticut Democrat, congratulated his colleague Yulee on the new insights he seemed to have acquired on the protection of American interests.

On April 3, Lincoln suggested to the House of Representatives that they give priority consideration to this joint resolution, but in vain. All the Illinoisans present (John A. McClernand, Thomas J. Turner, and John Wentworth) except one (Orlando B. Ficklin) voted for Lincoln's proposition. The opposition came from George S. Houston (Dem.-Ala.) backed by Howell Cobb (Dem.-Ga.), who managed to defeat the successive attempts made to take up the question put forward by Robert Smith (Democratic representative of the Alton District in southern Illinois) on April 10, and then by Thomas Butler King (Whig-Ga.). Yet another Illinoisan, Thomas J. Turner (a Democrat representing the Freeport District in the north of the state), renewed the attack and finally obtained passage of the joint resolution, which was signed by President Polk on May 9. Lincoln did not take part in the final debate on May 4, when George W. Jones (Dem.-Tenn.) tried to amend the resolution to make it still more favorable to growers. King, who led the defense of the resolution, convinced him that it was sufficient to guarantee growers stability and good average prices (higher than $200 a ton), thus encouraging American agriculture while at the same time protecting the United States from fluctuations in the world market.[21]

We can see that Lincoln was keeping up with the problems of his district. In the same way, he presented petitions from Illinoisans on various subjects, defending the interests of Isaac Funk, for example, and of Philo Hale Thompson, a Whig merchant from Pekin who wanted to have one of his friends named to the Land Office of that town. He got a reimbursement for his friend Anson G. Henry, who had advanced funds to Illinois volunteers headed for Mexico. He visited the General Land Office several times to press his constituents' claims to land and requested, with varying success, jobs for his friends. After Zachary Taylor's election, his services were called upon to divide some spoils, chiefly the posts of receiver and register in the Land Offices of Springfield, Pekin, Edwardsville, Vandalia, Kaskaskia, and, on that occasion, he did not make everybody happy.[22]

As if he wanted to persuade people that his spot resolutions had been a pure formality, "rather aggressively for a freshman, Lincoln maneuvered to have his name attached to the liberalization" of laws distributing bounty land to veterans of the Mexican War, even though he knew perfectly well that bounty lands given to veterans mostly benefited speculators.[23] But his position on public lands cannot be reduced to that aspect alone—as important as it was.

THE QUESTION OF PUBLIC LANDS

Always faithful to his dream, he took part in the unsuccessful struggle of Illinoisans in the Senate (Douglas) and in the House to have public lands ceded for the construction of a railroad between the Mississippi and the Great Lakes. After Ficklin, Smith, McClernand, and Wentworth, Lincoln presented a proposition to that end but independently, while the other representatives from his state, all Democrats loyal to Douglas, generally acted together to defend those kinds of interests.[24]

He argued for the constitutionality of federal aid to states for the improvement of rivers and harbors (which Polk had vetoed, thereby provoking the Chicago Convention of July 1847) and voted for a new bill affirming it. His intervention on the question of internal improvements brought him congratulations from Horace Greeley.[25] Thus his vision of public lands as a means of improving transportation and of economic development was not belied by the positions he took in Congress. As always, he was ready to compromise with the interests of the "old states" to gain land cessions for western states, and his attitude during the debate over the admission of Wisconsin as a state demonstrated it once again.

According to custom, each new state received from the United States a certain amount of public lands to enable it to finance the development of its transportation. These lands were distributed in the form of sections of 640 acres located inside rectangular bands, where they alternated, like squares on a chessboard, with other sections that remained the property of the federal government. The same procedure was applied to land cessions for the construction of railroads and canals in all the states that benefited from them.

Eastern representatives had consented to award federal land to Wisconsin only on condition that public lands not ceded to the new state (the "alternate sections") would be sold at $2.50 an acre instead of $1.25. In the debate, Caleb B. Smith (Whig-Ind.), chairman of the Committee on the Territories, had framed the question broadly and presented the point of view of the West. He had opposed all increase in the price of public lands occasioned by concessions to the states, including for the construction of railroads. By so doing, he expressed the traditional trans-Allegheny position that the settlement of western states should not be slowed down by the high cost of public lands.

While hoping that Wisconsin might benefit from a reduction of $1.25 in the price of public lands located in its alternate sections, Lincoln urged his colleague Smith not to make his general position— which he was ready to adopt, if it were realistic—a condition for ceding public lands to the states. He explained "in passing" that he believed a doubling of the price was not justified and suggested a compromise price of $1.50. But he repeated his main point: if the issue "did not look to persons residing east of the mountains as it did to those who lived among the public lands," their views must be taken into account, and conditions placed by the "old states" on cession of public lands to the new states must be accepted.[26]

Neither Lincoln's conciliatory position nor Smith's firmness could budge the eastern Whigs from wanting to reserve the public domain to raise revenue for the federal government, and, as always, they would give to western states only the strictest minimum. Jacob Collamer (Whig-Vt.), chairman of the Committee on Public Lands, would bend his economic policy only to benefit Mexican War veterans. Lincoln publicly attacked the Whig leader Samuel Finley Vinton (Ohio) for his unwillingness to accept a preliminary topographic survey drawn up at state expense as evidence of a state's intention to complete the construction of a railroad and for using that as a pretext to oppose cessions of lands to subsidize the construction of rail networks.

The Mexican War contributed still further to a stiffening of eastern attitudes toward the public domain. The increase in the debt offered a good excuse for refusing to alienate what had officially become in January 1847 the security for it.[27] The slave South and the industrial East both viewed with disfavor the wave of northern workers and masses of emigrants moving toward the unoccupied lands of the West. Industrialists feared a decrease in the availability of workers, slaveholders feared the closing of territories to the peculiar institution, and the combination of the two forces was invincible in Congress.

On the other hand, granting land to veterans was more than ever on the agenda. Congressmen felt keenly the pressure that veterans could exert on them at election time, although it was less than the influence that land speculators exerted by "stuffing their pocket books."[28]

The position that Lincoln adopted in debate on this question was not at all surprising for a representative who wished to appease the agitation caused by his hostility to a war that had been genuinely popular and who enjoyed cordial ties with Illinois land speculators. We will see that the first factor was the determining one in his attitude. Even the most fervent reformers of the laws on public lands, Greeley or George W. Julian, would wait for the memories of Buena Vista to fade a bit (until 1852) before expressing opposition (timid at that, a necessity of parliamentary bargaining) to the principle of these grants.[29]

Lincoln came down in favor of granting lands to Mexican War veterans and seized the opportunity offered by a discussion on an amendment to the law of February 11, 1847, organizing troop levies for the war, which had called for such distributions. On March 29, 1848, he proposed adding by way of amendments three propositions: the benefit should be extended to veterans who had joined up as privates and had been promoted to officers; it should be extended to "the volunteers of the war of 1812"; and the title holders should have the possibility of locating their claim "in parcels, and not be required to locate them in one body" as was required previously.[30]

The third proposal came from Lincoln himself and took up an idea that he had put forward in a proposition rejected by the House of Representatives on February 9. He wanted veterans to be able to use their titles flexibly and foresaw in particular their being able to acquire in that way lands for which they already had a right of preemption.[31] This measure was obviously intended for veterans of states where public lands still existed. He was, then, bending the system of bounties to veterans in a slightly democratic direction and proving his solicitude for the interests of Illinois squatters.

The first point, concerning officers promoted from the ranks, had been mentioned by Alexander Evans (Whig-Md.) on March 7. The adoption of a similar measure to benefit veterans of the Black Hawk War enabled Captain Lincoln to profit from grants of land in 1852 and 1855. Was Lincoln's espousal of this point an affirmation of the right of each American to rise in society?[32] Certainly, it was that, but he was at the same time taking Evans's position into account in order to gain his approbation for the second proposition, which came from Joshua R. Giddings, the Whig abolitionist from Ohio, and which carried a precise meaning.

Giddings had risen to condemn the "indecent haste" with which people eagerly compensated the authors of an aggression against a neighboring country while the heroes of 1812 had not all received from the nation the testimony of admiration that their defense of the country against an invader surely merited. Evans ridiculed Giddings, explaining that such cases did not exist. By affirming quite plainly the opposite and invoking the statement of his neighbor John P. Gaines (Whig-Ky.), Lincoln thus made a gesture toward Giddings while avoiding venturing onto dangerous ground.

However, Lincoln displayed these gems of parliamentary skill in vain. The Whig speaker (Robert C. Winthrop of Massachusetts) was no more favorable to his new-style amendment than was the leader of the Democrats (Linn Boyd of Kentucky), who had reported unfavorably on the original project.[33]

Giddings's noisy irruption into the debate on land grants to veterans testified to the invasive nature of the slavery question because the "Old Horse" from Ohio, in opposing the Mexican War by all means, was combating the extension of slavery. And, little by little, the question of slavery would weigh more and more in the deliberations on a subject traditionally looked at from the perspectives of state revenues, of industrial development, and of the needs of westward expansion.

Admittedly, traditional interests and problems remained important, as we have seen. Congressmen found time to discuss the fate of states that were put at a disadvantage because of the whims of geography and to whom were allotted poorly located or even nonexistent sections of land intended for the financing of their school systems (the sixteenth section of each township) before they realized that the question was already almost solved by an earlier law that Lincoln took the trouble of searching for in the General Land Office in response to a petition of Illinoisans.[34] He was inspired by the views of John A. McClernand, the only Illinoisan on the Committee on Public Lands, and we shall see that Douglas's righthand man in the House exerted a certain influence upon him.

But the first session of the Thirtieth Congress saw the appearance of projects tending to link the future of the public domain to the question of slavery, with abolitionists adopting a combative attitude. Thus, Amos Tuck (Whig-N.H.) presented a petition from the citizens of Philadelphia, asking that the proceeds from the sale of public lands be earmarked for the extinction of slavery. Lincoln voted in favor of receiving this petition. He was present on May 18, 1848, when William Duer (Whig-N.Y.) proposed setting aside a territory taken from the public domain to give homesteads to freed Negroes.[35]

LINCOLN AND SLAVERY IN CONGRESS

The issue of slavery, already irritating in 1846–47 and coming to the fore after the victory over Mexico and the settlement of the Anglo-American dispute over Oregon, largely dominated the Thirtieth Congress. The period of tension, marked by several incidents in Congress and in Washington, revealed to Lincoln the depth of the antagonism between North and South.

The opponents of slavery took the offensive (at least with words) in two directions: first, the abolition of the slave trade and if possible of slavery itself in the District of Columbia, and, second, the rejection of the extension of the peculiar institution into the territories, whether "ceded" from Mexico (expressed in the Wilmot Proviso) or located in

Oregon. The creation of the Free Soil party in August 1848 and its participation in the presidential campaign reflected the importance of the anti-extension sentiment in the country.

This offensive provoked a lively reaction from the South. Calhoun seized the opportunity to begin realizing his dream of bringing together congressmen from the South without distinction of party (January 1849). This first frown was sufficient to cause the advocates of the abolition of slavery in the District of Columbia to retreat (the Gott Resolution was tabled in February). The South raised its voice again after Zachary Taylor's death made Millard Fillmore president. His sympathies for the peculiar institution were revealed rapidly—to general astonishment. This period culminated with the Compromise of 1850, an impossible deadlock of contradictions between slavery and liberal capitalism.

What attitude did Lincoln take during the two sessions from 1847 to 1849? The most recent and the most complete study of that question finds an ambiguous attitude on the part of the future president, a position of "yes and no" on slavery and anti-slavery. The ultra-revisionist position of Riddle goes even beyond that of Beveridge and gives the impression of great confusion in Lincoln's mind.[36] Like a majority of Northern representatives, Lincoln was undeniably disoriented by the unfolding of events. His commitment to Taylor's candidacy and the active campaign he waged in favor of the politically uncertain and slave-holding former general, in the company of men as different as Robert Toombs, Alexander Stephens, William H. Seward, and Benjamin F. Wade, hardly did anything to clarify the situation. However, a careful examination of his votes in Congress in chronological order and by categories of questions allows us to draw a few definitive conclusions.[37]

Firmness against the Extension of Slavery Where It Did Not Exist

In 1854, in his famous Peoria speech against the Kansas-Nebraska Act, Lincoln recalled having voted "at least forty times" for the Wilmot Proviso during his term in Congress, when it was "constantly coming up in some shape or other."[38] There is no reason not to believe him, for that is probably the number of occasions on which he had to make a decision, if we include procedural votes, on which a roll call was not ordered each time.

During the first session, he voted against the Clayton Bill (developed in the Senate in collaboration with Douglas), which proposed extending the Missouri Compromise line to the Pacific Ocean. The adoption of this law would have resulted in opening to slavery the territories of New

Mexico and Utah, which was later done with the Compromise of 1850. Despite the maneuvers of the Polk administration, which attempted to bring this about by all possible means, Lincoln and almost all the representatives of free states imposed the logic of 1787 against that of 1820. The law finally adopted establishing the Oregon Territory would refer to the Northwest Ordinance and not to the Missouri Compromise in excluding slavery.[39]

The anti-extension men, therefore, approached the second session from a position of strength. During that session, Lincoln voted in favor of the resolution presented by Joseph M. Root (Whig-Ohio) to create territories in New Mexico and California that would exclude slavery; he voted against the Walker amendment (passed by the Senate) to extend the laws of the United States to unorganized territories, which would have had the effect of annulling the prohibition on slavery established by Mexican law; and he voted for a new version of the Wilmot Proviso. But this time the Senate blocked all attempts to organize the territories acquired during the war with Mexico without the recognition—at least tacit—of the possibility of extending slavery there.[40]

The firmness against the extension of slavery, which Lincoln demonstrated throughout his term, reflected the sincerity of his convictions and the depth of the movement taking shape in favor of Free Soil. Admittedly, the movement of history dragged him forward without his being aware of it very clearly, and he never made the decision to abandon his legalistic excess baggage before being forced to do so by events, but his evolution was clear. It is interesting to see Lincoln join the group of "young Indians," including the Georgia pro-slavery Whigs Toombs and Stephens, in supporting the rather unprincipled politician Taylor yet end up conducting a presidential campaign based on Free-Soiler themes!

Lincoln found it impossible, of course, to defend the general's candidacy in Massachusetts, where he was sent by the Whig party, unless he presented Taylor as an anti-extensionist. The four surviving speeches deal almost exclusively with this subject. Lincoln's argument is simple, almost simplistic. Even if Martin Van Buren, the candidate of the Free Soil party, seemed to some Whigs to be completely safe on this question, much more so than the slaveholder Taylor, the former president had no chance of beating Lewis Cass, the Democratic candidate, who would surely support Southern extensionism. A vote for Taylor was the only useful vote, and Lincoln, for his part, promised that the old soldier would behave like a good Whig. The comments of the Free Soil newspapers on his Taunton speech were revealing. Describing Lincoln's Whig audience, the Free Soil journalist asserted, with an astounding impartiality for the era, that the climate of apathy and discouragement that prevailed until the arrival of the congressman from Illinois was quickly dissipated, for "It was reviving to hear a man speak as if he believed what he was saying and had a grain or two of feeling up with it."[41]

The choice Lincoln made to support a slaveholder as the best candidate for president to stop extension of slavery might with good reason seem contradictory. Lincoln and many historians after 1862 realized that only the abolition of slavery would dry up the source of extension and extensionism. But such a conception remained that of a minority during the years 1840 to 1854. Abolition called into question the most sacred right, the right of property, protected by the Constitution, the foundation of the nation. It was in that sense that Lincoln wrote in 1845, "I hold it to be a paramount duty of us in the free states, due to the Union of the states, and perhaps to liberty itself (paradox though it may seem) to let the slavery of the other states alone."[42]

Abolition of property, even if only partial abolition, is indeed the most serious threat that could weaken liberty in a society founded on the private ownership of the means of production. Lincoln was passionately attached to the defense of liberty and of property. He was, therefore, genuinely in favor of maintaining slavery in the South. What is paradoxical, or rather contradictory, is that the form of private property to which he was attached, founded according to him on human labor freely accumulated by the free worker, was incompatible with the other form of property, that which deprived a man of all the fruit of his work and reduced him to the level of a beast of burden.

That form of private property was, however, incompatible with slavery only to the degree that the two forms entered into competition in the same territory. As long as North and South were considered watertight compartments in a federation of autonomous states, a Northerner did not face the issue of slavery except in the territories, where the two systems met. On that question, Lincoln was inflexible.

The choice to support Taylor was, therefore, perfectly reasonable on Lincoln's part, to the degree that he judged that the general was really opposed to extension and that everybody was convinced rightly that a slaveholder was in the best position to fight against abolition. This candidacy promised to accomplish the impossible: maintain the status quo under the leadership of a national hero who would rule with a firm hand. Moreover, the few months of the Taylor administration (he died in July 1850) seemed to indicate that this was his position at the beginning.

In 1848–49, then, Lincoln was only just starting to become aware of the contradiction between slavery as founded on the rights of private property and slavery as constituting a particular form of that right that was opposed to the form that predominated in the United States. This was only the beginning of the "irrepressible conflict" between the two modes of production that coexisted in the country.

Opposition to the extension of slavery would lead Lincoln to aboli- tion of the peculiar institution. After recognizing that the field of combat, in both general terms and long-range terms, was the *nation* (the House Divided speech), pressure of events would lead Lincoln to the Emancipation Proclamation after many hesitations. In the same way, on a more modest scale, Lincoln's anti-extensionism in Congress led him to a practical position of extremely modest and circumscribed abolitionism.

Moderation on Slavery Where It Existed

During the first session, only his attitude toward abolitionist petitions distinguished Lincoln from Southern congressmen. He invariably voted to receive them, even though he opposed taking under consideration bills inspired by them.[43]

He favored compromise in the case of fugitive slaves imprisoned in Washington, whose cause was pleaded by Giddings in incidents that demonstrated how strong the feelings on opposing sides of the slavery question were. As early as April 18, 1848, Giddings had presented, amid jeers, a resolution demanding an inquiry into the reasons for the jailing in the District of Columbia prison of eighty men, women, and children whose sole crime was "an attempt to enjoy that liberty for which our fathers encountered toil, suffering, and death itself, and for which the people of many European governments are now struggling." He was opposed by an amendment put forward, amid laughter, by Isaac E. Holmes (D.-S.C.) proposing to replace all of the text following the demand for an inquiry with the phrase "whether the scoundrels who caused the slaves to be there ought not to be hung."[44] The situation only got tenser as time went on.

Lincoln came down in favor of indemnifying the owner of a slave stolen by the English in 1814 and against the abolition of the slave trade in the District of Columbia and a fortiori against the abolition of slavery there.[45] After the campaign in the summer of 1848 and the rise of anti-extensionist pressure, Lincoln's position evolved. When a new case to indemnify a slaveholder appeared, Lincoln began by voting in favor of a "bill for the relief of the legal representatives of Antonio Pacheco," who had lost a slave during an Indian war, before voting, in vain, against it. Was this a significant change in Lincoln's position on the property rights of slaveholders?[46] Perhaps it was merely a defensive reaction in response to the bitterness of the strictly sectional debate because this position was contradicted by the rest of Lincoln's attitude. He always insisted that the emancipation of slaves should be compensated financially and should be voluntary. This might have been, then, a sort of parliamentary "war measure," foreshadowing another war measure taken by the commander in chief in 1862.

The debate on the abolition of the slave trade and of slavery in the District of Columbia revealed this attitude clearly. Lincoln voted against a bill by John G. Palfrey (Whig-Mass.) to abolish slavery in the District, against a bill by Giddings to call a referendum by the population of the District on the abolition of the slave trade in Washington, and against a resolution by Daniel Gott (Whig-N.Y.) to abolish the slave trade in the District.[47] None of these measures satisfied him, because they were too radical. He himself prepared an amendment—in reality a substitution—to Gott's resolution, which expressed the state of his thinking on the subject.

The violence of the debate, the emotional importance of the presence of a slave market (the famous Georgia Pen) which could be seen from the windows of the Capitol in Washington (which Lincoln would mention in 1854), and the beginnings of abolitionist agitation in his quite moderate district combined to create the conditions for a personal statement. Lincoln, therefore, introduced his own bill on January 10, 1849.[48] It would forbid importation (section 1) and exportation (section 2) of slaves in the District of Columbia, except for the needs of federal officeholders and elected officials passing through Washington on business related to their positions. It called for emancipation (section 3) of slave children born after January 1, 1850 in the District, along with their employment as apprentices up to a certain age. Slaveholders would be permitted to sell their slaves—at a price to be determined by a government commission—to the federal government, which would free them (section 4). The municipal authorities of Washington and Georgetown would take appropriate measures to arrest fugitive slaves and return them to their owners (section 5). The entire project would be submitted to a binding referendum in which only white males of twenty-one years of age or older would vote (section 6).

Lincoln's position was obviously quite moderate. Compensated and voluntary emancipation was his great idea, as it was Clay's, for it alone did not call into question the right of property. The only "bold" measure called for in his bill was the automatic emancipation of children born after 1849, and even that was accompanied by an apprenticeship that considerably cushioned the shock of emancipation. In sum, the final disappearance of slavery in the District (concerning only residents) could be expected in about 1950. Section 5 of Lincoln's bill induced the abolitionist Wendell Phillips to nickname him the "slave hound from Illinois."

Nevertheless, as moderate as it was, the bill was seen as a provocation by pro-slavery men, and Calhoun in his "Southern Address" placed Lincoln on the same level as Gott, Giddings, and other abolitionists. Only a complete capitulation could satisfy the pro-slavery forces, as was seen in 1850, 1854, 1857, and 1860. Lincoln was not a man of complete capitulations.

Three days after introducing this amendment, he announced his intention of introducing a bill to abolish slavery in the District of Columbia "by the consent of free white people . . . and with compensation for owners." Unless this was merely the revival in another form of the resolution of January 10, the gesture indicated the high point of his abolitionist zeal in 1849, but, because no trace of it has been found, it is impossible to know exactly what he proposed.[49]

We thus see that Lincoln combined a very firm attitude against the extension of slavery with a particularly conservative position on the possibilities of doing away, even locally, with the particular institution, but this conservative position was evolving in a progressive direction. Does that mean that the conservatism that he expressed had no repercussions on his anti-extensionism? One could answer that, on the whole and on the most important subjects, he did not differ from the most zealous abolitionists. But, as soon as the threat of extension became less obvious, or the debate itself no longer gave it prominence, Lincoln let considerations other than the fight against slavery guide his actions. He did not forget his responsibilities as a member of the Congress of the United States, for example, on the issue of organizing the territories. By the close of the first session, anti-extensionists had succeeded in organizing Oregon as a free territory. Toward the end of the second session, however, no progress had been made in the direction of organizing California and New Mexico into territories. In contrast to pro-slavery people, Lincoln voted in favor of the organization of California as a free territory on February 27, 1849. But five days earlier, in contrast to abolitionists and anti-extensionists (Giddings, Wilmot, and Gott, for example) he voted for the extension of the laws of the United States into that territory, doubtless refusing to contribute to obstructing the situation.[50]

During his term as a congressman, then, Lincoln modified his attitude on the slavery question. From being a minor problem for him, it became an important element in the political situation. It is in the light of this experience that one should approach new aspects of the question of public lands, aspects that cannot be analyzed without referring to the competition between free labor and slavery. One was the agitation in favor the homestead law, which, as one writer noted, made its appearance "by coincidence" at the same time as the debate on the extension of slavery.[51]

LINCOLN AND THE HOMESTEAD, 1849

The credit for authorship of the first national homestead proposal went to Lincoln's colleague Robert Smith, who on January 4, 1844, proposed giving eighty acres to the head of any impecunious family who would occupy them.[52] From then on, at each session, propositions to that effect appeared and were immediately rejected.

During the 30th Congress, the same scenario was repeated but with a variation. In the House, the chairman of the Committee on Public Lands, Jacob Collamer, reported unfavorably on all projects tending to diminish the revenues of the federal government.[53] In the Senate, his counterpart was a Democrat from Illinois, Sidney Breese, who defended the interests of his state and those of the veterans of the Mexican War with more vigor than he did his own projects for reducing the price of public lands.[54]

During the second session, attention focused on two bills. One by Horace Greeley of December 13, 1848, proposing "to secure homes" on public land for those who had none, did not come up for a roll call vote, and Lincoln had not yet arrived at the time of the first vote on January 5.[55] Collamer calmly killed that bill in committee.[56] The second came from the Democrat from Illinois who sat on the Committee on Public Lands, John A. McClernand, Douglas's lieutenant in the House. His resolution proposed "That the present traffic in the public lands should cease, and that they should be disposed of to occupants and cultivators on proper conditions, at such a price as will nearly indemnify the cost [to the Federal government] of their purchase, management, and sale."[57] If it had been adopted, this resolution would have had the effect of promoting consideration of all bills having the effect so described, which would have constituted a great step forward in the direction of the Homestead Act.

A roll call vote having been asked for, Lincoln and fifty-nine representatives voted against tabling the resolution (that is, in favor of considering it). A majority of 104 voted to table it (that is, against considering it). The opposition between Whigs and Democrats seems well confirmed by the analysis of party voting: 87 percent of the Whigs opposed the resolution, and 64 percent of the Democrats favored it. A majority of Whigs from all sections voted against the resolution, except those from the Northwest (one out of four who were present) and the Southwest (the sole Whig present voted for it). A majority of Democrats from all regions voted for considering the resolution, except those from the Middle Atlantic states (44 percent only) and the South (16 percent).

The opposition between the parties was particularly noticeable in the slave border states of the West. Clay's Whigs dominated in Kentucky, while agrarian Democrats—among whom was Andrew Johnson—were in a majority in Tennessee. Ohio furnished the most striking example of partisan division within one state, pitting Samuel Vinton's Whigs against the Democrats. Only the abolitionist Whigs Joshua R. Giddings and Joseph M. Root from Ohio deserted their party to vote with the Ohio Democrats, who stuck together as fiercely as their rivals.

Lincoln's vote was therefore interesting for demonstrating how much he clearly distanced himself from his party. Only ten Whigs voted as he did: Horace Greeley and two other New York Whigs (Harvey Putnam and Eliakim Sherrill); two from Indiana (Caleb B. Smith and Elisha Embree); Giddings and Root; William A. Newell from New Jersey; Patrick W. Tompkins from Mississippi; and the maverick Toombs from Georgia.

The analysis of party votes by geographical sections helps to clarify the choices, to qualify them by highlighting factors other than partisan affiliation, which appears to have been decisive only in the slave border states, New England, and Ohio. Although still important in the Middle Atlantic states (90 percent of the Whigs were against the resolution and only 56 percent of the Democrats), political affiliation was not decisive there because a majority in favor of rejection clearly existed in both parties. It was even less important in the Northwest (except for Ohio), where 75 percent of the Whigs and 100 percent of the Democrats favored the resolution; it was negligible in the South (84 percent of Democrats and 93 percent of Whigs opposed the measure); and of no importance (but the sample was quite small) in the Southwest.

If, then, vote by section and by party is taken into account at the same time, Lincoln was representative of the Whigs of the Northwest, who were decidedly anti-slavery, whether they were moderates (Embree, Smith, Lincoln) or abolitionists (Root, Giddings). If we add Greeley and his friends from New York, we find a nice sample of the founders of the Republican party among the eleven Whigs who voted for the McClernand resolution.

The Homestead, Land, and Labor, 1849

Many reasons make it impossible to deal with the problem of the Homestead as if it were merely one measure among many for distribution of public lands. First, in terms of chronology, the agitation in favor of the Homestead was a recent phenomenon on the national level. Appearing in Congress in 1844, it became important in national political life only after 1852 and triumphed in 1862. Its history, then, "coincides" exactly with the development of the crisis linked to the question of the extension of slavery. That alone justifies a separate study of the other problems linked to public lands and throws light on Lincoln's vote in favor of the McClernand resolution during the second session.[58] There is, for that matter, nothing surprising about this "coincidence," inasmuch as the adoption of a Homestead law and the extension of slavery were the two opposing ways of definitively settling the question of the status of the territories.

Another factor differentiated the Homestead from other measures concerning the public domain. It involved specific demands by the labor movement. For city workers, nothing could replace the Homestead because graduation involved the poorest lands and therefore demanded substantial financial resources to succeed on not very fertile soil, whereas preemption a posteriori benefited only farmers who were already on the spot.

Was the prospect of a farm in the West merely a dream that was swept away by the reality of the costs of cultivation in the 1850s?[59] Even if that were the case, the novice farmer who could save on the acquisition of land had a better chance of fulfilling his dream than one who had to pay a high price for it. In any case, the force of attraction of the West was inversely proportional to the price of land, and, once on the spot, pioneers often proved they were capable of facing difficult conditions. Now this force of attraction was an important factor in determining the level of wages in the East, a reality that was perfectly clear to people at the time concerned with ways of realizing the "American Dream."

Even when workers were not directly interested in the possibilities offered by the West, they would benefit indirectly by the easing of competition from eastern farmers who were victims of the rural exodus and the immense waves of immigrants who were beginning to flood the East Coast.[60] From that point of view, the slogan of the Homestead had an educational value against nativist xenophobia and contributed to labor unity. Very quickly the Homestead became one of the principal worker demands, along with the ten-hour law. Subsequently, George Henry Evans contrasted the Homestead and the ten-hour law, describing the first as the goal and the second as the means of worker emancipation. His National Land Reform Association was opposed to the creation of unions. The slogan of the Homestead, then, became the demand of those seeking the disappearance of the labor movement and became part of a program that was not specifically labor related.[61]

But although the Homestead was the specific demand of workers in regard to land, it was not exclusively a worker demand. Many small and middling farmers hoped their children might profit from it, and the eternal squatters of the frontier were obviously in favor of it. The movement advocating the Homestead made more rapid progress on the level of congressional representation in the West than in the industrial East because western congressmen wanted their region to become populated quickly.

The year 1848 saw a significant breakthrough on the part of the movement for reform of the public domain, which was directed by the National Land Reform Association of George Henry Evans. At election time, both Martin Van Buren (the Free Soil candidate) and Gerritt Smith (the abolitionist candidate of the Liberty party) agreed to add this principle of reform to their platforms, and about a hundred candidates for Congress agreed to sign a pledge to "prevent all further traffic in the Public Lands of the United States, and to cause them to be laid out in Farms and Lots for the free and exclusive use of actual settlers."[62] The similarity between this wording and the (more moderate) wording of the McClernand resolution is remarkable, and it is not surprising to find the Illinoisans once again united on this measure, given the place of that state in the battle for the Homestead.

Several Prairie State politicians figured among architects of the Homestead. The National Reformers of 1848 had chosen as their candidate for vice president William S. Wait, the Democratic leader of Bond County and a longtime defender of agrarian causes, to whom Lincoln had written in 1839 to explain the change in the calculation of the tax base.[63] The Democratic party in Illinois was completely, or almost completely, behind the idea of reform. Long John Wentworth, the representative and future mayor of Chicago, who wrote numerous editorials in his Chicago *Daily Democrat* in favor of the Homestead as the only means of settling the question of the extension of slavery in the territories without an open conflict with the South, reflected the position of Stephen A. Douglas, who first introduced a Homestead bill in the Senate on December 27, 1849. Another supporter was William B. Ogden, an important stockholder in the American Land Company from 1833 to 1837, one of those who helped create the Illinois and Michigan Canal in the 1840s, a future president of the Chicago and Northwestern Rail

Road, and a leader of the Republican party of Illinois, who would become a close collaborator of Lincoln's, a congressman, and then governor of Illinois. At the time, Ogden was president of the Free Soil League of Chicago, whose secretary, the Democratic boss Fernando Jones, likewise favored reform. Other supporters included Carl A. Helmuth, the editor in chief of the *Illinois Staats Zeitung,* a German-language Democratic newspaper, and John Locke Scripps, Lincoln's future biographer.

It is striking to notice the number of speculators and large landed proprietors among the partisans of the Homestead in Illinois. Alongside Douglas and Wentworth (the creator of a model farm at Summit Hill and leader of the Illinois Breeding Association), for whom land speculation complemented their political activities, can be found Fernando Jones, William B. Ogden (who specialized in investing funds from the Atlantic Coast in western lands), Nathan H. Bolles, and William Sampson, for whom political activities complemented land speculation.[64]

For these men, the principal virtue of the Homestead was to attract settlers into the West, which had the effect of increasing the value of their well-chosen and nicely located lands. With equal zeal, Douglas and Wentworth expended their energy defending the Homestead and promoting the development of railroads. We will return later to these contradictory links between land cessions for railroads and encouragement of small private property. But at the beginning of the 1850s, railroads and the Homestead seemed to both Douglas and Lincoln a sure means of rapidly populating the West with pioneers, which would bring prosperity and liberty.

At that stage, both the industrial East and the slave South opposed the Homestead equally staunchly. It was only after the creation of the Republican party and the beginnings of the disintegration of the Democratic party that majorities in favor of the Homestead appeared in the House of Representatives. Furthermore, the railroad lobby opposed the Homestead to the very end, thus permitting the South to block all legislation of that type until 1860.[65]

As we have seen, Lincoln's attitude toward the East was conciliatory on the question of public lands during his first session in Congress. He had urged Caleb B. Smith to consider the argument of Jacob Collamer, who was asking for an increase in the price of federal lands near the new railroad lines created by cessions of public lands. On December 21, 1848, he voted for the McClernand resolution along with Smith and against Collamer. On February 13, 1849, he attacked Vinton somewhat bitterly, denouncing his "utterly futile" fears concerning a possible squandering of the public lands to the advantage of the "new States."[66]

This constituted an incontestable evolution, as Lincoln was in a position to gauge during the course of the second session the tenacity of the
representatives of the industrial East who doggedly refused to help the
development of the Northwest.

It is difficult to push any further the analysis of Lincoln's evolution
on the question of public lands. It should simply be noted that he
showed during the second session a new independence with regard to
his party and the East. This position was taken after the electoral
campaign of 1848, when he had to debate against the supporters of Van
Buren and Gerritt Smith in New England (both of whom were in favor
of Homestead and Free Soil). We have seen that after that same campaign his anti-extensionism on the question of slavery had begun to be
coupled with a limited, moderate, and gradual abolitionism. The inter-
ruption of his congressional career at the end of his term reduces us to
making conjectures about the later evolution of his position on public
lands. There is hardly any mention of this problem in his preoccupations of the 1850s, because all of his energy was used to unify the North
under the banner of anti-extensionism after 1854. The temptation is
therefore great to conclude that his vote in December 1848 was linked to
his opposition to the extension of slavery at least as much as to his
permanent desire to see the Northwest become prosperous and populated.

FROM FRUSTRATION TO DISARRAY

Lincoln had every reason to be disappointed with his stay in Washington.
Several days after his speech against the Mexican War, the United States
achieved a victorious peace. The question of territories remained in
suspense, and only Oregon had been organized. Illinois did not obtain
the cession of public lands needed for building a railroad. The problem
of slavery in the District of Columbia remained intact.

The only satisfaction he had, the choice of Taylor by the Whigs
followed by his election to the presidency, quickly turned sour. Lincoln
did not succeed in getting the federal office he sought, that of commissioner of the General Land Office. Only after the opening of the papers
in the Robert Todd Lincoln Collection were historians able to appreciate
the determination with which Lincoln had fought against his rival
Justin Butterfield, another Whig lawyer from Illinois, for nomination to
that office. Lincoln enjoyed many advantages: his vigorous campaign
for Taylor, his professional qualities, and his acceptability to the Democrats because of his courteousness. He had even received the support of
the departing commissioner, Richard M. Young. Butterfield, a man in

poor health—he would die shortly afterward—was altogether unpopular among Illinois Whigs and had done nothing for Taylor's victory. But he enjoyed the support of Webster, and Lincoln fell victim to the deals for dividing up offices made among the factions controlling the Whig party. The strenuous campaign waged by Lincoln's friends against Butterfield, which went as far as libel, was completely useless, and Butterfield was named commissioner of the General Land Office.[67]

Both sides had tried to obtain the largest possible number of recommendations from important political personalities, not only in Washington but also in Illinois. Although Butterfield had contented himself with getting signatures from Whig officeholders and lawyers (he had in particular the unanimous support of the Chicago bar), it seems that Lincoln circulated petitions among farmers. He doubtless believed that the latter were best able to judge the respective abilities of the two candidates. Butterfield, upset by such behavior, did not share that opinion. He prided himself on having collected only signatures of lawyers, of "leading and intelligent whigs, who are presumed to know something about the nature of the office and the qualifications requisite to fill it." Butterfield's assertion that Lincoln campaigned among the farmers of Morgan and Sangamon counties was bolstered by the fact that Lincoln chose Levi Davis, the land speculator and cousin of Judge David Davis, as an intermediary between himself and Butterfield. Large landowners and resident speculators in fact exercised a great deal of influence in the region and were those most capable of mobilizing small landowners.[68]

One should not believe, however, that Lincoln sought the office of commissioner of the General Land Office because of the nature of the work. The reason for his choice was that it was "about the only crumb of patronage which Illinois expects," and the position of commissioner was modest enough that he could aspire to it and sufficiently important to be worth the trouble that would be necessary to obtain it.[69]

There is a certain irony in this last episode of Lincoln's congressional career. His political ambition did not receive its expected gratification yet Lincoln had retained the friendship of those who had been won over by his talents as a lawyer. One can consequently understand the remark in his third-person autobiography for Scripps: "Upon his return from Congress he went to the practice of the law with greater earnestness than ever before."[70]

The great question that had come to the fore during his term in Congress was not settled. The prospects for its solution were quite uncertain in 1849, and Lincoln's political preoccupations could easily take on considerable importance in his mind. The next year, the Compromise of 1850 would settle "forever" the problem of the extension of slavery.[71] This permanent solution lasted only four years, until the Kansas-Nebraska Act. During those four years, Lincoln, who continued to lead the Whig party in Illinois, gave three important speeches: funeral orations for Taylor and Clay and an election speech in favor of Winfield Scott, the Whig candidate in 1852, which did not resonate any less sadly.

After the death of Taylor, Lincoln expressed fears about the likelihood of settling "the one *great* question of the day" because with the general had died his popularity, from which Lincoln expected miracles.[72] Lincoln doubtless hoped for a firm and resolute attitude on the part of the old soldier, such as he had begun to demonstrate at the time of the dispute between Texas and New Mexico and had expressed in his plan for organizing the territories. Taylor had offered to give immediate statehood to California and to do the same thing very quickly for New Mexico, thus avoiding the issue of the Wilmot Proviso while guaranteeing concretely and effectively—given the brief length of time expected to elapse before the adoption of a constitution—that these states would be free.

Taylor's death in July 1850 was one of the factors making possible the adoption of the Compromise of 1850 in September. Douglas was without doubt its architect even more than was Clay, but history and legend have attributed it to Clay. Two years after the eulogy on Taylor, Lincoln gave one on Clay. It is striking to notice that although the orator, in two short passages, showered praise on Clay for the Compromise of 1850, he did not expand on this point, whereas he described in detail the other successes of the "Great Compromiser": the entry of the United States into war with Great Britain in 1812 and especially the adoption of the Missouri Compromise of 1820.[73] Lincoln did not discuss the substance of the Compromise of 1850 until 1854, in his speech in Bloomington on September 12, when he described

what are called the "compromise measures of 1850," which comprised among other things the following:

1st. The "fugitive slave law," which was a concession on the part of the North to the South.

2d. California was admitted as a free State, called a concession of the South to the North.

3d. It was left with New Mexico, and Utah to decide when they became States, whether they would be free or not. . . . The South had got all they claimed, and all the territory south of the compromise line had been appropriated to slavery; they had gotten and eaten their half of the loaf of bread.[74]

Lincoln's reservations about the Compromise of 1850 between its adoption and 1854 and the analysis he then made show how unenthusiastic his adherence to it was. But, to the degree that the compromise seemed effectively to put an end to "fraternal strife" and left the country "prosperous and powerful," Lincoln, like the majority of politicians in the North, was ready to be satisfied with it.[75]

Only the abolitionists continued to treat slavery as a major political question in their speeches, newspapers, and pamphlets. For the rest of the political class, it was time to return to normality, to continue business as usual. As one of the leaders of the Whig party in Illinois, Lincoln had to do "something in the way of canvassing" for Scott in 1852, although, because of "the hopelessness of the cause in Illinois," he admitted doing much less than for previous presidential campaigns.[76]

He seemed to invest as little of his intellect and emotions as he did of his time, as his speeches in the summer of 1852 demonstrate. Because Lincoln argued that the Compromise of 1850, whether "for praise or blame," had entered into the "history of the country" as the fruit of national thought and "belonged to neither party to the exclusion of the other," he rejected the claims by Douglas and the Democratic party that it was their property and denied their accusations that the Whigs were campaigning for their candidate by spitting on the platform that included adherence to the compromise. All of Lincoln's argument consisted of showing that Douglas was accusing the Whigs without any proof. By doing so, Lincoln demonstrated the truth of the senator's charges, for he never once defended the compromise.

With this point eliminated from the debate, what remained? A defense of Scott's military career, an interesting defense against imputations that the Whig platform was nativist, and the eternal declarations in favor of increasing the tariff all mixed with jokes ranging from ludicrous to vulgar.[77]

If Lincoln did not retire from politics between 1850 and 1854, it was doubtless because he retained a bit of political ambition, or rather because he did not want to lose the prestige that went with his last title, that of member of the National Committee of the Whig party. Like his party, he survived. Recalling this period in his autobiography for Fell he wrote in 1859: "I was losing interest in politics, when the repeal of the Missouri Compromise aroused me again."[78]

7

RECONCILIATION

Part 1: Go West, Young Man

GO FORTH INTO THE COUNTRY

The Lincoln-Douglas debates have rightly assumed a place of prominence in history. As these two men competed against each other, two visions of the world also met head on. However, in the context of this study, what needs to be stressed is that at stake in this conflict was the political, cultural, and symbolic representation of a critical part of the American people: the rural masses of what was then the Northwest. Until 1858, in the eyes of America, of immigrants, and of the entire world, Stephen A. Douglas represented that new power, "the Great West," "a growing, increasing, swelling power that will be able to speak the law to this nation."[1]

How Lincoln—along with Douglas—kept pace with the growth of the Northwest and what mark he left on the land of Illinois during the decade of the 1850s are the first questions we must answer. To do that, we must consider the connections of the future president with immigrants who longed for the Homestead, with railroads that opened the new land and acquired immense landed property, with land speculators, squatters, large landowners, and sharecroppers, and with the great agricultural revolution that would transform the prairie into the corn belt. But this analysis will not be sufficient to explain why Lincoln in 1858 helped his party obtain more popular votes than their Democratic rivals, and why the Republican party, of which he was one of the first and most important founders, won the 1856 election for governor and the 1860 election for president.

Everybody agrees that the Lincoln-Douglas debates played a decisive role in the evolution of the rural electorate of Illinois, who largely deserted the Democratic party for the Republican party. It remains to be seen how the subject of those debates, devoted exclusively to expressing two different points of view on the connection between slavery and free labor, could have been chosen by orators and accepted by the electorate as the touchstone of political orientation. All other current issues were deliberately put aside:

> immigration, the tariff, international policy, promotion of education, westward extension of railroads, the opening of new lands for homesteads, protection against greedy exploitation of those lands (a problem to which Congress gave insufficient attention), encouragement to settlers, and the bettering of agriculture, not to mention such social problems as guarding against economic depression, improving the condition of factory workers, and alleviating those agrarian grievances that were to plague the coming decades—with such issues facing the country, these two candidates for the Senate talked as if there were only one issue.[2]

The Appeal of Illinois Land

The population of Illinois doubled between 1850 and 1860, going from 851,000 to 1,712,000 inhabitants. The urban population tripled, going from 64,000 to 246,000, and Chicago, that "little mushroom town" of 1833, covered with smoke as early as 1849, was by 1860 an industrial metropolis with numerous metallurgical factories, which drained off the agricultural produce of Illinois by canal and railroad before loading it, through elevators with a capacity of 750,000 bushels, on ships headed for the East via the Great Lakes.[3]

The large number of immigrants, especially Germans and Irish, who crowded into Chicago were no less eager for land than those lucky enough to settle on the prairie upon their arrival in Illinois. Wentworth's reforming agitation was proof of that. And they could not help being dazzled by the biblical richness of the now-cultivated prairie as it was described at that time by the amazed Reverend J. P. Thompson: "one may ride on horseback through acres of corn without once seeing over the tops of the gigantic stalks, and where at harvest time the wondrous cutting-machine, drawn by horses, like the old scythe-armed chariot of Roman warfare, as it forces its mighty swath through the toppling grain, mocks at the puny efforts of the sickle, and the hot and weary day's work of a man." Only there can one understand what the Bible said of the "vast wealth of Job in lands, and corn, and stock."[4] How "easy" it was for a farmer to make a living! Even a worker could be happy in Illinois as easily as could a farmer. Did not two workers succeed in creating a factory? added Gerhard in 1857 before concluding his excellent guide with the most famous example of all, that of Douglas: "The poor schoolmaster has become a man of affluence and has filled various public offices with advantage to the state. . . . This is no dream—no fancy sketch—but the literal history, so far as it goes, of thousands of our western farmers."[5]

The pull exerted by Illinois on the poor farmers of the Northeast can be easily understood. They flocked en masse, reversing the balance of immigration toward the Prairie State, previously still weighted in favor of citizens from such areas as Kentucky and southern Indiana.[6] Farmers weary of the poor soils of New England, which, Lincoln said, "scarcely sprouts black-eyed beans,"[7] pushed on toward Illinois, and the proportion of people originating in the South and the slave border states fell from 17 percent to 10.5 percent in the population of the state. The proportion of foreigners grew from 13 percent to 19 percent.[8] For all these newcomers to Illinois, the Homestead was the promise of an easy settlement in the West. Among them, foreigners, especially the Germans, constituted a particularly active and militant group in favor of the Homestead. It was, in fact, in response to the Germans of Cincinnati in 1861 that Lincoln would make his first public declaration on the subject. It is therefore interesting to consider the ties between Lincoln and foreigners as an introduction to the study of his attitude toward that measure.

AMERICA FOR AMERICANS?

The sizable foreign immigration in the years from 1845 to 1860 at first swelled the ranks of the Democratic party, which since Jefferson had been the party of equal rights between American citizens and future citizens. But the attachment of foreigners, particularly Germans, to Free Soil, which was for them a vital issue, was demonstrated by the beginnings of defection in 1854 after the adoption of the Kansas-Nebraska Act. Germans in America, who were by and large anti-slavery, were not reassured by the defeat in the House of the Clayton amendment, passed by the Senate, which would have reserved the territories exclusively for American citizens.[9] However, their change of opinion could never result in positions that were concrete and durable unless a party appropriated them to develop a new policy. But the Republican party, absorbed in merging anti-Kansas-Nebraska Democrats, anti-slavery Whigs, Free-Soilers of various origins, nativists from the American party, and prohibitionists, took a long time before ridding itself of xenophobia. And Douglas managed to get the foreign electorate back under control, from the always-faithful Irish to the Germans, who at least favored the senator who declared support for the Homestead without restriction of nationality and opposed the prohibition of German beer and the Irishman's much-loved whiskey. Therefore, on the national level, Republicans did not increase their share of the German vote between 1856 and 1860.

Before 1940, historians erroneously conceived of the German vote as a block that, on the initiative of the leaders of the community, was transferred to the Republican party and thus made possible Lincoln's election in 1860 by giving him the extra votes he needed to defeat his opponents in the decisive states of the Northwest. But more recent research has demonstrated that five out of six Germans voted for Douglas in Wisconsin, where the Yankee element tipped the scales in Lincoln's favor. Furthermore, the majority of Germans in Iowa voted for Douglas in 1860 as they had voted Democratic in 1856, and they did so despite the position of their leaders. And the managers of the Republican party counted too much upon these quite discredited "leaders," who exerted little influence on electors likely to vote Republican because they had for so long been members of the Democratic party. Research on these questions emphasizes the importance of two positions taken by eastern Republicans: the Maine law organizing prohibition and the Massachusetts law granting the right to vote exclusively to those who were naturalized. It concludes that opposition of foreigners to these measures explains their vote against Lincoln.

A subtler analysis shows that although German Catholics voted against Lincoln, German Protestants and free-thinkers voted for him. This difference demonstrates the importance of slavery in the voters' considerations because the Catholic church was not opposed to slavery, as well as the impact of nativism directed as much against a "papist conspiracy" as against foreigners. The labor movement, both union and political, was almost entirely on Lincoln's side and campaigned under the banner of the Homestead and anti-extension.

A certain number of facts will enable us to qualify the revisionist conclusions just described. One must be prudent and take into account the existence of what Ronald P. Formisano calls " 'the law of available data' by which it is assumed that significant causes are those which can be measured. Saturation in traditional sources as well as a historian's sense of the relevant can keep quantitative analysis in perspective."[10] We know, in fact, that *all* the political observers at the time believed that the German vote would be decisive, and all sides struggled to obtain it, publishing newspapers in German, presenting German candidates, and lining up German speakers. The influence of the Republican campaign on "Germans" in general may need to be revised downward, but the extent of the influence of Germans, in particular militant ones, on the Republican campaign must be fully considered. Particularly is this so in Illinois, where the German vote was decisive and where the Republican party in 1856 and Lincoln in 1860 obtained it not only by renewed concessions on the issues of nativism and prohibition, but also by fighting fiercely for the Homestead.

The role of Germans must be further qualified. Eighty percent of Illinois Catholics voted Democratic; old rural communities voted less Republican (65 to 70 percent) than new ones (85 percent). In Chicago a violent reaction to the threats of prohibition (the "beer riots" of 1855) and to the nativism of local Republicans gave a majority of 70–75 percent to Democrats in 1856 in the German neighborhood called "Nordseite."

This preliminary study provides the necessary context for an analysis of Lincoln's attitude on the essential question, Should American land belong only to citizens? Should there be discrimination among workers of different nationalities on American soil? Should the Homestead be extended to foreigners?

Lincoln and Foreigners

Lincoln was not a xenophobe although his attitude was extremely rare at the time in Whig circles. William Herndon and Mary Todd Lincoln, for example, were fiercely anti-Irish, and Mary supported Millard Fillmore in 1856.[11] The young shopkeeper from New Salem had moved in Masonic circles; he gave the eulogy for the Master Mason Bowling Green at the invitation of Springfield Masonic Lodge No. 4. It is possible that he had met members of the Jewish community of Petersburg.[12] At any rate, he showed an open-mindedness rare for the period when, as president, he opposed Simon Cameron by advocating the naming of Jewish chaplains in the army and revoked Grant's order forbidding Jews access to military camps under his command. This benevolence extended to all foreigners, Irish as well as Germans, and to Catholics as well as Protestants.[13]

Thus Lincoln was not at all doing violence to his own feelings when he set out to cultivate the German vote. Campaigning for John C. Frémont in Belleville in 1856, he created a sensation by declaring merrily "God bless the Dutch," thus using the popular expression by which the Germans were known but which was studiously avoided by hypocritical xenophobes in their official speeches.[14] His letter to Theodor Canisius of May 17, 1859, was intended to make known officially his position against the Massachusetts law. Because of this opposition, he was the second choice of Germans at the Republican convention of 1860 (William Henry Seward was first, both leading Edward Bates, who was a nativist), and his German friends played a role in the nomination.[15]

Lincoln entrusted to Gustave Koerner the direction of efforts extended toward Germans. Koerner, a lawyer from Belleville, put him in touch with Canisius, editor-in-chief of the *Freie Presse* of Alton, and, on May 30, 1859, Lincoln confided to the latter the management of the *Illinois Staats Anzeiger,* which he had recently acquired. It was in the first issue of that newspaper that the letter to Canisius was published. Koerner was a moderate, a "Gray" liberal who distrusted more radical "Greens." He presented the traditional themes of agrarian Jacksonianism and claimed to draw on the tradition of 1830 more than that of 1848. An important role went to Friedrich Hecker, a hero of 1848 and a farmer in St. Clair County, who established himself, despite Koerner, as the principal organizer among Germans and was recognized as such by Lincoln but whom Lincoln stopped using at Koerner's insistence.[16] In the person of Koerner, Lincoln brought into his campaign a moderate anti-slavery man who had broken with Douglas in 1854, two years after being elected lieutenant governor of Illinois.

In 1860 Lincoln enjoyed several advantages with German voters. He was known as the main adversary to nativism within the Illinois Republican party. Indeed, he played the principal role in the tolerant direction taken by the party in 1856. The lateness of the formation of the party in Illinois limited the impact of the nativist wave, which was beginning to recede by then. All those of progressive tendencies and the most militant elements in the German community campaigned for the Republican party. Thus the caucus of German delegates at the Chicago Convention brought together the widest possible spectrum: Caspar Butz, a former Forty-eighter and representative in the Illinois house, who drafted the portion of the Republican platform dealing with foreigners in 1860; Koerner; Hecker; George Schneider, the founder of the *Illinois Staats Zeitung* and a collaborator of Lincoln's since 1856; Charles F. Haussner, creator of workers' and gymnastic associations, who after the war became a successful realtor; and Joseph Weydemeyer, a former Prussian artillery officer, friend of Marx, editor of the *Voice of the People* [*Stimme des Volkes*] in Chicago in 1860, general of a Missouri regiment, and principal correspondent of Marx and Engels on military questions in the Civil War.[17]

Lincoln, the Germans, and the Homestead

All shades of anti-slavery resistance were represented, from the moderate positions of Koerner and of the Arbeiterbund, which had finally taken a stand against slavery for the first time in 1859, all the way to the abolitionism of Weydemeyer. All these shades of opinion, all the newspapers—from the Quincy *Whig* to Koerner's *Belleviller Zeitung,* from Carl Schurz's *Anzeiger des Westens* to the Canisius-Lincoln *Illinois Staats Anzeiger*—campaigned energetically for the Homestead. The slogans *"Die Heimstätte-Bill"* and *"Land für die Landlosen"* sounded equally good in German and in English, even if the lawyer and landowner Koerner did not give them the same meaning as did the socialist Weydemeyer. The latter had, in fact, published in 1855 under the auspices of the *American Workers League* a pamphlet presenting the Homestead in a distinctive way, putting forward the slogan of "inviolability and indivisibility of state property, development of these lands by workers' associations under the control and with the help of the states."[18] The same unanimity in favor of the Homestead was also found among the Scandinavians, to whom Lincoln confided the education of his son Robert before sending him to Harvard and the majority of whom voted Republican.[19]

Consequently a question inevitably arises, Why did Lincoln not declare his support for the Homestead until February 12, 1861, when he responded "to Germans at Cincinnati" in very vague terms? On the one hand, and this is most important, Lincoln waited to be elected before revealing his position on any question except for the extension of slavery in order to avoid dividing the Republican party. He therefore remained silent on the tariff, writing to one Pennsylvania correspondent in October 1859 that, although he was personally in favor of protectionism, "it is my opinion that, just now, the revival of that question, will not advance the cause itself, or the man who revives it."[20] He did not reveal his protectionist views until February 15, 1861, in his speech in Pittsburgh, when he hid behind the Republican platform by endorsing its plank on the tariff.[21]

On the other hand, it is possible that his convictions had been strengthened by the enthusiasm of the crowds on his "journey to greatness."[22] The vagueness of his stands can be explained by his not wishing to commit his administration in advance on questions that were the primary responsibility of Congress, where the congressional bargaining among sections and party factions was supposed to bring about a unity of decision without executive arbitration (a traditional Whig stance). His duty, therefore, was to remain vague on the subject.

But it seemed important to him that the Republican president-elect declare publicly that he did not intend to imitate the retiring Democratic president, Buchanan, who had just vetoed a Homestead Bill finally passed by both houses.

Those were the conditions surrounding Lincoln's response to the question asked by the Germans at Cincinnati. The particular circumstances were equally interesting because they testified to the determination of one portion of the foreign-born workers in the Northwest and to the deliberate nature of Lincoln's declaration. The representative of the Germans, Frederick Oberkleine (or Oberkline) had expressed himself thus:

> We, the German free workingmen of Cincinnati, avail ourselves of this opportunity to assure you, our chosen Chief Magistrate, of our sincere and heartfelt regard. You earned our votes as the champion of Free Labor and Free Homesteads. Our vanquished opponents have, in recent times, made frequent use of the terms "Workingmen" and "Workingmen's Meetings," in order to create an impression that the mass of workingmen were *in favor of compromises between the interests of free labor and slave labor, by which the victory just won would be turned into a defeat.*[23]

Oberkleine concluded by encouraging the president-elect to stand firm and promised the backing—military if necessary—of those for whom he spoke.

To this speech, which was not on the program, Lincoln responded with a sketch of the problem of secession, a general declaration in favor of working men as the basis of all governments "for the reason that there are more of them than of any other class," an assessment of "Germans and foreigners" as "no better than other people, nor any worse." He also seized the occasion to assert his support for the Homestead, but in the vaguest terms. Two versions of his remarks were recorded: "I am in favor of cutting up the wild lands into parcels, so that every poor man may have a home," or "I think it [the Homestead Law] worthy of consideration, and that the wild lands of the country should be distributed so that every man should have the means and opportunity of benefitting his condition. [Cheers.]"[24]

It is immediately obvious that, although the question was unanticipated, Lincoln had carefully prepared his answer, seizing upon what he himself called "an allusion . . . to the Homestead Law," to give an indication of his personal position on the issue. Because the president enjoyed a certain freedom of movement in regard to the party platform, it is not insignificant that Lincoln decided to declare himself in favor of the Homestead. It was proof that he considered this a beneficial measure.

Why? It was not because of a change in his tolerant attitude toward speculators, as we will see. Reasoning by analogy to the evolution he experienced during his term in Congress, we can assume that at a certain point in his reflection on the fight against the extension of slavery, Lincoln concluded that the Homestead was necessary for that struggle. It was, after all, what Douglas had been repeating incessantly since 1850. Lincoln's silence until after the election of 1860 can thus be better understood. It was imperative for him to beat Douglas by forcing him to answer a precise question, the legal possibilities of extending slavery. Douglas, however, was willing to leave open these possibilities as a concession to the South. He depended on a series of extra-legal arguments and means as a way of insisting that extension would be avoided and of contributing to prevent it. Among those means, the Homestead held a major place, and Douglas had attached his name to the measure as early as 1849.[25] Lincoln would have had nothing to gain by standing on his opponent's chosen ground, from which Douglas enjoyed enormous prestige derived from his national stature and efforts.

A second argument spoke in favor of silence, that of the unity of the Republican party, and we will have occasion to return to this theme. But, on the other hand, it would have been dangerous to let Douglas monopolize the debate in favor of the Homestead. In particular, a grave risk existed of alienating the foreign vote, either by not campaigning for the Homestead or by campaigning for a Homestead reserved for Americans. But only the latter was acceptable to a large segment of the Republican party influenced by nativism, and Lincoln did not want to confront them head-on.[26] Lincoln resolved this thorny problem by (1) making no pronouncement on the Homestead, but (2) rejecting in the abstract any differentiation between American citizens and foreigners and (3) letting his friends—especially Germans—campaign for the Homestead.

After the election Lincoln did not disappoint the foreigners who put their trust in him, and the conclusion to his answer to Oberkleine was a call for immigration: "And inasmuch as the continent of America is comparatively a new country, and the other countries of the world are old countries, there is more room here, comparatively speaking, than there is there; and if they can better their condition by leaving their old homes, there is nothing in my heart to forbid them coming; and I bid them all God speed."[27]

Pioneers who heard that call in the 1850s found before them a land very different from that which Thomas and Abraham Lincoln had cleared in 1830. The last wolf hunt took place in 1852. The railroad had definitely triumphed over wild nature. Straddling the Mississippi, the rail crossed Rock Island, and its bridge pilings stood where Black Hawk took his first steps in the bluegrass of the Sauk village. His old enemy Shabbona, the Potawatomi chief who helped the whites in 1832, was now eighty. Duped by the government and exploited by land speculators, he maintained great dignity in his poverty and sat in majesty next to the abolitionist Republican representative Owen Lovejoy on the rostrum of honor during the debate between Lincoln and Douglas in Ottawa.[28]

Although wolves and Indians had disappeared, the pioneer of 1850 had to compete for land with even more formidable rivals. Large landowners, cattle kings, speculators, and railroad companies had, in fact, seized control of the best land and had possession of most of the prairie. Several years later, the pioneer would either have to buy his land from these large estate holders or rent from them.

THE LAST SALES OF PUBLIC LAND IN ILLINOIS

Thirty-five million acres, that was the area of Illinois, one of the most beautiful regions of the American public domain, an immense wealth that passed into private hands in the space of forty years. When Congress granted each state a land cession for founding agricultural colleges (the Morrill Land Act of 1862), Illinois had to receive its gift (480,000 acres) in the form of paper scrip because the Prairie State no longer had that quantity of public land within its boundaries. And when the Homestead Law was finally signed by the Illinoisan Abraham Lincoln, the fifty-nine beneficiaries from the Prairie State divided up between 1862 and 1880 fewer than five thousand acres.[29]

The pace of disposal of the public domain had accelerated considerably. Before 1841, sixteen million acres had been either sold (73 percent of the total) or distributed to the state, to veterans, or to others. From 1841 to 1848, five million acres were mostly sold, and, in the absence of separate statistics for those who benefited from rights of preemption, it can be assumed that a goodly portion went to small farmers taking advantage of the 1841 law. From 1849 to 1856, six million acres were bought by farmers, large and small, and six million by speculators. The rest, two million acres, was controlled by public and private institutions to which the federal government had ceded them and which had not yet sold them, except for about a hundred thousand acres that could still be bought at Springfield, site of the last Land Office still open. These lands, located in the eastern and southern portions of the state, were of

mediocre quality and sold at a discount in accordance with the Graduation Law of 1854.[30]

The federal government was especially prodigal in distributing sixty-
one million acres of public land to veterans between 1847 and 1855
(thirty-four million for the year 1855 alone), and, after 1850, most
purchases of public land in Illinois were paid for with land warrants.[31]
More often, these land warrants were sold to speculators for sums from
60 cents to $1 an acre. Rarely did an eastern veteran take advantage of
the opportunity he had to register his warrant himself. A westerner was
more likely to do so. Thus Captain Abraham Lincoln took the trouble to
register two warrants, one for forty acres in 1852, the other for 120 acres
in 1856, which he had received because of his service in the Black Hawk
War. But although most farmers who were veterans wanted above all to
enlarge their property and bought land near their farms, Lincoln wanted
to make a good investment. He therefore entrusted the task of registering
the first warrant to the lawyer Clifton H. Moore. Moore, a large landowner in Clinton County and an associate of David Davis's (they owned
jointly seventy thousand acres in the Northwest), was a colleague of
Lincoln's, like him a lawyer for the Illinois Central Railroad. Moore
registered the forty acres in Tama County, Iowa. They would be sold by
Lincoln's heirs for $500 in 1874. In 1859, Lincoln took the trouble of
registering his second warrant himself. The second parcel, of 120 acres,
was located in Crawford County, Iowa, 144 miles west of the first parcel,
in an area where Moore also speculated. It would be sold for $1,300 in
1892. According to Herndon, these lands had above all sentimental
value for Lincoln, who was proud of having earned them in the war and
who declared that he would never sell them.[32] However, Lincoln was
careful to see that this sentimental value would become more concrete
by virtue of a good investment.

Speculators also benefited from cessions of public land to the state of
Illinois (1.5 million acres) resulting from laws distributing swamps to
the states in which they were located. (The three Swamp Lands Acts of
1849–50 concerned 6.5 million acres in the United States that could be
acquired for 10 cents an acre.)[33]

What did Lincoln think of such speculations and of speculators?
Because he remained absolutely silent on the question, the answer must
be derived from examining his actual relationships with land speculation and speculators during the second great wave (following the one of
1836–37) that covered Illinois with voracious multitudes, including
several large and greedy predators.

Speculation, Speculators, and Estate Holders

Herndon and Henry C. Whitney insisted that Lincoln had never personally speculated, unlike most of his friends and fellow lawyers.[34] If this fact can be verified, ascertaining the motives for such a decision is important. If, as his friends imply, Lincoln refused to speculate on moral grounds, then it is possible to assert, given Lincoln's personality, that this moral rejection explains, at least in part, his attitude in favor of the Homestead. Despite its diversion from the beginning away from its objective, the Homestead had been intended by many as a means of fighting speculation. If, on the other hand, other motives made him disdain this means of getting rich, then his position on the Homestead must have been taken for other purely political reasons referred to earlier.

An examination of Lincoln's land transactions in the 1850s reveals no large land speculation. Only the purchase in October 1851 of two town lots in Bloomington, Illinois, for $325.08 (resold for $400 in 1856) resembles a speculation if the hypothesis that Lincoln intended to move to that town is rejected.[35] Indeed, his old friends Jesse W. Fell and David Davis fought hard to get the Illinois Central Railroad to pass through Bloomington (more precisely through Fell's property in North Bloomington, which would become the new town of Normal). Furthermore, it was from Levi Davis, David's cousin, that Lincoln bought the two lots in question several months after the Illinois Central Railroad was granted its charter by the state of Illinois in February 1851 at the end of a long legislative battle in which Lincoln played an important role from outside the General Assembly.[36] Had Lincoln waited, it is probable that this investment would have proved quite profitable.

Lincoln's other transactions were not at all speculations. In September 1854, he sold (for $1,200) a property of eighty acres that had been offered to him by his father-in-law ten years earlier.[37] Although he received a plot in the town of Lincoln, Illinois, in 1858, it was in compensation for a loss of $400 that he suffered for co-signing a loan. And his last acquisition was obviously not of a speculative nature: a plot in the Hutchinson Cemetery in Springfield. History prevented his "benefiting" from it because he was buried in Oak Ridge Cemetery at the expense of the state of Illinois.[38]

However, we know that, at the suggestion of the Republican leader from Chicago Norman B. Judd, he went to Council Bluffs, Iowa, in 1859 to evaluate the possibilities of speculating on the passage through that locality of the Pacific Railroad, a proposal that the Republicans had included in their platform. Although he refused to get involved in the affair—on the advice of his friend Ozias M. Hatch—he did agree to renew and increase a loan of $2,500 made to Judd in 1857 to finance this speculation and took a mortgage for $3,000 on seventeen plots in Council Bluffs and on ten acres along the route of the Mississippi and Missouri Railroad. At 10 percent a year—the legal maximum and the practical minimum—"the lending of money was not a rapid road to wealth, but it accorded far better with Lincoln's cautious temperament than the speculation in which he might have engaged."[39]

Lincoln had before him the example of his friend Fell, who was bankrupted in 1837 and forced for several years to lead a true pioneer's life, planting with his own hands an orchard and then a nursery, before returning—successfully—to speculation after 1845.[40] Doubtless it was more prudence than moral condemnation of speculation that led Lincoln to prefer lending at interest on a mortgage to land speculation. Indeed, his personal friends and acquaintances among the leaders of the Illinois Republican party included many land speculators, from cattle kings to great landed proprietors.

The most important of these was surely David Davis. The young prodigy of the bar, who came from a family of slaveholding planters from Maryland, settled in Illinois in 1835. Moving to Bloomington as a lawyer in 1836, he was a friend of Fell's and of John T. Stuart's, was elected to the Illinois legislature in 1844, and benefited from the political support of Lincoln to become in 1849, at thirty-four, judge of the Eighth Circuit on which Lincoln practiced. He was a colorful character, obese (three hundred pounds), with a young-looking face, a conservative, authoritarian manner, and a love of jokes.[41] He played an important role in Lincoln's nomination at Chicago, to the point that Davis's biographer titled his work *Lincoln's Manager.* Although Lincoln always knew how to organize his political career himself, it is nonetheless true that he listened to Davis's advice on political questions. He was Lincoln's close friend, as well as a great jurist whom Lincoln named to the Supreme Court of the United States.

David Davis's worst enemy, Asahel Gridley, was likewise Lincoln's "intimate political & personal friend," according to the president's own assertions. Gridley, who was the judge's great rival in land speculation in Bloomington, where he had purchased land ceded to the Illinois Central Railroad, was, perhaps for that reason, the only lawyer on the Eighth Circuit who stood up to Davis.[42] The spirit of the relations between them can be summed up in one anecdote: Davis bought the bankrupt Fell's Bloomington farm for the sole purpose of preventing Gridley from acquiring it.

Lincoln, like Fell (who was the best man at Davis's wedding and a

close friend of Gridley's), tried to preserve peaceful and amiable relations among the group of lawyers and landowners to which he belonged,
although as a lawyer only. To present a proposal for a charter in favor of
the Honorable John A. Rockwell (Whig-Conn.) for his Vermillion Coal
and Manufacturing Company, Lincoln called on Gridley's services as a
state senator. The terms of the charter were too favorable to Rockwell
(especially regarding the use of public land), and the former colleague
of Lincoln's in the Thirtieth Congress did not obtain what he wanted.
Lincoln was also linked to Gridley by their mutual interest in the
Illinois Central Railroad.[43]

Lincoln's relationships with land speculators appear, then, as a closed
network in which the threads of politics, law, industry, and railroads all
became intertwined. Moving from the Bloomington group (Davis, Gridley,
Fell, and Isaac Funk) to Springfield and its vicinity, we find Jacob Bunn.
Bunn, who joined Lincoln in signing appeals in favor of the Springfield
and Alton Railroad in 1849, was the leading merchant in Springfield,
where he also functioned as a banker. This land speculator, who owned
2,500 acres, was one of the Republican leaders in Springfield and served
as the front man for Lincoln in his purchase of the *Illinois Staats
Anzeiger.* [44] In neighboring Logan County, besides James N. Brown and
Richard F. Barrett, Richard J. Oglesby was one of the first to support
Lincoln for the Senate election of 1858. This Republican leader, future
governor, and then senator of Illinois, was the son-in-law of John Dean
Gillett, the cattle king who owned sixteen thousand acres of prairie in
that county.[45]

With Bunn and Oglesby we have left the circle of intimates to meet
political friends. When Lincoln recommended Bronson Murray, one of
the principal architects of the Illinois Central Railroad, who owned ten
thousand acres in Livingston and La Salle counties (in the north of the
state), he mentioned an "acquaintance and friend, of some years standing,
whom I would like to oblige."[46] As for Solomon Sturges, the Republican
banker from Chicago who owned, in association with Alvah Buckingham,
176,000 acres between the Ohio and the Nebraska rivers, Lincoln declined
his invitation to stay with him in Chicago while assuring him of his
agreement on the question of slavery in a letter of 1860.[47] More likely,
he stayed at a hotel or at the home of friends, such as the Judds. Indeed,
when Sturges raised a regiment to help the North during the war,
Lincoln's recommendation (which spoke of "a man of large means, and
of the highest character") did not refer to him as a friend, unlike his
usual custom when intervening in favor of those personally close to
him.[48] Was he really as friendly with Benjamin Franklin Harris, the
cattle king of Champaign County, as Harris declared in his auto-

biography? Harris asserted, in fact, that Lincoln often slept at his home when he traveled from Springfield to Urbana on the circuit, and that he had himself visited Lincoln in Springfield and then in Washington in May 1861.[49] Harris was an influential Republican who raised a company during the war. But the only document signed by Lincoln that Harris ever owned had no value as historic proof: the charter of the First National Bank of Champaign that Harris obtained in 1865.[50] However, one must recall Whitney's description of Vermilion and Champaign counties as forming a separate society in which "the social circle which revolved around the Judge was larger and more active . . . than elsewhere."[51] Harris, a justice of the peace who often served as a juror at Urbana, was doubtless part of this circle.

Lincoln's political relations extended to other states in the West. Thus he was in contact with a Republican leader from Indiana, Moses Fowler, to whom he sent a speaker during the 1860 campaign. Fowler, a banker, cattle king, and large stockholder in a slaughterhouse and meat-packing plant, was also linked to railroads in Indiana where he owned 45,000 acres, rented in part to fifty or so farmers, and for which he paid no taxes.[52]

The substantial role of large landowners in the Republican party reflects the important place that this class always occupied in Illinois politics. Whether they were originally Whigs (Funk, Harris, Fell, Davis, for example) or Democrats who had broken with Douglas after 1854 (such as Wentworth, William B. Ogden, or David Strawn, brother of Jacob and himself a cattle king of La Salle County, where he owned seven thousand acres), they were a powerful force that had to be reckoned with.[53] Lincoln's silence on the question of public land between 1849 and 1861 was perhaps motivated by the importance of this pressure group within his party. By associating with Davis, Fell, Moore, and others, Lincoln had an opportunity of observing closely the relationships between these large landowners and their tenants, which revealed the importance, long underestimated, of class conflicts in rural Illinois.

Class Conflicts

The myth of the frontier as a cradle of a social democracy based on small landed property rests on the reality of acquisition of property by thousands of farmers and agricultural workers. In the years from 1850 to 1860, this reality was universally recognized. The myth was not revealed as such until recent research stressed the large number of agricultural workers and sharecroppers without land and of perennially threatened squatters who were in conflict with the powerful for control of the soil.

As early as 1860, 6 percent of the population of Iowa consisted of agricultural workers (41,000), and the results of the first complete census (1880) revealed that 53 percent of the agricultural population of Illinois was comprised of tenants or sharecroppers and agricultural workers. More than half of those who worked the soil did not own any of it.[54]

When they wanted to acquire some, their interests directly confronted those of the large landowners. What if a squatter wanted to gather together quickly the sums needed to buy the patch of land that he occupied in order to claim his right of preemption before the land was put up for public auction? If he did not want to deal with loan sharks who lent money at 25 percent, he had to sell his livestock at a low price, and someone like B. F. Harris was there to buy it from him. What if one of Clifton H. Moore's or of David Davis's sharecroppers had trouble meeting the yields stipulated in his contract? His contract was terminated, and the land, improved by his work, was rented to another.[55]

It is impossible to imagine that Lincoln was unaware of all of these facts that were part of the daily life of his intimate friends. But Lincoln must have had the opportunity of dealing still more closely with the relationships between the haves and have-nots because of his quite special ties with the Illinois Central Railroad, the biggest landowner in Illinois. From 1850, when he represented a pressure group eager to obtain a charter for the I.C.R., until 1860, when he successfully argued before the Illinois supreme court to obtain a tax exemption for the company, Lincoln's career was tightly linked to the development of the enormous enterprise of building railroads and selling land. Given free travel on the I.C.R. lines and paid a fixed sum for numerous matters in which he used his political influence with the Republican adminis-tration of Illinois to help the company, Lincoln earned the largest fees paid by that company during the decade, $5,000 for another tax exemp-tion case in 1855. Lincoln served as the lawyer for the company in the six counties of the Eighth Circuit where it had lines or land and represented the company at least fifty times between April 1853 and October 1859.[56]

On one occasion Lincoln had to speak on the relationship between the I.C.R. and squatters. At the request of the company, he rendered an opinion on March 6, 1856, in answer to the question "Can there be any valid pre-emption on section of land, *alternate* to the Sections granted to the Illinois Central Railroad?" After analyzing the effects of the 1841 law on preemption, of the laws of 1850, 1852, 1853, 1854, and 1855 concerning the particular case of the I.C.R., he gave the following opinion: the legislature had established a deadline beyond which a person settling on alternate sections could not enjoy rights of preemption. Therefore, squatters who had arrived after March 13, 1852, on those lands never had preemption rights. Those who arrived before March 13, 1852, had lost their rights if they had not completed the normal procedure of "claim, proof, and payment." Finally, Lincoln indicated the procedure to be followed for annulling fraudulent or illegal claims that receivers or clerks of land offices had allowed.

This opinion was upheld by the subsequent jurisprudence of the Illinois courts. The question of the extinction of preemption rights, not only on its own sections (a point that Lincoln referred to in passing in his opinion), but also on the alternate sections that still belonged to the federal government, was a very important question for the company. Evicting squatters on odd (government) sections at a moment when "the public domain in Illinois was practically extinguished" was bound to provide an increased demand for I.C.R. land.[57]

Thus, in his professional life, Lincoln was led to assert the interests of a railroad company against those of squatters. Also in that capacity, he helped develop an important jurisprudence in favor of railroads by establishing the principle of limitation of responsibility of railroad carriers in the case of *Illinois Central Railroad vs. Morrisson and Crabtree* (December 1857). The case concerned the railroad's responsibility for the weight loss that livestock it transported suffered because of train delays. By separating the case of railroads from the common law of carriers, which held that the transporter was at the same time the insurer of the goods carried, Lincoln made possible a decisive step forward in the development of railroads in agricultural regions.[58]

The internal improvements supporter of 1837 was firmly resolved to take his place in the development of railroads in Illinois, even if the wheels of progress crushed some agricultural interests. From the point of view of production, the arrival of the railroad was beneficial, as Lincoln explained in an open letter praising the Springfield and Alton Railroad. The letter, which he drafted along with the most important figures in Springfield, contained arguments that were expanded shortly afterward in a published report. The question of who would profit from building the line, several shares of which Lincoln owned, was not brought up for the answer was obvious: all farmers, small and large, without distinction, because commodities could more easily reach the market.[59]

Lincoln was at the center of the whirlwind of changes brought on by the arrival of railroads. In 1852, he defended J. T. Stuart against a coalition of other investors so that his old friend might profit from the first sales of public land along the I.C.R., going so far as to write on Stuart's behalf to his successful rival for the General Land Office, Justin

Butterfield. And he sized up the immense land speculation that was developing. Grain that could finally be exported and livestock that could be more easily transported were being produced in ever-larger quantities. The price of land was rising at a dizzying rate. Towns mushroomed along the railroad lines. But progress was also moral and intellectual, as demonstrated by the crop of newspapers, literary clubs, and learned societies, or societies hoping to be so. It was by rail that Lincoln traveled to give his lectures on "Discoveries and Inventions" in 1858 and 1859. It was by rail that he and Douglas moved about during their famous debates in 1858. The Illinois Central Railroad transported 625,518 troops during the Civil War.[60]

Therefore, class conflicts seemed minor to Lincoln in comparison to the progress of civilization, even when he was confronted with the reality of class conflicts in railroad strikes and the activities of squatters' claim associations and when he himself played a role in them. But the professional and political circles in which he moved constantly presented him with institutions that seemed to serve as bridges between classes: the world of the circuit, freemasonry, the Republican party. And Lincoln himself, more than any other, seemed to symbolize such a bridge.

SOLUTION OF THE CONFLICTS

Judge Davis's Court

As a lawyer during the 1850s, Lincoln projected a double image. There was the lawyer for the I.C.R., more expensive than Rufus Choate, and there was the lawyer on the circuit who made, at the same time, $40 for five days of work in Champaign County. He was the man who argued 240 times before the Illinois supreme court, thus eclipsing all his colleagues in the state, as well as the man who described himself in a triple pun as "a mast-fed lawyer" and who whittled some wooden pegs with a pocket knife to hold up his suspenders before launching into the analysis of a document or into a plea couched in the "vocabulary of the people."[61]

Queer Mr. Lincoln, with his "well-worn and ill-fitting suit of bombazine," his gray shawl, his big, faded-green umbrella with a knob handle, and his carpet bag.[62] Who was he? To the Lawyer Whitney, he had the air of "an ordinary farmer," a little slovenly, who for ten years wore the same short coat he had bought in Washington in 1849. Charles W. Marsh, the farmer and manufacturer of agricultural machinery, who attended the Lincoln-Douglas debate at Ottawa, described him as dressed simply in a suit of traditional cut with the air of "a kindly old fashioned, professional man who was making a good living but putting on no style."[63]

Who was he? Eight months out of the year he lived on Eighth Street in Springfield, in a modest but spacious and well-furnished house. His wife tried to force him to use a butter knife and to let the maid open the door for visitors (she got along poorly with the servants because she was not used to being waited on by free women). The Lincolns gave lovely parties for Springfield society, who gathered under the sparkling lights.[64]

Four months out of the year, in his buggy, he rode the "mud circuit" along the rutted and swampy roads. Stopping in the evenings, he slept in an overflowing inn, two people to a bed, eight to a room, forty in the main room, after a bad supper eaten by the light of the first gasoline lamps, which were beginning to replace oil lamps. The rooms were cold, there were bugs, and the roofs leaked. In the morning, a basin in the yard and a towel hung on a nail were provided for all the clients to wash up with. After the sessions, held in "unkempt court-rooms, where, ten months in the year, the town boys played at marbles," the lawyers returned to the inn for an evening spent most often among men, drinking, smoking, and telling jokes. Sometimes Judge Davis presided over a session of his "orgmathorial court" in which the cases of the day before or the next day were treated in a farcical manner. Before such a session, of course, they made sure that no one undesirable was present: lawyers who did not belong to the group, clients, jurors, and witnesses had to stay in the common room, and any one who dared enter the sanctuary of the back parlor "was frozen out" on the spot by the awesome Davis.[65]

The "real Lincoln" could, no doubt, be found in the back parlor, if indeed that modern Grail could be found anywhere. There Davis's group got together: Leonard Swett, Henry C. Whitney, Stephen T. Logan, Ward H. Lamon, Isaac Arnold, and others joined by doctors, bankers, merchants, journalists, and prosperous farmers from the area. A mirror image of the Illinois bourgeoisie, the institution was a sort of Pickwickian freemasonry with its rites of passage, its esoteric language, its common thoughts and interests. The members took care of business, and they discussed metempsychosis and the last harvest, good investments and natural calamities. The cream of Illinois politicians was on the Eighth Circuit: Lincoln, Douglas, and some figures of lesser importance, lawyers who were preparing fine careers as senators in Wisconsin (Isaac P. Walker), California (J. A. McDougall), Oregon (E. D. Baker), Indiana (D. W. Voorhees), or even as members of Lincoln's cabinet (J. P. Usher).[66]

Illinois politicians were born in this fish pond of local worthies, landed proprietors, cattle raisers, doctors, schoolmasters, and, always and above all, lawyers who crowded into David Davis's "orgmathorial" courts and into Masonic lodges.

Asahel Gridley's Lodge

Although Lincoln was not a Mason, he was close to Masonry philosophically, and he lived surrounded by influential Masons. At Springfield itself, Lodge No. 4 counted among its eighty-one members in 1857 the best man at Lincoln's wedding, James Matheny (past master of the Grand Lodge of Illinois, of which John M. Palmer, from Carlinville, was the first orator); Lincoln's neighbor, James Gourley; Mason Brayman, a lawyer for the I.C.R. with whom he worked closely during the 1850s; and Newton E. Bateman, the state superintendent of schools (a close political associate). Lodge No. 43 at Bloomington included Asahel Gridley, and the one in De Witt County (No. 84) had Clifton H. Moore and Laurence Weldon. Isaac N. Arnold was a member of Chicago Lodge No. 18, which included more Germans than the Germania lodge (No. 182). "Long" John Wentworth belonged to the Oriental Lodge No. 33, and Stephen A. Hurlbut, Lincoln's envoy to Fort Sumter, took part in the activities of Lodge No. 60 at Belvedere. The other Judge Davis, Oliver L. Davis, participated in those of Lodge No. 38 at Danville. Finally, Lincoln's old friends, the lawyer L. M. Green and sheriff J. A. Rankin (the father of H. B. Rankin) were in Lodge No. 19 in Menard County.[67]

Illinois Masonry exerted real political influence (8,526 members were counted in 1857). Douglas, a model Mason, knew how to take advantage of it. Lincoln's good relations with Masonry were certainly exploited against Seward during the Republican convention in Chicago, notably by Swett and Arnold. The Masonic delegates' hostility toward the former leader of the Anti-Masonic party in New York doubtless played a small role in the selection of Lincoln.[68] But from the point of view of our subject, the study of the relationship between Lincoln and Masonry holds another interest. On a sociological level Masonry furnished the image of a society within a society that brought together in one institution a large fraction of the middle class of Illinois, many of whom were also in the Republican party.

The Grand Lodge of Illinois had always attracted a considerable portion of the elite. It had been founded in 1806 in Kaskaskia by a large landowner of Irish descent, John Edgar. Edgar was a slaveholder who owned the Kaskaskia mill and speculated on a large scale by falsifying land titles. This major general in the state militia had created a framework in which, for fifty years, the political leaders of Illinois (Elisha Kent Kane, William C. Dawson), supreme court judges (John Dean Caton), and influential persons from the country (such as Judge Bowling Green) could meet.

Changes in the 1850s were linked to the increase in the population of Illinois and attested to the capacity of the old leadership circles to welcome members from new levels into a structure that they controlled. The institution belonging to men such as Usher F. Linder, Isaac N. Arnold, John Wentworth, and Clifton H. Moore experienced a spectacular growth in the year following the Republican victory in the state elections. For the year 1857 alone, two thousand new members were signed up, an increase of 30 percent. Among the new initiates were eleven bankers, twenty-six lawyers, thirty-four ministers, sixty-nine doctors, eighteen engineers, twenty-five officials, and twenty professors. There were twenty-five innkeepers and 312 merchants as well. But around this nucleus were found 173 employees, 66 of whom worked with the railroads, 529 farmers, and 438 workers and artisans.[69]

These figures reveal the picture of an open society and not of a closed circle. But how many among the 529 farmers had as much land as Gridley or Moore? Did the sixty-six employees of the railroads know Mason Brayman's secrets? Which member of the Oriental Lodge of Chicago (the largest in the state, with 154 members) could pride himself on owning one-hundredth of the political influence of his brother John Wentworth?

In the same way, the small sharecropper being sued for debts or the agricultural worker who wanted his employer arrested for not paying his wages could dine at David Davis's table in a Peoria inn and listen eagerly to the conversations of Lincoln, Swett, Lamon, and company, learning information and ideas that "for some time after each session . . . formed the chief staple of conversation, in the stores and wherever men would gather." They were present during the defense pleas, losing not a scrap of the show; according to one of them "the most important incident in our lives, was the semi-annual meeting of the court; altho' in my county, its total sitting was comprised within two or three days." But the little group that gravitated around the stars of the legal profession was no longer there when Davis, assisted by the clerk and a lawyer who represented him, was both judge and party. He was no longer there when the "orgmathorial court" sat in session in the back parlor amid jokes and discussions of high politics, between a philosophical debate and a Negro folk song—of which Lamon was a specialist—while on the side matters of money, land, and political plums were settled.[70]

Abraham Lincoln's Republican Party

In the same way, the Republican party was organized in concentric circles, from the leadership core of Lincoln, Lyman Trumbull, and William Henry Bissell, out to the wide-awakes, a paramilitary organization of young anti-slavery workers and farmers. To lead these people on the move one had to be willing to mix with them. In the cohort of Young Republicans who marched in the streets, their torches and lamps dripping hot oil, encased in a wax cape with "Wide-Awake" spread across it, a son of a Democratic merchant from New York was preparing a career as a Republican federal official. Lincoln's young friend Elmer Ephraim Ellsworth, a law student from Chicago, organized a company of Zouaves, whose gleaming uniforms caused a sensation during parades, and the young farmers of Illinois rushed to imitate him by parading on village greens with old cannons and brand new drums.[71] But there were also "back-room Republicans," the real leaders, Oglesby, Funk, Fell, Davis, and Gridley, whom activists saluted as they paraded with their placards demanding the Homestead without considering how risky it was to entrust such men with the task of achieving such a goal.

In the same way, the huge crowds that pressed around the Wigwam in Chicago in May 1860, cheering the Republican candidate whose nomination was saluted by cannons, this crowd of workers, storekeepers, and farmers, more than twenty thousand drunk with joy and alcohol and all crying out Lincoln's name, did they know that behind the scenes of the convention, in the hotels and restaurants, a small group led by Davis, Swett, Lamon, and Judd had worked quietly for the Rail-Splitter? While the crowd of supporters of Old Abe shouted itself hoarse to drown out the cries of New Yorkers shipped in on special trains to back Seward, Davis and Jesse K. Dubois telegraphed to Lincoln: "We are quiet but moving heaven & Earth."[72]

The Rail-Splitter legend itself was created by Oglesby after consultation with the leading Republican leaders of the state. In the spring of 1860, Oglesby learned in a conversation with John Hanks that Lincoln and his cousin had cleared and enclosed a field near Decatur in 1830. The next day the future governor and the old pioneer went to the spot, found some thirty-year-old rails of locust and walnut, and triumphantly took back a pair of them, which Hanks presented with great fanfare to the state convention in Decatur.[73] A myth had been born. Carved in a thousand and one ways, Lincoln rails would spread throughout the country just as the log cabins of the Harrison campaign had earlier.

But there was a big difference between 1840 and 1860. In the first case, the slogan had been born from an attack against the general. A Democratic newspaper had decided to mock his presidential ambitions by the declaring that the old man would be satisfied if he were allowed to live in a log cabin with a jug of hard cider. The conditional was important because Harrison came from one of the first families of Virginia and his father, Benjamin Harrison, had been a signer of the Declaration of Independence. The log cabin and the jug of cider were symbols of the Spartan virtues of a soldier on the Indian-infested Marches.

In the case of Lincoln, on the other hand, there was no need to fabricate a myth for the purposes of the campaign. As he himself acknowledged when the rails were presented to him, it was true that he had split some near Decatur in 1830. Were they the same ones? In any case, he had split many more and of better quality.[74] The rails of 1860 symbolized manual labor, free labor, agricultural labor, and the man who split them was the model of the self-made man, the incarnation of the American Dream of a classless society.

The movement of 1840 was a foam on the surface of the waves, produced by demagogic agitation. But the crowds in 1860 were no longer being manipulated. Lincoln no longer needed to incite, as he had done for Taylor's campaign in 1848, a Rough and Ready Club in which Herndon brought together "all the shrewd wild boys about town, whether just of age, or little under age."[75] In 1860, a groundswell, a great movement of popular resistance to the demands of the South, carried Lincoln and his party to the presidency. The Republican party was certainly the heir of the old Whig party, but, by losing its national base, it lost a great deal of its faintheartedness. Moreover, as Lincoln himself noted in 1858, "nearly all the old exclusive silk-stocking whiggery is against us." An extraordinary pressure of events and the destruction of the old party was required before a man like David Davis could bring himself to join an organization in which the small farmers of Illinois were active. "I am naturally so conservative that it was a long time before I could wish the Republican party entire success," he said.[76]

That was how the Republican party differed from Judge Davis's court or from Asahel Gridley's lodge. Conflicts were resolved by a compromise between classes and not by the simple subordination of one to the other. The man of this compromise between the haves and the have-nots, Lincoln was able to become the symbol of the whole American nation because of his stand as a public figure on the question of slavery. But before tackling this point, it remains to be seen how, as a private individual, he was, more than any other, ideally suited for such an identification.

"DEAR MR. ABE LINCOLN"

"His life is an invincible attestation of the superiority of Free Society, as his election will be its crowning triumph," wrote the New York *Tribune* on October 23, 1860. Two years earlier, Charles Henry Ray of the Chicago *Tribune* had sent a disarmingly frank letter to Lincoln, urging him to agree to publication of a biography in which the modest origins of the Republican candidate would be stressed. Although he had been publicizing this fact, Ray was astounded to discover that it was indeed true. "My Dear Sir, It was my suspicion that Abe Lincoln was not born with a silver spoon in his mouth," he began before revealing his amazement at the "ridiculously small" wages earned by the Rail-Splitter during his youth.[77]

Was Mr. Abe Lincoln part of the world of people like Davis and Fell? These men, who were soon joined at the head of the Illinois Republican party by a new generation of estate-owning politicians such as John T. Alexander, knew him as a defender of the rights of property, knew "that Lincoln would be honest and just in the handling of property and of property owners."[78] Wasn't he personally a rich man? Of course, he owned no land, but since his return from Congress, he had invested his income prudently in the form of mortgage loans backed up by the rich loam of the Sangamon, by town lots, or by railroad land. In a period when crises were shaking the most solid fortunes, his 10 percent a year arrived regularly to augment his savings.

In 1854, when a Springfield blacksmith, Samuel Sidener, refused to pay interest, Lincoln had the town plot mortgaged by the debtor seized and sold, then bought it himself and sold it immediately. This is the only surviving recorded instance of such an incident for the entire eleven-year period during which Lincoln made loans.[79] At the same time, the most expensive lawyer in the United States took a case for $3 in 1854 dealing with a hog and was still involved in 1860 in a case dealing with a trifling debt ($16.80 of interest).[80] We can see here again the lawyer's special position, tied to the aristocracy but maintaining a daily contact with ordinary people.

A Groundwork of Honesty

During this period, Lincoln was recognized as a specialist in land law, both public and private, and was entrusted with such tasks as estimating damages caused by the digging of the Illinois and Michigan Canal and examining the validity of titles and geographical limits of a town's jurisdiction. In his daily practice he examined all sorts of legal questions linked to landed property: wills, protection of the landed estate of minor heirs, effective dates of transactions, validity of tax titles, fraudulent titles, and statutes of limitation. For his clients, he pondered how to raise a mortgage at the cheapest cost, to register preemption rights, and to order—or to prevent—an expulsion. He executed sales, made estimates before forced sales, obtained titles for his clients (if necessary going himself to pay the receiver of the Land Office in gold when clients lived elsewhere), and went so far as to serve as an intermediary in organizing a sale for a client friend.[81] In each case, his knowledge as a surveyor and the rigor and precision in the description of land titles that he always insisted upon were important factors in his success.[82] To them can be attributed his victory in April 1860 in the famous "Chicago Sandbar Case," which involved the ownership of land that had built up in the heart of the city on the banks of Lake Michigan.[83]

In civil as well as criminal cases, he regularly saw the darkest side of human nature as it was influenced by hunger for land. One title was contested twenty-two years after the sale, and one dispute over boundaries ended with a murder.[84] In a man not motivated by the same passion, such a spectacle must have reinforced the feeling that justice must be rendered in a completely impartial fashion, giving each his due. Besides, the impartial application of the law was sufficient to protect the interests of estate holders and speculators because the law was written by them, for them, and applied and controlled by them or their friends. This comes out clearly in Lincoln's written opinion concerning the validity of sales of swamp lands in Bureau County (January 31, 1859).

The facts of the swamp lands case were as follows: as soon as the marshes were given by the federal government to the state of Illinois, the latter had entrusted the surveying and sale of them to the counties. In theory, the income from these sales was supposed to make possible draining the swamps. In fact, the surveyors used the vagueness of the terms of the land cessions to include under the rubric of "swamp lands" all public land that had not yet been sold, and the income from the sales was used only in part for drainage work. Speculators took advantage of these excellent opportunities to round out their estates. Some, along with some other buyers, found themselves in difficulty and consulted Lincoln on the following point: Could the courts enforce sales contracts? Or, rather, were buyers obligated to honor their signatures? Lincoln preferred to pose the question this way in order better to define the point. His answer on this precise point was that the buyer could contest the sale only under circumstances specifically mentioned in the contract. After having thus answered the practical question that he had been asked, Lincoln turned toward the problems posed by the more general terms of the consultation. He therefore placed himself in the position of the buyer, that is, practically in the situation of the person who had just bought excellent land for 10 cents an acre and feared losing his property.

Suppose the purchaser takes *possession*—*how*, and *by whom* can he be got out? Will the United States undertake to put him out? Will the United States re-assume ownership, and sell, and give a Patent to some individual? Will the State do either of these things? Manifestly not. . . . Suppose, then, a stranger squats upon the land, and the purchaser thus loses it, unless he can dispossess the squatter. He brings his Ejectment; shows the acts of Congress, and the Patent of the United States to the State . . . [Lincoln indicated the procedure to be followed], and his case is made out. Suppose the squatter shall then offer to say, that by the acts of Congress, the proceeds of the lands were to be appropriated to the draining of the lands, and that this has not been done. Can a naked wrongdoer be allowed to alledge this? And if alledged, could it, at law, overturn the United States Patent? . . . A Bill in Equity, could not be for a moment maintained against the Patent, by a mere wrongdoer.

My opinion is, that the purchasers from the County, will never lose the land, unless it be by some fault of their own.[85]

A reading of these lines can leave no doubt: Lincoln did indeed belong to the same world as Davis and Fell. At the same time, because he did not speculate himself, he made it possible for social levels other than that of large landowners to identify with him.

In fact, faithful to his principles, Lincoln discouraged pettifoggery and often proposed amicable arrangements, even if it meant losing fees. On one occasion he settled a dispute between a farmer and his miller and on another refused to contest a property title. Each semester on the circuit, he was approached by a Mr. Gilliland, who claimed to have title to a piece of property and wanted to procure Lincoln's services. Each time, Lincoln listened patiently and kindly before refusing to take the case.[86]

Would such an attitude have been possible had Lincoln demonstrated the same greed for land and money as his colleagues and friends? The private man does not explain the public man unless it be to the degree that the influential proprietors at the Chicago Convention recognized Lincoln as one of their own. But the private man explains the fascinating nature of the Lincoln myth, resting on a reality that the young farmers of the Sangamon could almost touch "on the eve of '61." The president-elect, in fact, received with open arms all the young people who arrived, their girlfriends on their arms, to make or renew the acquaintance of the rail-splitter president and soil his carpet with their muddy boots.[87] But the real popularity of Lincoln and of his party had its roots in his stand on slavery, and that point remains to be discussed.

Part 2: This Species of Property

It is out of the question, given the limitations of the present study, to analyze completely the controversy between Lincoln and Douglas from 1854 to 1860 on the question of slavery and its extension. I will, therefore, limit myself to showing the elements of the Lincoln discourse that, in substance and form, corresponded to the relationship he wanted to create between himself and his party on one hand, and the rural population of Illinois on the other. However, this question must certainly be placed in the larger context of the conflict between two modes of civilization for control of a state whose original mission was the defense of property under all its forms. We must trace the outlines of the discussion as it unfolded in the North and reverberated in the South.

PROPERTY AND THE STATE

Douglas

Viewed from the broadest perspective, the debate between Lincoln and Douglas expressed the two possible responses on the part of the North to the extensionist ambitions of the South: firmness or conciliation. Stripped of its tactical aspects and the hesitations and errors of both men, it can be reduced to the following canvas: from 1854 (the Kansas-Nebraska Act) to 1857 (the Dred Scott decision) the controversy centered essentially on the issue of whether the geographical domain of slavery should be limited by law (Lincoln) or whether other "natural" factors (such as climate or will of the settlers) would make such a limitation useless or harmful (Douglas).

The results of applying the Kansas-Nebraska Act were barely beginning to appear in Kansas itself (a civil war had broken out) when the Dred Scott decision in March 1857 came to legalize the extension of slavery into all the territories, to deny civil rights to blacks, and to place Douglas's doctrine in danger by affirming the constitutional right of slaveholders to transport their property wherever they wished, although

Douglas had until then claimed that the population of a territory could decide the issue freely (the doctrine of popular sovereignty).

From then on, Douglas found himself on the defensive and proclaimed the "Freeport Doctrine," stating that the police powers of territorial assemblies could be used to prevent slaveholders from bringing their slaves into the territories. All they needed to do was to refrain from making regulations necessary for the preservation of this particular form of property. Such was the last refuge of the conciliatory attitude that had held sway in the North since 1800. Ironically, the repeated attempts by the North to find a constitutional compromise had finally resulted in this openly unconstitutional "doctrine."

The Lecompton Constitution, which made Kansas a slave state, was a further slap to Douglas. He had preached for so long that the application of the principle of popular sovereignty in the territories would resolve the issue of the extension of slavery there that he could not admit without loss of honor—and of his influence in the Northwest—that a rigged election could embody this principle. His split with Buchanan in December 1857 opened a decisive breach in the Democratic party, thus bringing the two sections face to face.

Immediately, a conciliatory attitude toward the "Little Giant" took shape in the Republican party, ready to welcome an ally in the fight against the Buchanan administration. And now the most influential man in the Republican party, Seward, backed by Horace Greeley's New York *Tribune*, the most widely read newspaper in rural Illinois, openly declared that Douglas was a reliable ally in the crusade against the extension of slavery! Herndon traveled to Washington and met with Greeley, Douglas, and Nathaniel P. Banks to determine the extent of the disaster. Lincoln worriedly asked Trumbull, "What does the New-York Tribune mean by it's constant eulogising, and admiring, and magnifying [of] Douglas?"[88]

Greeley's campaign continued. On June 1, 1858, Norman B. Judd wrote to Lincoln about the situation in the Republican party in Chicago and the northern part of the state: "There is no trouble immediately at home, but rumors from the rural districts show that some of the brethren have thought that the puffing of Douglas meant something."[89] Two weeks later, Lincoln, named Senate candidate by the Republican convention at Springfield, gave his famous House Divided speech.

Lincoln

Lincoln reacted by stiffening his position, and his emergence as the intransigent adversary of the conciliatory Douglas gave him a national stature. As the issue of extension developed, the issue of slavery itself was increasingly brought up. One could not repeat in every possible way that the extension of slavery was harmful without ending up explaining how slavery itself was an evil. For if slavery was not an evil, why be opposed to its extension? And because the Dred Scott decision legalized its extension into the territories, why not into the states?

Neither the arguments on "the natural limits to slavery" nor the assurances given by the South that it did not wish to introduce slavery into Nebraska, or New Mexico, or, of course, into Illinois could make Lincoln believe that the South's continued control of the federal government would not be translated into the extension of the peculiar institution across the entire country. What was needed was to retake the government from the South, that is, return to the period before 1800 (the election of Jefferson), and before 1793 (Eli Whitney and the cotton gin). Between 1776 and 1790, the revolutionary state and the newborn federal state had been founded on the idea of the "ultimate extinction" of slavery. That is the meaning of the House Divided speech.

In the course of his argument, Lincoln had to define the conception of property, which he opposed to slave property, and show its foundation in labor. In so doing, he sought support in the labor movement against the slave aristocracy and in the ideology of liberal capitalism against the theories of a society of hierarchical castes. In the rest of this section, I will focus on the way in which he opposed the liberal ideology to the slave ideology in terms that corresponded to the state of mind of the rural masses of Illinois.

But calling into question a form of property opened a breach in the general system of the defense of property, which explains Lincoln's position in favor of the fugitive slave law and later, during the Civil War, his hesitating and temporizing on abolition, his refusal to ratify military emancipation proclamations or to apply the Confiscation Act. Likewise, although the old form of the federal state, molded to the exigencies of the protection of slavery, became incompatible with the conduct of the war, its destruction raised with extreme acuteness the issue of its replacement because it was indispensable that the state continue to guarantee the defense of private property. That was the origin of the poignant issue of reconstruction, which tortured Lincoln well before the end of the war was in sight.

As early as the period from 1854 to 1860, the contradiction between calling slave property into question and defending private property was expressed in Lincoln's confusion toward the Negro question. In response to the Dred Scott decision, he formulated for the first time his definition of the equality between blacks and whites, thus giving his interpretation of the Declaration of Independence. Speaking of a black woman, he explained, "In some respects she certainly is not my equal; but in her natural right to eat the bread she earns with her own hands without asking leave of any one else, she is my equal, and the equal of all others."[90] It would be hard to express more vigorously the principle of the equality of all wage-earners before capital. But by placing on the same level all distinctions such as "color, size, intellect, moral developments, or social capacity," Lincoln rejected any other possibilities for equality between blacks and whites. He believed that there was "a physical difference between the white and black races which . . . will for ever forbid the two races living together on terms of social and political equality." This rejection of blacks, which went hand in glove with the fear of servile insurrection that Lincoln felt from 1845 on and the reasons for which were furnished in his condemnation of John Brown's expedition, admittedly corresponded to a condition of civilization particularly important on the frontier.[91] But it constituted a weakness that Douglas would exploit relentlessly. Above all, the fear of insurrection would paralyze the military activity of the North until the administration decided to emancipate and enlist slaves. Only this organized insurrection enabled the Thirteenth and Fourteenth Amendments to become "the supreme law of the land." These are, briefly sketched, the problems linked to Lincoln's conviction that slavery was an evil. A corresponding pattern can be found on the side of the South.

The South

If slavery was not good, why permit it into the territories? And if it was not permitted into the territories, why not suppress it in the states? If the federal government, built to defend property in the South as well as the North, fell for the first time into the hands of men who refused to defend the peculiar institution by permitting it to spread, what guarantees did slaveholders have that the federal government could carry out its role as defender of slave property in the South?

The debate over secession among supporters of slavery would turn entirely on this question, one faction of Southern leaders regarding the Union as still capable of fulfilling its function as a defender of slave property, another group terrified at the idea of the offices of postal workers, U.S. marshals, district judges, commanders of army posts, and tariff collectors in Southern states being given to anti-slavery Republicans. All the hesitations, the retreats, the concessions of the North, all the assurances given of maintaining the right of slaveholders to work their Negroes for their own use, all that could not convince planters that this government would be theirs. Everything that remained of a conciliatory spirit among Republican leaders, along with the sabotage organized by the Buchanan administration, resulted in only one thing: permitting the South to secede under the best conditions. Rare was the slavery supporter who remained attached to the Union, rarer still were those with the honesty of Herschel V. Johnson, Douglas's running-mate in 1860, who recanted the secessionist positions he had held in 1850 for a simple reason: "I had become satisfied that Slavery was safer in than out of the Union."[92]

It can thus be seen how much the question of property was at the center of the great American conflict. It was likewise of paramount importance in Lincoln's argument before the farmers of Illinois. In form and substance, Lincoln would cause the "mystic chords" in the hearts of his listeners to vibrate, chords that drew their evocative strength from the relationship of the pioneer to his land, to the property he had earned by his own labor.

THE FARMER AND THE POLITICIAN

The Allegory of the Hogs

As soon as the Kansas-Nebraska Act was passed, it became the main subject of political discussion in Illinois as elsewhere. Lincoln, having entered the arena to support the Whig Richard Yates running for Congress from the Springfield district, found himself contending with John Calhoun, Douglas's lieutenant. And the former deputy surveyor of Sangamon County (Lincoln) attacked the former head surveyor of said county (Calhoun) in a manner that certainly must have fascinated their former clients:

> To illustrate the case—Abraham Lincoln has a fine meadow, containing beautiful springs of water, and well fenced, which John Calhoun had agreed with Abraham (originally owning the land in common) should be his. . . . John Calhoun, however, in the course of time, had become owner of an extensive herd of cattle—the prairie grass had become dried up and there was no convenient water to be had. John Calhoun then looks with a longing eye on Lincoln's meadow, and goes to it and throws down the fences, and exposes it to the ravages of his starving and famishing cattle. "You rascal," says Lincoln, "what have you done? what do you do this for?" "Oh," replies Calhoun, "everything is right. I have taken down your fence; but nothing more. It is my true intent and meaning not to drive my cattle into your meadow, nor to exclude them therefrom, but to leave

them perfectly free to form their own notions of the feed, and to direct their movements in their own way!"[93]

In the same vein, on October 4, 1854, Lincoln, in shirtsleeves in the stultifying heat of the great hall of the Illinois house of representatives, gave his first significant speech on slavery in response to an appeal that Douglas had given the previous day in favor of the Kansas-Nebraska Act. The audience was made up of many farmers who had come for the State Agricultural Fair. Obviously, Douglas, followed by Lincoln, had come to "cajole and captivate the rustic classes," as Whitney expressed it.[94] And the crowd strained to hear what the orators had to say about the extension of slavery. Why? It was not for that reason that they had come to Springfield, but to learn how to increase their productivity by making use of progress in machines and in plant and animal breeding. The organizers had not looked kindly on the intrusion of politics into the fair's proceedings, which shifted the center of interest from the flooded fields where it had been for the last several days toward the smoke-filled room of the statehouse.[95] Why then had they come to listen to Douglas and Lincoln? Was it merely a distraction, a sideshow like those found at all fairs? Perhaps a study of Lincoln's argument will enable us to answer that question because now, as an active anti-extensionist, he knew that the future belonged to those who would be able to find the words, images, and ideas capable of winning over to his cause these "rustic classes."

No image could better bring Lincoln's audience to grasp the inanity of the arguments in favor of the doctrine of popular sovereignty in the Kansas and Nebraska Territories. *"Even the hogs would know better,"* Lincoln concluded after repeating his allegory, now improved by the addition of hogs.[96] Indeed, these animals, as stupid as they might be, could not understand why the fence had been removed if not to allow them to enter. In substance, the idea that "Abraham Lincoln has a fine meadow" had been engraved for a long time in the collective consciousness of Illinois pioneers, who saw the West as the promise of more land for themselves and their children. And they knew better than anyone—except perhaps surveyors and lawyers—what enclosure meant. The idea that rights have a tangible reality, that an "imaginary" line drawn by a surveyor on a deed is worth more than the most sturdy rails, the consciousness that a legal limit is a reality in the same way as is a geographical barrier, such were Lincoln's principal arguments, and they were perfectly adapted to the ideas and feelings of his audience.

The counterattack could come from two directions: the thesis of the natural limits of the slavery system, which would be one of the main subjects of debate from 1858 to 1860, and the tactic of assimilating the debate on slave property with the debate on property in general. The latter was the basis for the accusation of "radicalism" brought against anti-extensionists and abolitionists by their common opponents, pro-slavery people and compromisers. But it was also the seed of a corruption that Lincoln avoided like the plague, the introduction of slavery as an acceptable form of property in the North.

Lincoln's commitment to capitalist property was not expressed exclusively through cold and tedious logic. The very texture of his feelings revealed his attachment to this aspect of the American Dream. This can be sensed when he declared to Joseph Gillespie that slave property "was the most glittering, ostentatious, and displaying property in the world, and now, if a young man goes courting, the only inquiry is how many negroes he or his lady-love owns. The love for slave property is swallowing up every other mercenary possession."[97] The extension of "this species of property" had to be halted for it could not in any way be considered as honorable as any other.[98] "This would be true if negroes were property in the same sense that hogs and horses are. But is this the case? . . . There are 400,00 free negroes in the United States. . . . At $500 each, their value is $2,000,000. Can you find *two million dollars worth* of any other kind of property running about without an owner?" And the metaphor, drawn out to its extreme, successfully reaches its limit of usefulness because the whole point was that slaves were not animals. The Southerner who refused to welcome a slave trader at his table would not act the same way toward "the man who deals in corn, cattle or tobacco."[99]

Two Contradictions

At this stage in his thinking, Lincoln was faced with two contradictions. He was not ready to resolve the first one: while disputing the *sacred* nature of the right of property in slaves because this form of property disgusted him, he continued to assert at the same time that he stood "fairly, fully, and firmly" behind the Constitution, which established precisely all the guarantees of the inviolability of that right.[100]

The second contradiction also appeared in a constitutional guise if one were willing to accord to the principles of the Declaration of Independence, as Lincoln insisted, a status comparable to those embodied in the Act of 1787. Citing the text of 1776 to contend that the powers of the government derived from the consent of the governed, Lincoln was "arguing against the EXTENSION of a bad thing, which where it already exists, we must of necessity, manage as we best can." What equality could be claimed for Negroes based on the Declaration? "Let it not be said I am contending for the establishment of political and social equality between the whites and blacks. I have already said the contrary," Lincoln reminded his hearers.[101] He needed the Declaration in order to affirm that blacks were men like whites, but he took pains to declare the ways in which blacks and whites shared a common humanity. At the very most, he could list the qualities of blacks that "made them more than *hogs or horses.*" They had "mind, feeling, souls, family affections, hopes, joys, sorrows."[102] Obviously, all of this was not enough to establish any sort of equality and remained perfectly acceptable for Douglas, who did not deny that blacks were superior to animals and founded his morality on a hierarchy of three levels: the white, the black, and the crocodile.

During the 1858 debates, under the pressure of Douglas's questions, Lincoln put forward two distinct explanations of what he meant by equality. The first rested on the idea that the inalienable rights of man, as affirmed in the Declaration, were abstract rights that could progressively become concrete as civilization advanced. Lincoln often cited Clay in support of this idea.[103] The second, formulated in the same speech as the previous one, was based on the equality of all men as workers.[104] Never disputed by Douglas, who accused Lincoln of changing the subject when he brought it up and who himself remained silent on the question, the opposition that Lincoln established, not between abstract liberty and slavery but rather between independent or wage labor on the one hand and slave labor on the other, was the most important for his audience. Indeed, Lincoln would now be able to answer with greater precision the questions that Illinois raised concerning the future of land and labor. Faithful to his style, Lincoln continued to use the allegory but, although the image of the fence retained all of its importance, the relationship to the land he put forward was no longer one of mere ownership of abstract property, but rather one of occupying and actively working the soil.

The Allegory of the Thistles

The stakes for Lincoln as well as for Douglas and their audiences were the western lands. "These broad prairies, with only the Heavens to bound my vision" were filled by "that stream of intelligence which is constantly flowing from the Old World to the New, ... clearing our wildernesses and building cities, towns, railroads and other internal improvements, and thus [making] this the asylum of the oppressed of the whole earth," asserted the senator, a zealous defender of the idea that the manifest destiny of the United States was to "make this continent one ocean-bound republic."[105] According to Douglas, it was up to the inhabitants of the territories to legislate as freely on the question of slavery as on any other sort of property. There should be no prior exclusion of slavery from the territories.

Lincoln combated the idea that "slavery is one of those little, unimportant, trivial matters which are of just about as much consequence as the question would be to me, whether my neighbor should raise horned cattle or plant tobacco ... ; that when a new territory is opened for settlement, the first man who goes into it may plant there a thing which, like the Canada thistle, or some other of those pests of the soil, cannot be dug out by the millions of men who will come thereafter."[106] He had moved from a spatial image (the allegory of the hogs) in which the land was only a territory, a closed field abstractly consecrated to liberty, to an organic image, that of a living struggle between two forms of work on the same soil.

Indeed, because he had set forth the thesis of the equality of men as workers, Lincoln could address his audience directly by depicting the danger that the extension of slavery posed for the free worker. Taking up Douglas's racist argument against "negro equality," he promised that "every white worker" would regret it "when he is elbowed from his plow or his anvil by slave niggers." But he was careful to make clear that it was "the institution" that debased the labor of whites.[107]

Slavery would go everywhere it was permitted to go. The idea that there existed natural limits to its extension was refuted by history, and Lincoln could draw on his own experience. By so doing, he renewed ties with his own origins and spoke a language perfectly clear to his listeners, who had emigrated as he had from Kentucky. Where would they have gone if, on arriving in Illinois fleeing slavery, they had found Douglas's doctrine holding sway?[108] We have already seen how this vision reflected the young Lincoln's experience. It has been discussed on the theoretical level, but the facts that Lincoln called on were stubborn.[109]

"The Eternal Struggle"

When Lincoln tried to give substance to his famous expression that his confrontation with Douglas was only an episode in "the eternal struggle between these two principles—right and wrong—throughout the world," he declared that "the one is the common right of humanity and the other the divine right of kings. It is the same principle in whatever shape it develops itself, ... 'You work and toil and earn bread, and I'll eat it.'"[110]

It is obvious that such an assertion threatened the very foundations of capitalist society. That is why Lincoln was careful to explain, in another famous passage, that he was not calling into question that system. First of all, he said, hired laborers made up no more than one-eighth of the nation's work force. But above all, those who "have not of their own land to work upon, or shops to work in" have the possibility of acquiring them after several years of hired labor.[111] The whole philosophy of the American Dream was here expressed.

But whether Lincoln wanted it or not, celebrating the principle that a man should not be deprived of the fruit of his labor was revolutionary, and the Republican orator was accused of favoring strikes. Courageously, Lincoln did not hesitate to declare in regard to a strike in Massachusetts in 1860, *"I am glad to see that a system of labor prevails in New England under which laborers CAN strike when they want to."*[112]

In a limited way, even before the beginning of armed conflict, the struggle against slavery led Lincoln, as conservative as he was, to an attitude favorable to the working class. The connection that he made between political democracy and social liberalism was translated into a willingness to allow the power struggle between classes to produce the necessary adjustments in case of conflict, which included the right of workers to organize.[113] That is the most that the labor movement can expect from economic liberalism. But we will see that the firmness of Lincoln's logic of opposition to slavery—compare his attitude to Seward's in his famous Senate speech on labor and capital of February 29, 1860—led him to a stand on the problems connected with labor on the land that was in certain respects "atypical."[114]

RECONCILIATION

It is natural to conclude this study by examining the only major speech that Lincoln ever devoted to the relationship between the land and labor, a speech addressed to the Wisconsin State Agricultural Society on the occasion of the Milwaukee Fair on September 30, 1859. The text is extremely rich and can be studied with profit from several points of view.[115] However, its principal interest lies in the approach adopted by Lincoln, and nothing can reveal it better than an analysis of the outline of the speech, which can be summarized as follows:

PREAMBLE
Fairs have a civilizing mission of bringing people together, of recreation, and of progress. The choice of a politician to deliver the customary address indicates to him the course to follow: he must present several

practical suggestions on the one hand and put forward problems of general interest on the other.

I. PRACTICAL SUGGESTIONS
  A. Defense of "thorough cultivation"
    1. Strictly economic point of view: analysis of yields; how to increase them; economies of means and growth of profits.
    2. Moral point of view (just as important) and economic implications: satisfaction of a job well done; the value of property flows from the value accorded to the work which acquires it; the good worker "will keep up the enclosure about it, and allow neither man nor beast to trespass upon it." Lack of care leads to enormous waste; example of mammoth farms that have failed.
  B. Prospects offered by the steam plow
II. QUESTIONS OF GENERAL INTEREST
  A. Preliminary remarks
    1. The pro-slavery "mud-sill" theory: Every society rests on the permanent subjugation of a laboring class, either hired or slave; the slave is better treated.
    2. The opposite theory: Society in the free states is comprised of three classes: idle capitalists, hired workers, and independent workers (farmers or artisans); there are mixed groups (independent workers employing others). The class of independent workers is the most numerous. It is open to hired laborers and if some do not accede to that status "it is not the fault of the system, but because of either a dependent nature which prefers it, or improvidence, folly, or singular misfortune."
  B. The essential question: work and education
    1. Facts of the problem
      a. The old system: Coexistence of an educated and idle minority with an ignorant and laboring majority; many working bees, a few drones.
      b. New conditions: The majority is now educated, therefore it must work. "How can *labor* and *education* be the most satisfactorily combined?"
    2. Possible solutions
      a. The pro-slavery response: "The education of laborers is not only useless, but pernicious, and dangerous." Their "heads are regarded as explosive materials, only to be safely kept in damp places, as far as possible from that peculiar sort of fire which ignites them."

    b. The free labor response: "In one word Free Labor insists on universal education."
    3. Preferred solution
        a. The Wisconsin audience had chosen de facto.
        b. Agriculture made possible a harmonious combination. It offered a multitude of subjects for study, the progress of the sciences made this study both possible and easy.
        c. Only intensive agriculture made possible this combination.
PERORATION
    If farmers practice the art of intensive agriculture, they "will be alike independent of crowned-kings, money-kings, and land-kings."

    In the course of his career, Lincoln had never said as many things in favor of agriculture as in these few pages. Admittedly, the first flattering words of the preamble saluted the fair as a remedy to rustic barbarism for whom "stranger" had for too long meant "enemy." It was the urbanity of agricultural shows that attracted Lincoln. Admittedly, agriculture was pleasant only in those aspects that brought it close to (and not in those that differentiated it from) the world of science and technology. His passion was for the steam plow, not for the furrow it plowed. Nevertheless, before this audience of farmers Lincoln managed to declare that farmers were the most numerous class, and therefore that agricultural interests should take precedence over others; that in a way, farmers, along with artisans, formed the bedrock of free society; and, finally, that the way to complete and eternal independence was open to them if they would just cultivate their garden carefully. Allowing for demagogy, this Jeffersonian tone nonetheless demands an explanation.
    Why this reconciliation? And, first of all, why this praise of intensive agriculture? Lincoln compared it to extensive agriculture solely because of his desire to contrast free labor and slavery. That is what stands out in his logical approach: modern agriculture requires education, slave society requires ignorance; modern agriculture needs a free society. In other words, let slavery spread into the territories and the states and you can say goodbye to your agricultural societies.
    From that point of view, the question is not whether Lincoln was right to present increasing yields as the goal of American agriculture. Historically, it developed not by increasing yields but by increasing the productivity of labor. In fact, Lincoln's argument works in both cases. Mechanized, scientific agriculture presupposes, in a first stage, an educated labor force. The antagonism between the progress of civili-

zation and the maintenance of slavery is sharply defined. This antagonism is not abstract, but rather is embodied in the competition between the slave plantation and individual agriculture. There was a warning behind Lincoln's words: the degradation that, according to him, accompanied extensive agriculture opened the way to another, more serious degradation. That is why Lincoln stressed the sentiment of the dignity of work and the ambition for education that characterized his audience to win them to his firm opposition to the extension of slavery.

Thus, his entire approach was founded on the desire to find a way of bringing the rural masses into the struggle against slavery. His technical talk on the methods of agricultural cultivation constituted one means. Lincoln was trying to associate in the minds of his hearers a production technique (mechanized agriculture) with a form of social organization (individual ownership of property).

But even in the area of agricultural mechanization, things are not linked so mechanically. It is necessary, first of all, to point to an error: Lincoln contrasted intensive agriculture and large estates. There is no theoretical basis for such an opposition. It is true that "mammoth farms," to which Lincoln referred, have often been failures.[116] Yet it was not because of a lack of mechanization but because of the rarity, expense, and mobility of agricultural labor. Most large farms had indeed been divided and cultivated profitably by individual farmers, as Lincoln explained, but he forgot to point out that these farmers were tenants or sharecroppers. In fact, from that point on, capital dominated American land by means of money rents and mortgages, leaving the still-intact shell of small individual farms to become gradually emptied of its content.

Moreover, at the very moment when agricultural enterprises were becoming transformed in this manner, cattle kings were concentrating land and capital into their hands and employing dozens of workers. When Lincoln asserted that "the ambition for broad acres leads to poor farming," he was certainly not thinking of his friend David Davis, on whose land another friend, Bronson Murray, made the first comparison tests of harvesting machines in Illinois on behalf of the agricultural society of the state; or of his friend B. F. Harris, whose bulls won contests from 1855 on, well before the famous "Bob Burns," "Abe Lincoln," and "John Williams" carried off the trophy in Chicago in 1867; or of his friend Fell, who was one of the pioneers of education in Illinois, with the special aim of raising the prices of plots of land located near educational institutions that he had helped to found.[117]

But if he was not thinking about it, his audience, who knew the cost of machines, stallions, and studies, doubtless could not help but think that "money-kings" and "land-kings" existed even in a democracy. To this mute questioning that had its origin in the fall of the last crowned heads, Lincoln had only two answers.

First, and most important, he addressed himself to the small farmer by saying: "Many independent men, in this assembly, doubtless a few years ago were hired laborers." From this point of view it is incorrect to talk of the "American Dream" in the sense that what Lincoln said was perfectly true. Speaking to those who had just acquired property, Lincoln was obviously addressing as well the tenant and the agricultural worker; they would have their land. This promise would be largely kept and before too long.

Second, there was his plea in favor of intensive agriculture, which was supposed to guarantee the independence of those who practiced it. But fewer than twenty years later, the effects of the growth of the ratio of capital to labor in agricultural production would be felt for the first time on a large scale in "agrarian" agitation. The route that Lincoln set out for the farmer was that of free competition, and, in real life, things do not always happen as they do at agricultural fairs. At agricultural fairs, the speaker can conclude his speech and introduce the awards ceremony by saying, "Some of you will be successful, and such will need but little philosophy to take them home in cheerful spirits; others will be disappointed. . . . Let them adopt the maxim, 'Better luck next time.'" This time, we were indeed confronted with the "American Dream"; the awakening would be painful.

CONCLUSION

Lincoln's reconciliation with the land was favored by the transformation of agriculture by mechanization and science, but his motive was the struggle against slavery. It alone could lead the friend of Davis, Fell, Gridley, Moore, and others to take a position in favor of the Homestead. It alone could enable the very urbane Lincoln to speak to the rural masses in their own language. It alone could bring this conservative to embark on a path toward recognition of the labor movement.

A young lawyer who studied with Lincoln and Herndon in Springfield between 1849 and 1854 has left us a recollection that stands as a symbol. He had found several seedlings that "had sprouted in the dirt that had collected in the office." The seeds were part of samples sent by the agricultural section of the Patent Office to members of Congress so they could distribute them among farmers, but Lincoln had, it seems, neglected this duty. The little packets were finally sent out with Free Soil and Republican literature.[118]

CONCLUSION

Lincoln's election put an end to sixty years of Southern domination of the federal government. For the first time, the rural masses who had given Jefferson the victory in 1800 had transferred their allegiance to the industrial Northeast.

The Republican party was the architect of this upheaval. The party, although formed of old materials, was a new force, uniting the industrial bourgeoisie of the Northeast, a large portion of urban workers, and the great mass of farmers, both large and small, in the same movement of resistance to the extension of slavery. The South's desire to extend the peculiar institution to the territories brought about this new alliance, enlarged still further by secession that placed Douglas and his partisans in the Union camp.

Twenty-five years earlier, for completely different motives, the man who would symbolize in history this new orientation of rural people had chosen to look east. Driven from Kentucky by slavery, which left neither land nor work for "poor whites," the Lincoln family had settled just on the other side of the Ohio River, in Indiana. There, Lincoln had been able to judge how little room the institution of slavery allowed for his ambitious dreams, nourished by his fierce desire to escape work on the land and by the narrowness of rural horizons. He achieved independence in Illinois by breaking, at the same time, with farm and family. Forced to earn his living in an essentially rural region, he had to find a relationship with the land other than manual labor: storekeeper, surveyor, lawyer, his social rise was accompanied by intellectual improvement. Having become a politician, he very quickly took his distance from the rural world. He had, in fact, chosen to make his career in a political party that was in the minority in the countryside and by developing an economic vision in contradiction with agricultural interests as understood by the majority. The stand on taxation taken by this man who wanted to be the "DeWitt Clinton of Illinois" could not help but alienate rural taxpayers. His devotion to protectionism was echoed by only a small group of agricultural producers.

His social and political success was accompanied by an estrangement from the class from which he sprang, which was interpreted as haughtiness. He developed ties with bankers, land speculators, and estate owners and little by little lost the habit of amusing himself among country people. His aversion toward things agricultural contributed to creating this gulf. But the new relationship with the land, which he established as a surveyor and lawyer, enabled him to maintain, especially after the failure of his career as an Illinois legislator, a certain intimacy with ordinary people, their preoccupations and their way of thinking, an intimacy compatible with his new social standing.

The strength of these ties would appear in an obvious way each time his defeats (in 1842 and 1848) revealed the frailty of his ties as a politician with his electors. During his stay in Congress, Lincoln became the victim of the contradiction between his orientation to the East and the expansionist spirit of his district. Despite all his efforts to fulfill his role as the representative of private interests, notably agricultural ones, he was not in agreement with his electors on the general issues of the day. Without his being aware of it, his stay in Washington provided the remedy along with the disease: the growing place of the issue of slavery in the life of the nation. For the most part, Lincoln, troubled by the development of the situation, moved toward a fixed point, opposition to the extension of slavery, and began a movement, admittedly still quite hesitant, toward the positions that the Republican party would adopt.

Lincoln then lived through a period of confusion linked as much to the Compromise of 1850 as to the personal setback that he had suffered. His old motivations dulled, he tried to satisfy his ambition in his professional career when the threat of an extension of slavery in the territories, until then protected by the Missouri Compromise, awoke in him a passion without which nothing great can be accomplished.

The story of his reconciliation with country people is the story of this passion and the way in which he brought them to share it. The substance, the form, and the circumstances of his dialogue with the rural masses of Illinois brought about a return to his roots, to the superiority of the free lands of the Northwest over the closed economy and society of the South. As a public man, Lincoln projected the silhouette of a defender of free labor, small farmers, workers, and artisans. The private man contributed the colors of simplicity and fairness. The coincidence of biography and the cleverness of politicians added the veneer of legend.

The desire to be understood even led him to tackle subjects that were for the most part foreign to him, such as agriculture. The low priority it held in his thinking would be revealed by the lack of interest he showed during his presidency in the great innovations his administration made in the realm of agriculture. His commissioner of agriculture, Isaac Newton, was chosen more on political than scientific criteria, and Lincoln defended him to the end against the almost-unanimous specialized press and agricultural associations. The president apparently played no role in the adoption of the Morrill Act, which laid the foundations of agricultural education, and even forgot to mention it among the accomplishments of his administration in his message of December 1862.[1] One can see that his 1859 speech was motivated only by his concern to be listened to by the people of the Northwest even though his interest in agronomy cannot be doubted.

At the center of this communion with the people was a shared idea of property and labor, antagonistic to that of the South. Alongside this radical opposition between two civilizations there existed contradictions within Northern society that numerous institutions and specifically American historical conditions managed to obscure. Thus the election of 1860 carried to the presidency a man who was the advocate for both the Homestead and the Illinois Central Railroad and vested him with the historical mission of settling, in and by civil war, questions essential for the future of American civilization: slavery, the agrarian question, and the form of the Union.

Under pressure of events and radicals, constrained by the necessities of conducting the war, moved increasingly by an intimate feeling of his providential mission, Lincoln ended by issuing his Emancipation Proclamation. Drafted like a description of a piece of land, it defined, with many details, the regions where slavery was abolished. "All Lincoln's Acts appear like the mean pettifogging conditions which one lawyer puts to his opposing lawyer. But this does not alter their historic content, and indeed it amuses me when I compare them with the drapery in which the Frenchman envelops even the most unimportant point," Marx wrote before drafting for the First International an address to the American president, communicating the support of the labor movement for his work of emancipation.[2]

With slavery abolished and the Homestead passed, the great question of expansion to the West was settled in the terms in which it had been stated since 1787: free workers, not slaves, would cultivate the lands in the West wrested from the Indians.

LINCOLN AND THE INDIANS

The passage of the Homestead, the creation of a federal army, and the opening of the Pacific railroad were the decisive steps toward the final solution of the Indian question, made still more pressing than before by the discovery of mineral riches in the West.

Once more Lincoln was faced with the irrepressible conflict between two forms of property, two civilizations, two relationships with the land. Receiving the chiefs of five Indian nations in Washington on March 27, 1863, three months after the Emancipation Proclamation, he explained to them: "The pale-faced people are numerous and prosperous because they cultivate the earth, produce bread, and depend upon the products of the earth rather than wild game for a subsistence."[3] The chiefs indicated their approval. Perhaps they would, as in 1862, pose for Mathew Brady in the garden of the White House with Mary Todd Lincoln.[4]

What irony in the remarks of the Great White Father, of the good brother of the red and white family! In fact, several months earlier, American troops had destroyed the Indian cultures in Minnesota following a Sioux revolt. The Sioux had risen up against the corruption of the Indian system, which the Republican administration had inherited with no thought of changing. Bankers, land speculators, agents of the railroads, Indian traders, liquor salesmen, and corrupt officials had divided the spoils and exploited the Indians with ferocity. Lincoln was powerless before the collusion of the administration and Congress with those committing fraud. He had been able to resist only the most outrageous demands against the Indians and to organize inquiries into only the most openly scandalous cases.[5] Once the revolt was put down and the Sioux were imprisoned at Camp Lincoln, military authorities pronounced 303 death sentences, a number that the president, after a patient study of the files, reduced to thirty-nine (thirty-seven cases of murder, two cases of rape, with the other combatants pardoned).

Lincoln accepted the deportation of the Winnebagoes from Minnesota following the Sioux revolt (in which they had not participated) and signed the order putting 54,000 acres of stolen Winnebago land up for sale. His armies campaigned in the Dakotas from 1863 to 1865, and he even asked the British for the right of pursuit when the Sioux sought refuge in Canada.[6]

The charitable Lincoln became commander-in-chief of the army that distinguished itself at Sand Creek by massacring women and children for the same reasons that, as a simple soldier, he had followed the Illinois militia as it marched toward Bad Axe. Americans' hunger for land was insatiable, and the social order founded on private property in the soil was so incompatible with the collectivist civilization of the Indians that there was no common ground. Lincoln and Commissioner of Agriculture Newton had this in mind when Lincoln expressed their certainty that agriculture was "especially when linked with private property, the cornerstone of civilization," as a modern historian expressed it.[7]

America crushed the Indians during the years of civil war, with a conscience made even clearer and more triumphant because the principle of private property, founded on working the land, was sanctified by the struggle against slavery, which was practiced by some Indian tribes although in a totally different context. In the same message in 1863, Lincoln mentioned the Emancipation Proclamation and the Homestead and congratulated himself on "extinguishing the possessory rights of the Indians to large and valuable tracts of land."[8]

What future was in store for the Indians? Lincoln's advice, urging them to cultivate the soil, cannot be understood apart from the constant preoccupation, from that time on, of white people, whether "friends" or "enemies" of Indians, to bring about their assimilation through Christian education and the destruction of the tribal system of collective land ownership, a policy embodied in the Dawes Allotment Act of 1887.[9] With the very foundation of their civilization thus destroyed, Indians would find themselves thrown as individuals into free competition with railroads, banks, and estate owners. But Lincoln could not yet see all of that, committed as he was to the fulfillment of the ultimate progress in the civilization of private property: the liberation of black slaves.

Herndon remembered the debate subject that Lincoln as a young schoolboy had found in the *Kentucky Preceptor:* "Which has the most right to complain, the Indian or the Negro?"[10] In 1863, Abraham Lincoln gave an unambiguous answer. But, alas for the Negro, it was neither complete nor final, for, as soon as man's ownership of man was abolished, the issue of man's ownership of land arose. And in that area, the lot of the black, who did not become the owner of the land that he had tilled for a quarter of a millennium, was scarcely better than the lot of the Indian, driven from the land he had owned even longer.

AGRARIAN REFORM IN THE SOUTH?

The distinction between property in land, considered as sacred, and property in a slave, considered anachronistic and immoral, had been at the center of Lincoln's thought and of that of the Republican party. It had led to emancipation. But, as soon as emancipation was attained, the distinction would no longer favor the Negro and would become the principal obstacle to his social emancipation.

Consider, for example, the development of the ideas of Salmon P. Chase, who told a Baltimore loyalist, the Reverend Richard Fuller, worried about his plantation and his slaves, "that, as a loyal man, he was Proprietor of the *land*. How about the negroes? he asked. They were free, I [Chase] replied. He thought his right to them was the same as his right to the land."[11] This opposition, which seemed unfair to the loyalist, could work in favor of the rebel. Lincoln acknowledged as much when he defined the limits of the Confiscation Act of 1862. He deemed unconstitutional the provisions of the law which stipulated *permanent* confiscation of rebels' land. According to the lawyer-president, the guarantee of Article III, section 3, line 2 of the Constitution referred to property in land: "The Congress shall have Power to declare the Punishment of Treason, but no Attainder of Treason shall work Corruption of Blood, or Forfeiture except during the Life of the Person attainted."[12] A year earlier, he had written in a "Private & confidential" letter to Orville H. Browning, "Can it be pretended that it is any longer the government of the U.S.—any government of Constitution and laws,— wherein a General, or a President, may make permanent rules of property by proclamation?"[13]

However, in one of his own images, he had been forced, like the Catholic captain who had resigned himself to abandoning to the furious waves the figurehead of his ship in distress, to "throw the Virgin Mary overboard" and emancipate the Negroes.[14] After having long believed that permanent cohabitation of whites and blacks on American soil was impossible and favored efforts to set up "black colonies," notably in South America, Lincoln recognized the unrealistic nature of these proposals. The fact that they seemed unrealistic at the very moment when emancipation would have given them a chance of succeeding shows how much those plans conflicted with solving the slavery issue.

As soon as emancipation became a concrete issue, agrarian reform immediately appeared as an issue. Should American land be given to Negroes? Lincoln favored the experiment at Sea Island, South Carolina, a sort of paying Homestead for several hundred black families ("so as to give them an interest in the soil"), including most notably the Fuller Plantation.[15] He signed the law creating the Freedmen's Bureau, one of the missions of which was to distribute confiscated land to freed blacks. At the same time, he redoubled efforts to see that former slaves would continue to cultivate the plantations as free workers in keeping with his

Emancipation Proclamation of January 1, 1863, whether the lands had been confiscated and placed under the control of the Freedmen's Bureau or were plantations on which the owners agreed to pay wages.[16] His policy then already showed the two divergent directions of Reconstruction: agrarian reform or restoration of the Bourbons. History has decided. The Kentucky courts are still burdened with cases concerning land titles.

What would Lincoln have done if an assassin's bullet had not ended his days on Good Friday of 1865? Would he have undergone the same "transubstantiation" as Andrew Johnson, the lawyer of the Homestead and of agrarian reform?[17] The same question without an answer faces us with the issue of the Homestead.

"THE HOMESTEAD LAW IN
AN INCONGRUOUS LAND SYSTEM"

The title of the article by Paul Wallace Gates expresses perfectly how contradictory the measure of 1862 was with the system of management of public lands that had been in place since the beginning of the nineteenth century.[18] The spirit of the Homestead was essentially that of agrarian reform, and its application, to a certain degree, was an agrarian reform. At the same time, however, the institutions in charge of managing public lands were not reformed. Congress and the land offices remained under the control of the same social forces and economic pressure groups that had created the conditions making the reform necessary.

Between 1862 and 1970, almost 250 million acres were distributed by virtue of the Homestead Act to more than three million persons. The figures are impressive, but we must consider as well the immense quantity of land distributed under the old system, particularly in the years that immediately followed the adoption of the Homestead. During the years of the war alone (1861–65), only 26,552 persons benefited from the Homestead. They occupied 3,421,000 acres. During the same period, railroads received, directly or through the states, 76,544,000 acres. States received 17,427,000 acres for the construction of public buildings and schools, not counting grants to support construction of railroads.

In the period from 1862 to 1871, railroads received grants of land representing 155 million acres, of which 94 million became essentially their property. At the same time, the states were receiving 38 million acres to that end. Between 1865 and 1900, they obtained again more then 38 million acres of Indian reservations which would be divided into parcels and sold, and about one hundred million acres of federal lands still unsold.[19]

Thus, even before the end of the nineteenth century, the die was cast. Free competition between the Homestead system and the system of the railroads and speculators could only end to the benefit of the latter. Even had the ratio been much less disproportionate between the eighty-one million acres distributed by the Homestead between 1862 and 1900 and the more than 200 million under the old system during the same period, the laws of concentration would have had their normal effect.

During the war itself there appeared the first organized opposition to the government's policy in favor of railroads, to Republican estate owners, and to the methods employed by railroad companies to appropriate for themselves an ever-larger share of agricultural revenue. Illinois was among the first states touched by this "radical agrarianism."[20]

The same Abraham Lincoln appended his signature to both the Homestead Act and the Pacific Railroad Act. There would never again be a Homestead Act or a measure of equal scope in the history of the United States, but numerous laws favorable to railroads would be signed by presidents who never had any other claim to fame.

A lawyer for railroads and a defender of the landless would never again be united in the same person. Lincoln's successors, for example, Johnson, Grant, or Garfield, were not able to preserve the heritage whole. Robert Todd Lincoln, the eldest son of the sixteenth president, was the lawyer for the Pullman Company during the strike in Chicago in 1894, which was broken by the first Democratic president since Buchanan, Grover Cleveland.[21] During his first term, Cleveland had named a former Confederate general, Joseph Eggleston Johnston, as commissioner of railroads. Some symbols need no commentary: "For if, on the one hand, the tragedy of the years 1861–1865 eliminated slavery and with it the feudal, anachronistic civilization of the old south, on the other hand, it initiated the prodigious industrial expansion of the northern states that resulted in the clearest crystallizations of the capitalist economy. Beyond his personal characteristics, Abraham Lincoln's ambiguity rests on this historical situation."[22] And the permanent reconstruction of the Union to guarantee this expansion could not be accomplished without Southern generals.

This return to "normalcy" should not conceal, but rather bring to the fore the incongruous nature of the Homestead Act and, ultimately, of the Emancipation Proclamation, proof of how a conservative leader under the influence of exceptional circumstances such as war may go further than he would have wished. It in no way diminishes the man or his achievements to indicate the limits of this movement.

Lincoln apparently wanted from posterity only a quite modest eulogy. But, recalling his 1858 comparison between slavery and that plague of cultivation at the time, the Canada thistle, his remarks take on a special resonance. One day, speaking to his lifelong friend Speed of the possibility of his death, Lincoln declared, "I want it said of me by those who know me best, that I always plucked a thistle and planted a flower when I thought a flower would grow."[23] A long time passed before that moment came, but Lincoln then certainly became "the man for the hour."[24]

HISTORIOGRAPHY

The "French images of President Lincoln" that we possess are, for the most part, in the nineteenth century, the reflection of French popular opinion after the death of the American president, and, in the twentieth century, the reflection of the work of American historians.[1] Popular works by Claude Aragonnès, *Lincoln héros d'un peuple* (1955); Louis de Villefosse, *Abraham Lincoln* (1956 and 1969); and Jean Daridan, *Abraham Lincoln* (1962) fit the second category even if, like the last one cited, they shed new light on certain aspects of French diplomacy during the Civil War.

VOX POPULI

We must turn our attention, then, to the United States to discover original conceptions and versions of French views. From Washington to Springfield, passing through New York and Chicago, statues, museums, piously preserved relics, and all the well-marked trails lead to the reconstructed village of New Salem, cradle of the Lincoln myth (Maurine W. Redway and Dorothy K. Bracker, *Marks of Lincoln on Our Land,* 1957), the rustic temple where the people worship in Lincoln a Christ of the frontier. This vision of Lincoln as "the racy product of American soil" greatly holds sway in the popular consciousness.[2]

The poets were not mistaken. Walt Whitman could not sing about Lincoln without first recalling:

Pictures of growing spring and farms and homes, . . .
And all the scenes of life and the workshops, and the workmen
homeward returning.[3]

And for James Russell Lowell, who recognized the unique character of the sixteenth president, Nature, to create him,

> her Old-World moulds aside she threw,
> And, choosing sweet clay from the breast
> Of the unexhausted West
> With stuff untainted shaped a hero new.[4]

The same spirit inspired Carl Sandburg, who was able, after years of scholarly research, to preserve for his hero the enthusiastic freshness that had inspired him as a child: "In the corn-fields, plowing, . . . his bare feet spoke with the clay of the earth; it was in his toenails and stuck on the skin. . . . In the short and simple annals of the poor, it seems there are people who breathe with the earth and take into their lungs and blood some of the hard and dark strength of its mystery." And Lincoln himself is identified with corn: "He was growing as inevitably as summer corn in Illinois loam," Sandburg wrote of the young shop-keeper from New Salem. Or again: "During the hot summer weeks in Illinois, as the corn was growing knee-high, Lincoln and Douglas had their coats off" to write together "an almanac of American visions." In *The Prairie Years* Sandburg sang "the epic of wheat" and of corn in the Northwest and the emergence of Lincoln as one and the same song.[5]

This image of Lincoln is still dominant in the American consciousness, that of an agricultural divinity who "had died to save Man's barns from Jefferson Davis' raiders" in the phrase of Lloyd Lewis (*Myths after Lincoln*).[6] Roy P. Basler (*The Lincoln Legend*) analyzed the mechanism by which this image familiar to all Americans was formed.[7] After World War II, television and films would add to the Lincoln folklore, which had been already popularized through song, theater, and children's books.[8]

Although this tradition has its roots in the widespread popular emotion aroused by the death of Lincoln, it was nourished by a line of biographers and historians for whom Lincoln, the man of country people, embodied the needs and the interests of the rural world. Another school would insist, on the contrary, on the difference in social status, of attitude, and of "nature" between Lincoln and his people. In almost all cases, those who highlighted in this way a certain distance from the common people of the countryside were on Douglas's side in the 1854–60 controversy. On this point likewise, the interpretation that one has of Lincoln is "a touchstone of American historiography," according to David M. Potter.[9] It is significant to note that the raw materials for these two traditions came from Lincoln and Douglas themselves.

VOX DEI

Although the connection between "Abraham Lincoln and the Self-Made Myth" appeared for the first time in the Chicago *Journal* in October 1854, just after his speeches in Springfield and Peoria, Lincoln himself in 1859 and 1860 gave out the autobiographical elements that enabled journalists and writers hired for that purpose to lay the foundations of the myth.[10] Despite attaching little importance to the modesty of his origins, Lincoln was enough of a politician to understand all the advantages that could be derived from it. It is true that "None knew better than he that splitting rails did not qualify a man for public duties," but he had nonetheless experienced the Harrison campaign in 1840.[11]

His autobiography written for Jesse W. Fell on December 20, 1859, was sent by Fell to a lawyer in Pennsylvania, Joseph J. Lewis, who derived from it a long article in the Chester County *Times* of February 11, 1860, in an extremely Whig tone and presenting a distinguished and protectionist Lincoln. Probably inspired by Fell, Lewis completed the portrait of the pioneer that Lincoln had drawn of himself and asserted that his candidate "was fully up to all the mysteries of the woods, [and] to the deeper mysteries of prairie farming."[12]

This article and the books by John Locke Scripps and William Dean Howells furnished the basis of the biographies for the 1860 campaign: thirteen in English, three in German, and two in Welsh. Scripps's biography, a million copies of which were printed, stressed the Decatur rails, the symbol "of the rights and the dignity of free labor," and presented Lincoln as a model employee for Offutt, then as a man whose social success did not change him in the least, who dressed simply and spoke simply. Recalling his career as an Illinois legislator, Scripps wrote loftily: "The details of State legislation afford but few matters of interest to the general reader, and for that reason it is not proposed to follow Mr. Lincoln through this portion of his career."[13]

The other important Lincoln biography in 1860, by Howells, was not as modest and tackled Lincoln's actions between 1834 and 1842. He began first by clearing Lincoln of any participation in the "more visionary of these schemes" of public works while saluting his encouragement of "whatever project seemed feasible." He noted that Lincoln came out in favor of granting charters to agricultural societies, improving roads, the education of the greatest number, and low salaries for public officials. He further stressed his stands in favor of squatters and debtors. He drew attention to Lincoln's proposal in Congress to give veterans the possibility of locating their land warrants in parcels. Lincoln was determined to justify—as he had done in his autobiography for Scripps—his position on the Mexican War of 1848, and Howells took notice of it. But, as to the rest, Howells and Lincoln (who reviewed the manuscript and twice, in 1864 and 1865, borrowed the copy in the White House library) carefully chose the aspects of the Republican candidate's political career that corresponded to what the rural and working electorate would expect from him. The Lincoln of 1860 presents here, in a way, the image that he hoped to give of his political life. Howells's biography completed that image by drawing the portrait of the poor people's lawyer and of the public figure who remained simple despite his greatness.[14]

These were the finest jewels in the crown that the Republican party offered its candidate in 1860. These works and the more mediocre editions with picturesque names like "Wigwam" or "Wide-Awake" had their counterparts in 1864. For example, there was the work of O. J. Victor, *The Private and Public Life of Abraham Lincoln,* by the author of the life of Walter Scott and of Garibaldi in the collection of *Beadle's Dime Biographies* (Kit Carson, Pontiac, McClellan), in which, beside the simple grotesque tribute (his congressional career in 1848–49 was "brilliant to a singular degree"), began to appear, as in William Makepeace Thayer's book, myths tied to the folklore of the frontier.[15]

This campaign hagiography would be found again in the funeral orations and the biography-necrologies that began to appear in 1865. Among them, the book by J. G. Holland is the best and the only one based on personal research.[16] In the same spirit, members of his administration left the recollection of a great man close to the people. After the memoirs and the biographies of George S. Boutwell, Lucius E. Chittenden, Carl Schurz, Theodor Canisius, James R. Gilmore, and others, Allen T. Rice and O. H. Oldroyd gathered recollections from people who, when they reached that point, all stressed Lincoln's profound link to the land and those who worked it.[17]

Older friends or relations, such as Henry B. Rankin, and journalists who had served in the Union army and felt a real admiration for Lincoln, such as Francis F. Browne (who wrote a work of real history) added to a portrait spread by popularizers like Thayer, a specialist in campaign biographies for the Republican party, or like Norman Hapgood.[18] The edifying value of the life of the self-made man was rapidly recognized abroad, and the model image was spread throughout the entire world by works such as the one published by the Society for Promoting Christian Knowledge in 1916, with the revealing title, *Abraham Lincoln, Farmer's Boy and President.*[19] It would be possible to lengthen this list indefinitely because works of this kind constitute the bulk of Jay Monaghan's

Lincoln Bibliography: 1839–1939, which compiled more than four thousand publications on Lincoln.[20] It would, moreover, be wrong to believe that the source had dried up.

Isaac N. Arnold's *The History of Abraham Lincoln and the Overthrow of Slavery* (1866) holds a special place in this family of biographies. Begun while Lincoln was still alive by his personal friend and political supporter within the House of Representatives of the United States, it was dedicated to the Thirty-seventh and Thirty-eighth Congresses. Arnold attributed to Lincoln views on Reconstruction that were closer to those of the radical Congress than to the positions of Andrew Johnson and supported his thesis by emphasizing at length Lincoln's democratic spirit, already evident well before his appearance in 1854 as "an actor who, hitherto comparatively obscure, was soon to become the most prominent figure in American history." Without saying a word about the internal improvements scheme of 1837, Arnold reviewed Lincoln's career before 1854 and set great store by his stands against slavery in 1837 and 1849. Especially in depicting the lawyer of the poor, the pure product of the upper Mississippi Valley, he emphasized what would become an article of faith of the hagiographic school: "Noblest son of the Republic, he was transferred, with no change of manner, from the rude life of the frontier to the capital."[21] Frederick Jackson Turner was also in this tradition when he wrote: "He represents the pioneer of the period; but his ax sank deeper than other men's, and the plaster cast of his great sinewy hand, at Washington, embodies the training of these frontier railsplitters."[22]

This identification of Lincoln with the pioneer spirit would be called into question by a biography generally considered the most stilted of the filiopietistic school, the monumental historico-biographical study by the president's two private secretaries, John G. Nicolay and John Hay: *Abraham Lincoln: A History* (10 vols., 1890). Certainly, the two Republican politicians heard the farmers of central Illinois say "that the brown thrush did not sing for a year after he died." But, ironically, they recall on the same page that Lincoln was not a Freemason, even if Masons around the world had taken him for one of theirs, and the general impression that emerges from their narrative of the years in Indiana and Illinois is that the rustic was all wrong to think he was entitled to identify himself with Lincoln: Lincoln "felt too large for the life of a farmhand on Pigeon Creek"; he was different from "the common run of Southern and Western rural laborers" because he possessed "an innate self-respect, and a consciousness that his self was worthy of respect." His famed wrestling prowess in New Salem was nothing more than an "ignoble scuffle," and after 1832 "having been, even in so slight a degree, a soldier and a politician, he was unfitted for a day laborer." Moreover, Lincoln was a Whig because "the better sort of people in Sangamon County were Whigs, though the majority were Democrats, and he preferred through life the better sort to the majority." "The election of Mr. Lincoln to the Legislature may be said to have closed the pioneer portion of his life. . . . From this time forward his associations were with a better class of men than he had ever known before," and he would enjoy the greatest benefit on the level of self-esteem and the civilized nature of his habits.[23]

Their vindication of Lincoln's legislative career, in both the state legislature and Congress, left no stone unturned. Although they had access to the Robert Todd Lincoln Papers, Nicolay and Hay did not hesitate to present Lincoln as a Tom Thumb lost in the political forest of Washington in 1849 when he wanted to be named commissioner of the General Land Office. It is even more significant that they presented, several pages further on, a realistic and piquant portrait of the "men who go there from small rural communities in the South and the West," who, dazzled by the lights of Washington, fall on the Democratic spoils to obtain the charity of a public office. They had, after all, defined their task as follows: "We ought to write the history of these times like two everlasting angels who know everything, judge everything, tell the truth about everything and don't care a twang of our harps about one side or the other. There will be one exception: we are Lincoln men all through."[24]

Thus, on the question of Lincoln's relationship with land and labor, Nicolay and Hay opened the way to revisionism by contrasting the politician and the man of the people, the cultivated city man and the ignorant rustic. The whole dimension of Lincoln as a lawyer eluded them. Before they wrote, Lincoln, as Christ-like as he was, had been embodied still in the frontier farmer, the symbol of the "common man." With Nicolay and Hay, he became for the first time a man out of the ordinary, in every sense of the term.

Revisionism would soon find an abundant source of revelations about that contrast throughout the biography by William H. Herndon and Jesse W. Weik entitled *Herndon's Lincoln: The True Story of a Great Life* (3 vols., 1889). Herndon believed he was writing a biography diametrically opposed to that by Nicolay and Hay, whose first efforts had seemed to him a mutilation of his hero. Motivated by personal rancor against Mary Todd Lincoln and her son, often moved by a bizarre desire to clarify certain indecent events, Herndon nonetheless produced the richest and most interesting work of all the biographers who had known Lincoln personally. Herndon, whom Albert Beveridge praised as "almost a fanatic in his devotion to the truth," gathered the most important collection of documents on Lincoln outside of those of Robert Todd Lincoln and Oliver R. Barrett, the last being now dispersed.[25] Used with care (and David Donald's *Lincoln's Herndon* is an adequate instruction manual), *Herndon's Lincoln* remains one of the major sources.

Writing at the height of agrarian agitation, Herndon favored populism and the greenbacker movement demanding a softening of credit. Alcoholism had led to his bankruptcy as a lawyer at the end of the 1860s, and he had just failed at a farming experiment. He had inherited from his father in 1867 a six-hundred-acre farm above the Sangamon River several miles to the north of Springfield, which he had baptized "Fairview." Book-learning alone was poor preparation for the role of a gentleman-farmer. He had failed lamentably and had to resign himself, at the age of fifty-three, to begin cultivating the land with his own hands during a period of depression for agricultural prices after the 1868–72 crisis. Thus Herndon's social position was quite different from that of the Republican notables Nicolay and Hay. His political evolution was even more different. Having become a "radical" on the question of slavery in 1856–57, he had grown apart from Lincoln after 1859 and had lost all real influence in the Illinois Republican party at that time. An ardent defender of the Homestead, he publicly endorsed Douglas's position on that subject.[26]

Herndon's *Lincoln* is of the people and out of the ordinary at the same time, a tree that touches the sky and sends its roots deep into the ground. Herndon, who had held a hoe in his hands, understood perfectly Lincoln's hatred for manual labor, dreary, stupid, and exhausting. Whereas Hay and Nicolay spoke as pretentious city dwellers, Herndon's account was not tainted by contempt for the rural masses. Close to nature throughout his life, he stressed what seemed to him Lincoln's peculiar lack of interest in flowers and country and woodland things. Where Nicolay and Hay spoke of "respect," Herndon said "freedom without familiarity," "courtesy without condescension," and he presented Lincoln's ambition as linked at the beginning to the aspirations of the entire community of New Salem, natural in a way. He tried to demonstrate this community of feelings by showing Lincoln as a surveyor who did not speculate, as a lawyer who did not become a real estate agent and who kept his distance from the railroad companies. He showed Lincoln at the Centralia Agricultural Fair after the Jonesboro debate in 1858 and being welcomed enthusiastically by the common people of Coles County in 1860, an honest, simple, sympathetic man, at one with the American people during the war.[27]

By so doing, Herndon gave life to the saintly image of the Rail-Splitter, "substituting for Lincoln's aureole the battered tall hat, with valuable papers stuck in its lining, which he had long contemplated with reverent irritation," as Lord Charnwood expressed it.[28] But, at the same time, he presented a Lincoln consumed by ambition, a wily politician who married well in order to rise in society.[29] These aspects, which seemed minor to Herndon, would enable Lincoln's enemies, and then modern critics, to define more precisely the important period from 1809 to 1860.

THE DEVIL'S ADVOCATES

In Herndon's lifetime, and with his well-paid blessing, the documents that form the basis of his collection were used by Ward Hill Lamon to "write" a biography of Lincoln: *The Life of Abraham Lincoln* (1872). Lamon, a lawyer from Danville, Illinois, had very quickly become Lincoln's bodyguard, and devotion to truth compels us to say that he acquitted himself of the task until April 1865 much better than he did that of guarding his master's memory after that date. In fact, Lamon, a Kentuckian sympathetic to the South and a marshal in Washington during the war, whose position had brought him into difficulties with Congress, did not hesitate to sign his name to a biography written by one of Lincoln's most astute enemies, Chauncey F. Black, a Democrat and son of Buchanan's attorney general. The reader cannot help being startled at pages on which Black settles Buchanan's and Calhoun's scores against Stephen A. Douglas.

But revisionist historians must have looked closely at the Black-Lamon work, for the thesis presented in that 1872 volume would be found in their books in a different style. We encounter an already "whiggish" Lincoln in 1832, an irresponsible supporter of unlimited public works (even if he was merely following the opinion of the majority of farmers), a defender of the Bank of the United States, "Mr. Biddle's profligate concern." "It must by this time be clear to the reader that Mr. Lincoln was never agitated by any passion more intense than his wonderful thirst for distinction," declared Black-Lamon. Lincoln the second-rate politician was manipulated by David Davis, his secret counselor at the White House, and chosen by the Republicans because of his political insignificance and the publicity value of his image as "Honest Old Abe," which he carefully cultivated and "beside whose 'running qualities' those of Taylor and Harrison were of slight comparison."

Black's hatred for Douglas was so strong that he went so far as to assign to Lincoln the superior role in the debates of 1854 and 1858.[30] Not having the same reasons for hating the "Little Giant," historians of the revisionist era, which Herndon had opened without knowing it, would reconstruct little by little Lincoln's story—and thus America's history—by adopting Douglas's point of view.

Herndon's revelations had indeed shaken the Lincoln myth irreparably. It required the genteel zeal of Ida M. Tarbell to sanitize, "Tarbellize" Beveridge would call it, the materials Herndon had collected and still show a Lincoln who might have become an influential agricultural leader of southwestern Indiana in her *In the Footsteps of the Lincolns* (1924), halfway between her *Early Life of Abraham Lincoln* (1896), which was a sort of response to Herndon, and the final version, a little more critical, *Life of Lincoln* (2 vols., 1928).[31] The works of William E. Barton and Louis A. Warren fit into this Tarbellian lineage to the degree that they still tried to preserve a certain harmony between Lincoln and the rural world.[32]

Besides the Tarbellian school, and while the hagiographic wave continued to pour uninterrupted from the presses of five continents, two original works appeared that deserve our attention before dealing with the revisionist school.

Godfrey Rathbone Benson, First Baron Charnwood, and Herman Schlüter, an American socialist leader, certainly occupied marginal positions in relation to the main current of Lincoln biography. Lord Charnwood, an alumnus of Balliol College, Oxford, liberal member of the House of Commons, and mayor of Litchfield, published his *Abraham Lincoln* in London in 1919 in the collection "Makers of the Nineteenth Century." Writing from a European perspective and a little surprised at first by the mediocrity of the personalities in the first acts of the Lincoln tragedy, he discovered a political man whose ambition—so sharply stressed by Herndon, whom Charnwood admired—was from the beginning "a clean and a high ambition." For the first time the years between 1834 and 1842 were described as a period of "discipline."[33] The moderation shown by Charnwood, who was careful to keep his distance from Herndon without, however, neglecting his contribution, can be explained by his sincere admiration for the man who was able to understand, better than had Douglas, the historical importance of the issue of slavery and who succeeded during the Civil War in rising to meet his task.

Herman Schlüter, a correspondent of Engels, was the author of *Lincoln, Labor and Slavery: A Chapter from the Social History of America,* published in New York in 1913 by the Socialist Literature Company. Taking explicitly the standpoint of "historical materialism, first brought into the science of history by Karl Marx and Friedrich Engels," he saw in Lincoln the "representative of the lower middle class (known in Europe as the *petit bourgeoisie)"* and pointed out in Lincoln's many speeches on social mobility his "glorification of the lower middle class, the men who are neither capitalists nor wage-workers."[34] The first serious study of Lincoln's theoretical texts on labor and property took exclusively the point of view of the urban working classes, therefore neglecting Lincoln's relationship with workers in the country, and especially with the petite bourgeoisie, although Schlüter recognized that Lincoln's views on it are essential for understanding his social discourse. The reason is that Schlüter was only moderately interested in Lincoln himself and did not aspire to write a biography. Following William H. Sylvis, Terence V. Powderly, and George E. McNeill, he took a pioneering approach to the history of the American labor movement, intending to write one chapter of that history (its relationship to slavery). He analyzed Lincoln's thought from that point of view.

Finally we come to Beveridge, the last amateur and the first professional historian. Like Herndon, this Lincoln biographer had the honor of his own biography.[35] Born on October 6, 1862 on a remote farm in Ohio, he would distinguish himself as an Indiana senator (1899–1912). A Republican, he later became a leader in Theodore Roosevelt's Progressive party. After a period of great political and literary success (he wrote a biography of John Marshall), the years of writing his unfinished *Abraham Lincoln* were marked by bitterness. He found nothing of the hero of his youth in the in-depth study that he was the first to make of Lincoln's political career in Springfield and in Congress.

In Lincoln's childhood and adolescence, Beveridge saw above all the poverty and the boredom from which he had himself suffered, and he devoted himself so passionately to reviving the civilization of Indiana that his first chapters seem sometimes to be "a rivulet of text in a meadow of footnotes." He depicted sympathetically Lincoln's efforts to rise above his condition, and he labored to explain the young worker's commitment to Henry Clay, who "was only second to Jackson in popularity."[36] Fascinated by the possibilities of improving river navigation, concerned to receive his wages in a sound and stable currency, surrounded by partisans of "Harry of the West," it was natural for Lincoln to break with his Democratic family. Beveridge's biography of John Marshall had revealed how much he, as a good Republican, disliked the agrarian Jeffersonian-Jacksonian current.

But, curiously, there is a reversal when Beveridge deals with Lincoln's career in the Illinois legislature. A certain distrust begins to penetrate his development of the contrast between the lobbies of the Vandalia capitol and the simplicity of New Salem. Although he still defended Lincoln's attitude toward the Springfield bank from 1835 to 1837, he presented him as the "trustworthy supporter" of the bank in 1840, this time from a negative point of view, and concluded by showing "that conservatism which so strongly marked his entire career in the Legislature." The ambiguity of "progressivism," that Republicanism highly colored with populism, appeared in these pages, from which Lincoln emerged as the ardent defender of "vested interests" while still acquiring the bases of an admirable political liberalism by fighting against Jacksonian despotism.

The tendency became even greater, and Beveridge took a new turn in the seventh chapter, "Congress and Decline," for the expansionist nationalism of Teddy Roosevelt's close collaborator was scandalized by Lincoln's opposition to the Mexican War. On his return to Springfield, it is hard to understand how the partisan politician with the narrow views that had been presented to us could have accomplished a "return to the grass roots," testifying to "Lincoln's belief in the people as the origin of all that is wise, right, and attractive."

That false-sounding Lincoln already interested Beveridge much less than did Stephen A. Douglas, whose daguerreotype graced the frontispiece of the second volume as Lincoln's had illustrated the first. For Beveridge can rightly be counted among the founders of the revisionist school, for whom the Civil War was attributable to the malicious fierceness of the abolitionists and anti-extensionists. The second volume of Beveridge's *Lincoln* is already a *Douglas*, in whom he recognizes a personality superior to Lincoln's.[37] Noting in passing that "when estimating the factors that finally merged into the Republican Party, serious account must be taken of the agrarian and industrial elements," he nonetheless defended, on the whole, Douglas's position on the relationship between "the west and slavery."[38]

Reading Tarbell had inspired Sandburg to write *Abraham Lincoln: The Prairie Years,* in which the son of Swedish immigrants, a former milkman, stagehand, truck driver, brick-yard worker, agricultural laborer, hotel dishwasher, and apprentice carpenter, had drawn an idyllic vision of the great Republican president.[39] *The Prairie Years* appeared in 1926, the year preceding Beveridge's *Lincoln.* Five years later, another poet, Edgar Lee Masters, seized on Beveridge to write the only biography that is hostile to Lincoln from start to finish, *Lincoln: The Man* (1931).

The discovery of Beveridge had transformed Masters, until then a Lincoln admirer. For the first time, he saw a possibility of reconciling himself with the opinion of his grandfather, the Democratic politician Davis Masters of Illinois, who had persisted, against all odds, in the poor opinion of Lincoln he had formed in the 1840s. At the same time, in the midst of an economic crisis and the defeat of the Republican party, Edgar Lee Masters produced a political work, dedicated to Thomas Jefferson, which took its place in Roosevelt's campaign against Hoover. The rural masses had once again changed sides. The Democratic party looked indisputably like their last hope in 1931. The ambiguity of Beveridge, a renegade from the Republican party who had not joined the Democrats, had no place in Masters's work. His conclusion on Lincoln was that "from the first he was a centralist, a privilegist, an adherent of the non-principled Whig Party, which laid the foundation of the Republican Party of 1854, and which has grown into the reckless, ignorant and unscrupulous imperial organization of the present time."[40]

Identifying the party of Coolidge and Hoover with that of Lincoln and Lincoln's party with the federalism of Hamilton and Webster had as its logical consequence assimilating Roosevelt to Douglas, Jackson, and Jefferson. This identification was, moreover, definitely in the spirit of an era when the voice of Charles Beard—an admirer of Beveridge— drowned out the modest remarks of Vernon L. Parrington, who, in a way, thought Lincoln was closer to Jackson and Jefferson than to the Adams family.[41]

Masters's book is interesting in that it brings out the contrast between the Whig politician, with his eyes turned to the East, and the Jacksonian masses of 1830–45. Up to a point, there is some truth in his hasty generalization that "it began with Samuel Lincoln settling in Hingham; it was climaxed with the Sixth Massachusetts Regiment being the first to respond to Lincoln's call for troops to subjugate the South."[42] But what Masters did not see was the shifting of the political center of gravity from the Great Northwest toward the Northeast. Lincoln foresaw, for reasons of his own, a real movement of rural population in favor of a collaboration with the East in preference to the South. The question of slavery disappeared as if by magic from the painting where it had for more than a half-century concealed all the other aspects of the landscape.

For the period from 1830 to 1860, revisionist logic culminated in the admirable work of Reinhard H. Luthin, *The Real Abraham Lincoln* (1960), which highlighted all of Lincoln's conservative, aristocratic, and partisan aspects and presented him generally as far removed from the preoccupations of country people.[43] In the same way as his study of the distribution of federal offices during the war (*Lincoln and the Patronage*) had concluded that Lincoln was a political maneuverer, in the same way as his *The First Lincoln Campaign* (1944) pictured the Republican party as a coalition of the "outs" eager to get "in," Luthin explains that the "real Abraham Lincoln" was "a politician to the bone."[44] But Luthin's book is interesting for another reason. More than Beveridge, Luthin was a civilizationist and integrated into his reflections the discoveries of John J. Duff, Willard L. King, and others. His analysis of the differences between the land laws of Kentucky and of Indiana, for example, and of the division of Sangamon County are remarkable for their conciseness and subtlety.

To whom should the first revisionist declaration be credited if not to Stephen A. Douglas himself, just as the source of the Lincoln legend can be found in the autobiographical writings? Let us listen to him attack his opponent with humor at Ottawa during their first debate in 1858: "I have known him for nearly twenty-five years. There were many points of sympathy between us when we first got acquainted. We were both comparatively boys, and both struggling with poverty. . . . I was a school-teacher in the town of Winchester, and he a flourishing grocery-keeper in the town of Salem. (Applause and laughter.) He was more successful in his occupation than I was in mine . . . for his business enabled him to get into the Legislature." Then "he subsided, or became submerged, and he was lost sight of as a public man for some years."[45]

A special place should be given to the principal revisionist historian who was a Lincoln specialist, James G. Randall, whose *Lincoln, the President* (4 vols., 1945–55) did not reach the same vision of the pre-1860 Lincoln as had his disciple, Luthin. On the contrary, Randall stressed the Milwaukee speech of 1859 and Lincoln's professed preference for small farms, declaring him more Jeffersonian than Hamiltonian. How to explain this atypical view? The answer lies perhaps in Randall's major thesis for the 1854–60 period. According to him, Lincoln and Douglas were very close to each other. If Lincoln had occupied the senatorial seat of his rival, he would have acted as did Douglas and would have been right to do so. This underestimation of the role of anti-slavery sentiment in the evolution of Lincoln and America is also found in Randall's interpretation of the Homestead Act, which he viewed as "a measure frankly devoted to welfare."[46]

THE PLEA FOR THE DEFENSE

After Beveridge, only Benjamin P. Thomas continued to see in Lincoln a man of the frontier, a democrat of the Whig party, in *Abraham Lincoln, a Biography* (1952). "Just as the West became a major determining factor in American national life, so it exerted a compelling influence on Lincoln." Heir of the real and living frontier democracy according to Turner's image, Lincoln was able to avoid "the most flagrant of the frontier's faults" such as xenophobia. Insisting on the fact that the division between the Whig party and the Democratic party was "not primarily along class lines," he inferred that the Whigs were not at all different from the Democrats in their attitude toward country people and credited Lincoln with a continuing attachment to the popular roots of his democratic philosophy.[47]

Harry V. Jaffa (*Crisis of the House Divided*, 1959) and Don E. Fehrenbacher (*Prelude to Greatness*, 1962) returned to the decade of 1850–60 to study in detail the Lincoln-Douglas rivalry and revised revisionism by showing the importance that the slavery issue held for the population of Illinois, and the strength of Lincoln's argument. Their conclusions were taken up by Stephen B. Oates in *With Malice Toward None: The Life of Abraham Lincoln* (1979).

This change in historical perspective did not translate itself, however, into a reconsideration of the revisionist conclusions on the 1830–54 period, nourished by such specialized studies as Charles H. Coleman (*Lincoln and Coles County, Illinois*, 1955), who emphasized the difference in social status between Lincoln and his family; Donald W. Riddle (*Congressman Lincoln*, 1957), showing an uncertain representative in 1848–49; and Benjamin Quarles (*Lincoln and the Negro*, 1962), showing Lincoln's conservatism on the Negro question.

An immense quantity of material accumulated in closely related areas: social histories of Illinois by Theodore C. Pease and Arthur C. Cole; studies by Arthur C. Boggess and William V. Pooley on the settlement of Illinois; by Robert M. Haig on the taxation system; by John H. Krenkel on public works; by Frances M. Morehouse and Willard L. King on Fell and Davis; and the collection of publications of the University of Illinois Studies in the Social Sciences, including the works of G. W. Dowrie and Richard Bardolph. The Illinois state historian, Paul M. Angle, edited the best travel accounts and traced the development of Springfield. Similarly, the works of Paul W. Gates and the contributors to the *Mississippi Valley Historical Review*, such as Allan G. Bogue and Theodore L. Carlson, stressed the social contradictions and the economic development of the Prairie State.

Lincoln studies (properly so called) had followed all possible trails. In particular, *Personal Finances* by Harry E. Pratt (1943) opened the way to more scientific research on Lincoln's social status. A whole line of authors explored the activities of Lincoln the lawyer. Among them, John J. Duff, in *Prairie Lawyer*, emphasized the nature of the cases Lincoln handled and the social ties created through his practice, while John P. Frank, in *Lincoln as a Lawyer* (1961), sought to demonstrate the mechanism that Marx, a lawyer himself, had noticed a century earlier: "where another man, acting for the sake of so many 'square feet of land' declaims about 'the struggle for an idea,' Lincoln, even when he is acting for the sake of an idea, speaks only in terms of 'square feet of land.' "[48]

Gabor S. Boritt seized all of these facts to take up an area of Lincoln's life completely unexplored before then: his thought and action in the realm of economics. In *Lincoln and the Economics of the American Dream* (1978) can be found for the first time an in-depth study of Lincoln's economic thought. In particular, Boritt devoted an entire chapter, "Et in Arcadia Ego," to Lincoln's attitude toward agriculture, the first exercise of this kind since an article by Earl D. Ross, "Lincoln and Agriculture," which appeared in *Agricultural History* in 1929. Ross had deplored Lincoln's lack of interest in both agriculture and social conflicts existing in the countryside during the 1861–65 period.

Boritt presented a Lincoln for whom agriculture and the issue of public lands were problems subordinate to his general orientation in favor of the development of commerce and industry. He noted, however, that Lincoln knew how to manage the interests of his "predominantly farming constituency" between 1830 and 1860, as well as later. According to him, from 1834 to 1862, Lincoln was a Whig embarrassed by his party's views on the question of public lands, a pragmatic supporter of all means of developing the West, from preemption to distribution. Boritt interpreted Lincoln's silence on graduation after 1839 as a support for that measure, his silence on the Homestead as marking a lack of interest, and pointed out for the first time his vote on the McClernand resolution as proof of his favorable position toward the Democratic program. It was his concern for not breaking with his party that motivated Lincoln, halfheartedly, to denounce Benton's plans and appreciate Clay's.[49]

Such an interpretation ignores all of Lincoln's stands on the taxation of land unless one interprets the "Rebecca Letters" as a simple demagogic game or considers the 1839 reforms as democratic.[50] At no time did Boritt take into account Lincoln's ties with speculators. If he thus effaced the contradictions between town and country, between large and small, it was in order to present a Lincoln, who, from the beginning was entirely guided by a highly moral desire to encourage "the opportunity to rise in life." According to him, the reversal of priorities in 1854, when Lincoln abandoned for a time his economic preoccupations to devote himself to the struggle against the extension of slavery, only "raised his Dream to its highest plane."[51]

There is a profound truth in this observation, and the pages that Boritt devotes to the relationship between property and labor are remarkable.[52] But it is difficult to deny that the "dream" had appeared in a fairly contradictory form during the preceding period; that the strength of the feeling that carried Lincoln toward common people was inhibited by other aspects of his personality and of his situation before 1854; that genuine conflicts occurred between classes before and after 1854; and that Lincoln's positions on these questions cannot be analyzed as an unchanging whole resting on the idea of the American Dream.

It is true that, overall, despite all the chaos, the crises, the absurdities of exuberant development, the Whig party—and, from this point of view, the Democratic party was its equal—played a progressive role during this period. But it should be remarked that it had to disappear before the Homestead and emancipation could be born, just as the Lincoln of the 1830s gave way for the birth of the man on whom more has been written in the English language, except for Jesus Christ.

It was the transformation of 1854 that remains a mystery for those who cannot conceive that the same man (or the same class) can transform himself into his opposite. Lincoln's radical ambiguity resides, at the same time, in the 1854 break and in the persistence after that date of the ambivalence, at that stage, of the class he represented. Astonished to find in Teddy Roosevelt, Herbert Hoover, or Dwight D. Eisenhower the successors of Lincoln, to rediscover in the sixteenth president the author of the Rebecca Letters, the revisionist had tried to prove that the great man was small. By trying to "mend this break" of 1854 as he himself put it, Boritt put himself in the position of demonstrating the opposite. In both cases, the essential importance of the issue of the extension of slavery per se was neglected.

It is not to disparage Boritt's work—which constitutes, rightly considered, the only original and complete view that American historiography has produced since Beveridge—to put the issue of slavery back in the place that Lincoln gave it after 1854, the first place.

ANOTHER ROUTE

In a large volume full of oddities, Henry Clay Whitney stuffed together pell-mell his reminiscences on Lincoln and his own views on people and things. His *Life on the Circuit with Lincoln* (1892) brought up more issues than it resolved.

Contrasting the millionaire David Davis, who was patrician, aristocratic, rich, and sensual, with a Lincoln who was democratic, plebeian, poor, and ascetic, Whitney did not help us to understand their friendship. He ended, as many had, by comparing Lincoln to Christ, but his remarks on Davis at the time of his death were much less flattering:

"doubtless his sad-eyed tenants were happier than he; and the end came: he had to be content with a few feet of the earth of which he had for fifty years monopolized and ruled over so much."

The question doubtless bothered the lawyer Whitney in his old age. His preface was dated from Chicago, on May 1, 1892, six years after the Haymarket massacre, one year before the Pullman strike. Confronted with the now-obvious antagonism between railroad barons and middle classes, Whitney began to be sorry that the rich man could not always prove that he had acquired his goods through real personal labor, for that weakness was the only thing that might help spread socialist propaganda, and he recalled the happy times when Lincoln talked of property without the words *strike* and *lockout* being pronounced.[53]

The American Dream transformed into a nightmare brought up the question of its reality at the beginning, on the midwestern prairie that was still the Far West. This is the trail we have followed to discover Lincoln, conscious, however, as was Herndon, citing Holland, that "Men caught only separate aspects of his character—only the fragments that were called into exhibition by their own qualities."[54]

NOTES

ABBREVIATIONS USED IN THE NOTES

Beveridge	Albert J. Beveridge. *Abraham Lincoln, 1809–1858.* 2 vols. Boston: Houghton Mifflin, 1928.
CW	Abraham Lincoln. *The Collected Works of Abraham Lincoln.* Edited by Roy P. Basler. 9 vols. New Brunswick: Rutgers University Press, 1953–55.
EWT	Reuben Gold Thwaites. *Early Western Travels, 1748–1846.* 32 vols. Cleveland: The Arthur H. Clark Co., 1904–7.
Herndon	William Herndon and William Jesse Weik. *Herndon's Lincoln: The True Story of a Great Life.* 3 vols. Chicago: Belford-Clarke Co., 1889.
Nicolay and Hay	John G. Nicolay and John Hay. *Abraham Lincoln: A History.* 10 vols. New York: The Century Co., 1914.

INTRODUCTION

1. James G. Randall, "Has the Lincoln Theme Been Exhausted?" *American Historical Review* 41 (1936): 270–94.

2. Clyde C. Walton, "An Agonizing Reappraisal: 'Has the Lincoln Theme Been Exhausted?'" in *Lincoln Images: Augustana College Centennial Essays,* ed. O. Fritiof Ander (Rock Island: Augustana College Library, 1960), 99–105.

3. Earl Schenck Miers, William E. Baringer, and C. Percy Powell, eds., *Lincoln Day by Day: A Chronology, 1809–1865,* 3 vols. (Washington: Lincoln Sesquicentennial Commission, 1960).

4. Walton, "An Agonizing Reappraisal," 105.

5. See the historiographical essay at the end of this volume.

6. Isaac N. Arnold, *The History of Abraham Lincoln and the Overthrow of Slavery* (Chicago: Clark and Co., 1866), 67.

CHAPTER 1: KENTUCKY

1. Autobiography written for John Locke Scripps, circa June 1860, *CW*, 4:61–62.

2. "It is a great piece of folly to attempt to make anything out of my early life." Letter from Scripps to Herndon, 24 June 1865, Herndon-Weik Collection, Library of Congress, cited by J. G. Randall, *Lincoln the President*, 4 vols. (New York: Dodd, Mead, 1945–55), 1:4.

3. Scripps to Herndon, 24 June 1865, Herndon-Weik Collection; Herndon, 1:2.

4. Louis A. Warren, *Lincoln's Youth, Indiana Years, Seven to Twenty-One, 1816–1830* (New York: Appleton, Century Crofts, 1959), 34; Thomas Cooper, *Some Information Respecting America Collected by Thomas Cooper*, 2d ed. (London: J. Johnson, 1795), 24.

5. Nicolay and Hay, 1:16.

6. Dennis Hanks to William Herndon, 13 June 1865, Herndon-Weik Collection, in Emmanuel Hertz, *The Hidden Lincoln, from the Letters and Papers of William H. Herndon* (New York: Viking Press, 1938), 274–75. Cf. Abraham Lincoln, "Autobiography Written for Jesse W. Fell," 20 December 1859, *CW*, 3:511: "he was killed by Indians, not in battle, but by stealth, when he was laboring to open a farm in the forest."

7. The exact date of Abraham Lincoln's death remains unknown. The discovery of a document in which Mordecai affirms that his father died in May 1786 is perplexing. See *Lincoln vs. Reed*, reproduced in Louis A. Warren, *Lincoln's Parentage and Childhood* (New York: The Century Co., 1926), 297. In fact, in the same document, Mordecai presents himself as the "heir at law," that is, the sole legal heir because of the law of primogeniture, and it is as such that his case was heard. But the law of primogeniture had been abolished in Virginia in October 1785. Ida Minerva Tarbell, *The Early Life of Abraham Lincoln* (1896; reprint with Introduction by Paul M. Angle, South Brunswick: Barnes, 1974), 18.

8. Lincoln, "Autobiography" for Scripps, *CW*, 4:61; Warren, *Parentage and Childhood*, 283.

9. Warren, *Parentage and Childhood*, 47.

10. R. Gerald McMurtry, *The Kentucky Lincolns on Mill Creek* (Harrogate: Lincoln Memorial University Press, 1939), 29, 19, 9–10; Warren, *Parentage and Childhood*, 43, 47; Warren, *Indiana Years*, 5–6.

11. Cooper, *Some Information*, 38.

12. McMurtry, *Kentucky Lincolns*, 24. The hypothesis finds some confirmation in the discoveries of William E. Barton, *The Lineage of Lincoln* (Indianapolis: Bobbs Merrill, 1929), 70, who noticed the coincidence of land sales by Mordecai and of purchases—among which Mill Creek—carried out by his brothers. The size of these sales, however, does not permit the affirmation that Abraham's inheritance was divided equally.

13. Warren, *Parentage and Childhood*, 51, 54, 315–16; £1 equaled $4.85. The lack of precious metal forced inhabitants of the American West to use all kinds

of money until the 1850s. At the beginning of the nineteenth century it was common to count in pounds, shillings, and pence. The Kentucky dollar was worth 6 shillings. Beveridge, 1:23–25.

14. Rev. Louis A. Warren here colors with humor his deep teleological convictions. Warren, *Parentage and Childhood*, 166. Later research (*Indiana Years*, 5) led him to believe that Thomas Lincoln had already cultivated the soil, as a tenant farmer, before that date.

15. The spot is now called Muldraugh, or Muldrow, Hill. Mammouth Cave is located in the region. F. A. Michaux, *Travels to the West of the Alleghany Mountains . . . in the Year 1802*, 2d ed. (London: B. Crosby and Co., 1805), 141. Michaux reached it from the valley of the Rolling Fork, which he described as a carpet of dark greenery.

16. Beveridge, 1:26–27; Warren, *Parentage and Childhood*, 115.

17. Abraham Lincoln to Samuel Haycraft, 4 June 1860, *CW*, 4:70. He retained precise memories of the topography and of the inhabitants. See Beveridge, 1:30; Warren, *Parentage and Childhood*, 142.

18. Ida Minerva Tarbell, *The Life of Abraham Lincoln*, 2 vols. (New York: Macmillan, 1928), 1:20.

19. William Dean Howells, *Life of Abraham Lincoln*. Reprint of the original 1860 edition corrected by Lincoln (Bloomington: Indiana University Press, 1960), 21.

20. Cooper, *Some Information*, 25.

21. McMurtry, *Kentucky Lincolns*, 17–20; Warren, *Parentage and Childhood*, 189–90.

22. McMurtry, *Kentucky Lincolns*, 19, 34–35. The surveys of plots, which were the responsibility of the buyers, took as their point of departure a marker defined in the "original deed" established by the first buyer of federal land of the region. In fact, these "original deeds" were often faulty.

23. Paul Wallace Gates, "Tenants of the Log Cabin," *Mississippi Valley Historical Review* 49 (1962–63): 3; Michaux, *Travels*, 175.

24. See Michaux, *Travels*, 163: "This incertitude in the right of property is an inexhaustible source of tedious and expensive law-suits, which serve to enrich the professional gentlemen of the country." The term *picrocholes* to refer to quarrelsome neighbors comes from the works of Rabelais.

25. Beveridge, 1:19; Theodore Calvin Pease, *The Frontier State, 1818–1848* (Springfield: Illinois Centennial Commission, 1918), 47; George Dangerfield, *The Awakening of American Nationalism, 1818–1828* (New York: Harper & Row, 1965), 111n.

26. The phrase comes from the first debate with Douglas at Ottawa, 21 August 1828, *CW*, 3:29.

27. Herndon, 1:106; Warren, *Indiana Years*, 168. "Whig Protest in Illinois Legislature Against the Reorganization of the Judiciary," 26 February 1841, *CW*, 1:248. The text, which attacks the Democrats' reorganization of the supreme court of Illinois, contains a reference to the situation in Kentucky and condemns the efforts of the general assembly of that state to modify

to the advantage of debtors the composition of the supreme magistrature of Kentucky.

28. Gates, "Tenants of the Log Cabin," 8.

29. Isaac Bush was the brother of Sarah Bush, who became Thomas Lincoln's second wife. Beveridge, 1:24–25; Warren, *Parentage and Childhood,* 113–14, 323–27.

30. Beveridge, 1:26; Barton, *Lineage of Lincoln,* 293.

31. One character is missing from this picture: the locator or land hunter who was hired by the owner of a land warrant to choose a plot, to draw up a survey, and to have it registered with the Land Office. Mordecai Lincoln devoted fifteen years before finally recovering in 1812 the 2,268 acres that a locator, John Reed, had fraudulently appropriated by imitating the signature of his client Abraham Lincoln and registering the property in his own name. Warren, *Parentage and Childhood,* 11; Barton, *Lineage of Lincoln,* 265–67.

32. Gates, "Tenants of the Log Cabin," 6–10. The episodes of Kentucky's long march toward statehood are recounted by Robert M. McElroy, *Kentucky in the Nation's History* (New York: Moffat, Yard, 1909), 116–46, who describes well Virginia's obstinacy on this point. Many contracts made provision for annullment matched with a promise of reimbursement in case a "prior and better claim" appeared. The acts of sale of Mill Creek are an example of such a provision.

33. Gates, "Tenants of the Log Cabin," 27–31.

34. Warren, *Parentage and Childhood,* 121. It was perhaps not mere accident. The land of Knob Creek was naturally fertile enough that the value of the improvements that Lincoln had been able to make in two years did not exceed three-fourths of the value of the property. Indeed, this clause of three-fourths of the value could have brought into play one of the provisions of the law of 1812 that permitted the occupier to keep his land. See Gates, "Tenants of the Log Cabin," 13. The property was, moreover, modest, and Thomas was vulnerable because of the lawsuit he had initiated about Nolin Creek.

35. Beveridge, 1:26, 34–35; Warren, *Parentage and Childhood,* 335–36; Dangerfield, *American Nationalism,* 210. *Green vs. Biddle* remained merely a threat: the courts in Kentucky having refused to apply it, the Supreme Court reversed its decision in 1831 in *Hawkins vs. Bailey's Lessee.* See Gates, "Tenants of the Log Cabin," 26.

36. Charles M. Segal, ed., *Conversations with Lincoln* (New York: G. P. Putnam's, 1961), 348. Borrett's recollections were first published in 1865.

37. Warren, *Parentage and Childhood,* 158–59, 283.

38. The sum in dispute amounted to $4.90; Warren, *Parentage and Childhood,* 52, 162–64; Beveridge, 1:22–23.

39. Warren, *Parentage and Childhood,* 289; CW, 3:470. In Paris, Kentucky, a carpenter earned a dollar a day in 1818, meals included. Thomas Hulme, "A Journal Made during a Tour in the Western Countries of America" [London, 1828], in *EWT,* 10:68. A migrant worker who had to move about by foot was considered the equal of a "nigger." William Faux, *Memorable Days in America* [London, 1823], in *EWT,* 11:282–83.

40. Warren, *Parentage and Childhood*, 234, 288–89.

41. Speech at Alton on 15 October 1858, Lincoln-Douglas Debates, *CW*, 3:312.

42. John Locke Scripps, *Life of Lincoln*, ed. Roy P. Basler and Lloyd A. Dunlap (Bloomington: Indiana University Press, 1961), 29–30; R. Gerald McMurtry, "The Lincoln Migration from Kentucky to Indiana in 1816," *Indiana Magazine of History* 33 (December 1937): 395.

43. *Voyage au Kentouckey et sur les bords du Genesée en 1820* (Paris, 1821), 173.

CHAPTER 2: LINCOLN AND INDIANA

1. Speech in Indianapolis, 19 September 1859, reported in the Indianapolis *Atlas* of the same date, *CW*, 3:463.

2. Federal Writers' Project, *Indiana: A Guide to the Hoosier State*, 3d ed. (New York: Oxford University Press, 1947), 9, 11–12. Knob Creek is fewer than a hundred miles from Little Pigeon Creek, Lincoln's home in Indiana.

3. Herndon, 1:75–76.

4. Autobiography for Scripps, *CW*, 4:64: "Hanks had not gone to New Orleans, but having a family, and being likely to be detained from home longer than at first expected, had turned back from St. Louis."

5. *CW*, 2:320.

6. *CW*, 1:260.

7. Herndon, 3:601.

8. Autobiography for Fell, 20 December 1859, *CW*, 3:511–12: "I was losing interest in politics, when the repeal of the Missouri Compromise aroused me again."

9. David M. Potter and Don E. Fehrenbacher, *The Impending Crisis, 1848–1861* (New York: Harper Torch Books, 1976), 49.

10. Speech in Indianapolis, 19 September 1859, and speech in Janesville, Wisconsin, 1 October 1859, *CW*, 3:465–67, 484–85.

11. *CW*, 3:415, 456, 465, 484–85.

12. In Illinois, the pro-slavery forces were so strong that the Constitution of 1818 was ambiguous. Pease, *The Frontier State*, 70.

13. Francis M. Van Natter, *Lincoln's Boyhood: A Chronicle of His Indiana Years* (Washington: Public Affairs Press, 1963), 131.

14. Jacob Piatt Dunn, *Indiana: A Redemption from Slavery* (Boston: Houghton, Mifflin, 1905), 427–29.

15. Van Natter, *Lincoln's Boyhood*, 133. William Faux collected in 1819 the testimony of a rich Indiana farmer who complained that he could not bring back his slaves from Kentucky, see *Memorable Days*, in *EWT*, 11:199.

16. Pease, *The Frontier State*, 77–91, cites especially the arguments of the pioneer Morris Birkbeck, who managed to convince the free farmers of Illinois that the introduction of slavery would bring them ruin, dishonor, and an end to neighborly relations that were the very soul of rural communities.

17. Dunn, *Indiana*, 441.

18. Van Natter, *Lincoln's Boyhood*, 132–34; Flint, in *EWT*, 9:218.

19. Speech at Cincinnati, 17 September 1850, *CW*, 3:455–57.

20. Warren, *Indiana Years*, 86–87, 121, 139–40, 206. The trustees were elected administrators who oversaw the finances of the congregation.

21. G. D'Haucourt, *La vie agricole et rurale dans l'Etat d'Indiana à l'époque pionnière* (Paris: Mouton, 1961), 125; testimony of John Romine, collected by Herndon on 14 September 1865, Herndon-Weik Collection, reproduced in Hertz, *Hidden Lincoln*, 360.

22. D'Haucourt, *La vie agricole*, 48, 390.

23. Warren, *Indiana Years*, 41; Law of 10 May 1800; Roy M. Robbins, *Our Landed Heritage: The Public Domain, 1776–1936* (Princeton: Princeton University Press, 1942), 18–19.

24. Faux, *Memorable Days*, in *EWT*, 11:163; Adlard Welby, *A Visit to North America and the English Settlements in Illinois* [London, 1821], in *EWT*, 12:225.

25. Beveridge, 95n; Warren, *Indiana Years*, 158–59; Van Natter, *Lincoln's Boyhood*, 123; D'Haucourt, *La vie agricole*, 50n.

26. Warren, *Indiana Years*, 51, 64, 228. The crisis of 1819 was particularly severe in Kentucky. According to tradition, Thomas had to pay several of the Widow Johnston's debts before being able to convince her to leave. The Sparrows maintained that they had lost their land by fraud.

27. Herndon, 1:40, 54, 61; Hertz, *Hidden Lincoln*, 365–68.

28. Elyas P. Fordham, *Personal Narratives of Travels in Virginia, Maryland, Pennsylvania, Ohio, Indiana, Kentucky; and of a Residence in the Illinois Territory: 1817–1818* (Cleveland: Arthur H. Clark Co., 1906), 168.

29. Warren, *Indiana Years*, 144–46, 176.

30. Bess Ehrmann, *The Missing Chapter in the Life of Abraham Lincoln* (Chicago: Walter M. Hill, 1938).

31. Warren, *Indiana Years*, 19–20; D'Haucourt, *La vie agricole*, 15, 76–77; Logan Esarey, *Internal Improvements in Early Indiana* (Indianapolis: Indiana Historical Society, 1912).

32. Henry J. Raymond, *The Life and Public Services of Abraham Lincoln* (New York: Derby and Miller, 1865), 19.

33. Warren, *Indiana Years*, 20, 221–22; Ward Hill Lamon, *The Life of Abraham Lincoln, from His Birth to His Inauguration as President* (Boston: James R. Osgood, 1872), 21; Van Natter, *Lincoln's Boyhood*, 10.

34. Logan Esarey, *A History of Indiana* (New York: Harcourt, Brace, 1922), 132; Federal Writers' Project, *Indiana*, 399; Nicolay and Hay, 1:30.

35. *CW*, 1:378–79, 386–89.

36. Faux, *Memorable Days*, *EWT*, 11:228; William M. Cockrum, *Pioneer History of Indiana* (Oakland City: Press of Oakland City *Journal*, 1907), 433, 464–65.

37. Herndon, 1:23.

38. Autobiography for Scripps, *CW*, 4:62.

39. Speech at Indianapolis on 19 September 1859, reported by the *Atlas*, *CW*, 3:463.

40. Francis B. Carpenter, *Six Months at the White House with Abraham Lincoln: The Story of a Picture* (New York: Hurd and Houghton, 1866), 113–14.

41. Howells, *Life of Abraham Lincoln*, 21.

42. Letter to Herndon, 3 May 1866, in Hertz, *Hidden Lincoln*, 294.

43. Herndon, 3:509; Beveridge, 46.

44. Autobiography for Scripps, *CW*, 4:62; Howells, *Life of Abraham Lincoln*, 22.

45. "My Childhood's Home I See Again," *CW*, 1:379.

46. Lamon, *The Life of Abraham Lincoln*, 27; Herndon, 1:26.

47. Warren, *Indiana Years*, 52–54.

48. Warren, *Indiana Years*, 57.

49. Letter to Andrew Johnston, 18 April 1846, *CW*, 1:378.

50. *CW*, 1:377

51. Herndon, 3:584.

52. Henry Clay Whitney, *Life on the Circuit with Lincoln* (Boston: Estes and Lauriat, 1892), 497–98.

53. Whitney, *Life on the Circuit*, 567.

54. *CW*, 1:370.

55. Autobiography for Fell, *CW*, 3:511–512.

56. Autobiography for Scripps, *CW*, 4:62.

57. *CW*, 4:62.

58. Warren, *Indiana Years*, 136; Reinhard H. Luthin, *The Real Abraham Lincoln* (Englewood Cliffs: Prentice-Hall, 1960), 9; D'Haucourt, *La vie agricole*, 233, 238, speaks of Lincoln's case as typical.

59. D'Haucourt, *La vie agricole*, 233. Teachers were rarely able to teach more than the rudiments of the three Rs.

60. Herndon, 2:332.

61. Beveridge, 1:68, 47.

62. "Pendant que, déployant ses voiles, / L'ombre, où se mêle une rumeur, / Semble élargir jusqu'aux étoiles / Le geste auguste du semeur." Victor Hugo, *Les Chansons des rues et des bois*, II: "Sagesse," in Hugo, *Oeuvres poétiques complètes* (Paris: Jean-Jacques Pauvert, 1961), 783.

63. William H. Smith, *The History of the State of Indiana from the Earliest Explorations of the French to the Present Time*, 2 vols. (Indianapolis: Western Publishing Co., 1903), 1:352; D'Haucourt, *La vie agricole*, 121–24; John B. Conner, *Indiana Agriculture, Agricultural Resources, and Development of the State* (Indianapolis: W. B. Burford, 1893), 7; Percy W. Bidwell and John I. Falconer, *History of Agriculture in the Northern United States, 1620–1860* (Washington: Carnegie Institution, 1925), 123–24; Esarey, *History of Indiana*, 86.

64. Letter of 27 March 1842, *CW*, 1:282.

65. *CW*, 3:471–82.

66. Testimony gathered by James Quay Howard (whose notes furnished the basis of Howells's documentation), in *The Lincoln Papers*, ed. David C. Mearns, 2 vols. (Garden City: Doubleday, 1948), 1:159.

67. "Abraham Lincoln as I Knew Him," *Sunset Magazine* 29 (October 1912): 430–38, reproduced in *Journal of the Illinois State Historical Society* 14 (1921): 76.

68. The basic work on Lincoln's reading is David C. Mearns, "Mr. Lincoln and the Books He Read," in Arthur E. Bestor, David C. Mearns, and Jonathan Daniels, *Three Presidents and Their Books* (Urbana: University of Illinois Press, 1955), 45–88.

69. *Hominy*, Lincoln explained jokingly during the war, came from the Latin *homini*, meaning "for human consumption."

70. Lexington, 1812, cited by Van Natter, *Lincoln's Boyhood*, 87.

71. Already knowing how to write when he arrived in Indiana, Lincoln seemed a child prodigy, and he was often called upon by his family and his neighbors to write their correspondence (Scripps, *Life of Lincoln*, 30–31). Indiana was one of the states in which the proportion of illiterates was the greatest, and the "poor whites" from the South and the "hard-shell" Baptists were the most backward groups (D'Haucourt, *La vie agricole*, 220, 225, 229); Hertz, *Hidden Lincoln*, 351.

72. *CW*, 2:437.

73. *CW*, 2:437.

74. *CW*, 2:440.

75. *CW*, 2:440.

76. *CW*, 2:441.

77. Lamon, *Life of Abraham Lincoln*, 135.

78. Charles H. Coleman, *Abraham Lincoln and Coles County, Illinois* (New Brunswick: Scarecrow Press, 1955), carefully details the ties between Lincoln and his family between 1830 and 1860. "Say to him that if we could meet now, it is doubtful whether it would not be more painful than pleasant." Letter to John D. Johnston, 12 January 1851, *CW*, 2:97.

79. Herndon, 1:36; see letter to Thomas Lincoln and John D. Johnston, 24 December 1848, *CW*, 2:15; autobiography for Scripps, *CW*, 4:61.

80. D'Haucourt, *La vie agricole*, 230; Testimony gathered by Herndon on 8 September 1865, in Hertz, *Hidden Lincoln*, 351.

81. Estimate based on figures furnished by Smith, *History of Indiana*, 1:353.

82. Beveridge, 1:65.

83. Edgar Lee Masters, *Lincoln: The Man* (New York: Dodd, Mead, 1931), 11.

84. J. T. Hanks to Lincoln, Robert Todd Lincoln Collection, reproduced in Mearns, *The Lincoln Papers*, 1:267–268.

85. Beveridge, 1:86.

86. Warren, *Indiana Years*, 101.

87. Estimates based on figures given by Warren, *Indiana Years*, 98. In a radius of a mile around the Lincolns' farm was a population of about eighty persons, or a density of fifteen inhabitants per square mile.

88. Warren, *Indiana Years*, 54; Faux, *Memorable Days*, in *EWT*, 11:213, 226, 231; Welby, in *EWT*, 12:229, 233–34.

89. D'Haucourt, *La vie agricole,* 102, 236; Faux, "Memorable Days," in *EWT,* 11:212–13; Woods, in *EWT,* 10:317; Fordham, *Personal Narratives,* 65. Herndon, 1:64–65, 117. Beveridge, 1:52. Lamon, *The Life of Abraham Lincoln,* 480. Hertz, *Hidden Lincoln,* 351–52.

90. See his speech to the Springfield Washington Temperance Society, on 22 February 1842, *CW,* 1:271–79, where he denounced as ineffective preaching that blamed the sinner.

91. Hertz, *Hidden Lincoln,* 350, 352; Lamon, *The Life of Abraham Lincoln,* 55. Lincoln said he had never "denied the truth of the Scriptures" nor "spoken with intentional disrespect of religion in general, or of any denomination of Christians in particular" (*CW,* 1:382–84). This shows his characteristic prudence, cleverness, and honesty. For unwanted side effects, see Peter Cartwright, *Autobiography of Peter Cartwright, the Backwoods Preacher,* ed. W. P. Strickland (Cincinnati: L. Swormstedt and A. Poe, 1860), 50–51: a sinner seized by the "jerks" chokes on his flask of whisky and dies during a camp meeting. Mental hospital reports use the term *religious excitement* with the same frequency as *alcoholism* to describe patients, see Reports of the Illinois State Hospital for the Insane, Illinois General Assembly Reports, Twentieth Assembly, 1855, 196–99.

92. Hertz, *Hidden Lincoln,* 300–301, 324–25, 350–53, 366, 384, 425. See Herndon, 3:445: "he was never a technical Christian."

93. Beveridge, 1:94.

94. "The sweet violet you enclosed, came safely to hand, but it was so dry, and mashed so fla[t], that it crumbled to dust at the first attempt to handle it. The juice that mashed out of it, stained a [place] on the letter, which I mean to preserve and ch[erish] for the sake of her who procured it to be se[nt,]" Letter to Speed, 27 March 1842, *CW,* 1:283. Fanny, Speed's wife, had picked the violet.

95. See Herndon, 1:47, 62–63: Lincoln and Allen Gentry put to flight a band of slaves who had attacked them while they were asleep during their trip to New Orleans. See Autobiography for Scripps, *CW,* 4:62. Other examples of his feats can be found from the New Salem period.

96. "Too much so," his mother said. See Hertz, *Hidden Lincoln,* 352.

97. Article in the Indianapolis *Journal* of 10 February 1879, cited by Warren, *Indiana Years,* 234; Whitney, *Life on the Circuit,* 48.

98. Testimony of H. E. Dummer (lawyer and later congressman) and of Leonard Swett in Hertz, *Hidden Lincoln,* 385, 299; Herndon, 3:534; Elizabeth Crawford to Herndon, 21 February 1866, in Hertz, *Hidden Lincoln,* 293; Nathaniel Grigsby to Herndon, 21 January 1866, Herndon-Weik Collection, cited by Beveridge, 1:68.

99. Herndon, 1:104.

100. Lincoln gave this text to the bailiff of a court in Springfield; *CW,* 8:420; Hertz, *Hidden Lincoln,* 400.

101. Mearns, *The Lincoln Papers,* 1:169. Mearns refers to Lincoln's "earthy fables."

102. *CW,* 3:360, the text was published in the *Illinois State Journal.* On the connotation of needle and thread in America at that time, see chapter 10 of

Huckleberry Finn. Linking inventions with sexual curiosity makes Lincoln a forerunner of Freud.

103. J. Edward Murr, "Lincoln in Indiana," *Indiana Magazine of History* 13 (1917): 335–39; letter to James W. Grimes, 12 July 1856, *CW,* 2:348; Herndon, 3:436.

104. Herndon, 1:38; monograph on "Lincoln as an Individual," in Hertz, *Hidden Lincoln,* 413–14.

105. Herndon, 3:589.

106. The *Illinois State Register,* 23 November 1839, spoke of "assumed clownishness." Cited in Herbert Mitgang, *Lincoln as They Saw Him: A Press Portrait* (New York: Rinehart, 1956), 17.

107. See Nicolay and Hay, 1:17, 57.

108. The point is important because the work also contained the Declaration of Independence, the Constitution, and the Northwest Ordinance of 1787. Van Natter, *Lincoln's Boyhood,* 97–99.

109. Beveridge, *Abraham Lincoln,* 1:79; D'Haucourt, *La vie agricole,* especially 148. Infares were feasts for a newly wed couple, usually a few days after the ceremony.

110. Testimony of Herndon himself and of David Turnham, in Herndon, 1:24–25. In *La vie agricole,* 162, D'Haucourt gives three supporting references.

111. D'Haucourt, *La vie agricole,* 163–64; John Bradbury, *Travels in the Interior of America, in the Years 1809, 1810, and 1811,* 2d ed. [London, 1819], in *EWT,* 5:313.

112. Beveridge, 1:86, 95; Warren, *Indiana Years,* 175, 192, 205. He made loans at 200 percent; see Van Natter, *Lincoln's Boyhood,* 29.

113. Warren, *Indiana Years,* 145–57.

114. Lincoln ascribed great importance to this incident. See the testimony of William H. Seward reported by Josiah Gilbert Holland, *The Life of Abraham Lincoln* (Springfield, Mass.: Gurdon Bill, 1866), 34, and of Swett in Allen Thorndike Rice, *Reminiscences of Abraham Lincoln by Distinguished Men of His Time* (New York: North American Publishing, 1886), 458.

115. Beveridge, 1:84; Herndon, 1:62.

116. Warren, *Indiana Years,* 149; Tarbell, *Early Life,* 76.

117. Herndon, 3:423–24.

118. *EWT,* 10:61. Minus the cigar, this describes Lincoln exactly in his shop in New Salem or his office in Springfield.

119. Warren, *Indiana Years,* 136–37; Welby, in *EWT,* 12:236; Woods, in *EWT,* 10:246.

120. Esarey, *Internal Improvements in Early Indiana,* 61, 85, 87–88. Little Pigeon Creek was dry in summer.

121. Lincoln passed through there on his way from Knob Creek. See McMurtry, "Lincoln Migration," 396, 400; Beveridge, 1:18–19.

122. Fordham, *Personal Narratives,* 163.

123. Warren, *Indiana Years,* 145–47. After having worked for Taylor, Lincoln worked for himself for a while with a small boat that delivered passengers to steamboats in the middle of the river.

124. Woods, in *EWT,* 10:241. Speculation in urban sites was all the rage at the time. Often, the original town contained more taverns than inhabitants and soon collapsed.

125. Fordham, *Personal Narratives,* 216.

126. Fordham, *Personal Narratives,* 168, 216.

127. F. Garvin Davenport, *Ante-bellum Kentucky: A Social History, 1800–1860* (Oxford, Ohio: Mississippi Valley Press, 1943), 21–36.

128. See Fordham, *Personal Narratives,* 168; Flint, in *EWT,* 9:142–43.

129. Faux, *Memorable Days,* in *EWT,* 11:193; Clement Eaton, *Henry Clay and the Art of American Politics* (Boston: Little, Brown, 1957), 69–70.

130. Hulme, "A Journal," in *EWT,* 10:65–66.

131. Flint, in *EWT,* 9:218–19. They occasionally were forced to flee with their lovers to the other side of the Ohio to get married.

132. Ruth Painter Randall, *Mary Lincoln: Biography of a Marriage* (Boston: Little, Brown, 1953), 158; Justin G. Turner and Linda Levitt Turner, *Mary Todd Lincoln: Her Life and Letters* (New York: Alfred A. Knopf, 1972), 52.

133. Fordham, *Personal Narratives,* 168–69.

134. Bradbury, in *EWT,* 5:291–92; Benjamin Smith, ed., *Twenty-four Letters from Labourers in America* (London: E. Rainford, 1829), 22.

135. Luthin, *The Real Abraham Lincoln,* 90.

136. See Herndon, 1:66.

CHAPTER 3: THE ASCENT

1. Scripps, *Life of Abraham Lincoln,* 42–43.

2. James Stuart, *Three Years in North America,* 2 vols. (Edinburgh, 1833), 2:342, cited in *Prairie State: Impressions of Illinois, 1673–1967, by Travelers and Other Observers,* ed. Paul M. Angle (Chicago: University of Chicago Press, 1968), 95.

3. Sarah Margaret Fuller, *Summer on the Lakes in 1843* (Boston, 1844), cited in Angle, *Prairie State,* 219.

4. Harriett Martineau, *Society in America,* 2 vols. (New York, 1837), cited in Angle, *Prairie State,* 175.

5. Arthur Clinton Boggess, *The Settlement of Illinois, 1778–1830,* Chicago Historical Society's Collection (Chicago: The Society, 1908), 5:190.

6. Boggess, *Settlement of Illinois,* 189–90; Pease, *Frontier State,* 178–79 for the years 1832–36. Boggess, *Settlement of Illinois,* 144, describes an 1829 workers' meeting in Wheeling, Virginia, to organize a mass migration to Illinois.

7. Boggess, *Settlement of Illinois,* 187: in 1825, 72,817 inhabitants; in 1830, 157,445 inhabitants.

8. Pease, *Frontier State,* 173. The names are those of present-day counties.

9. Flint, in *EWT,* 9:186.

10. George W. Ogden, *Letters from the West* [New Bedford, 1823], in *EWT,* 19:56.; Pease, *Frontier State,* 7. See the description of variety no. 5 of the soils of Illinois in Samuel R. Brown, *The Western Gazetteer, or Emigrant's Directory*

(Auburn: H. C. Southwick, 1817), 23: "Timbered land, moderately hilly, well watered, and of a rich soil."

11. John Reynolds, "Treatise of Agricultural Resources of Southern Illinois," *Transactions of the Illinois State Agricultural Society* 2 (1856–57): 361; Boggess, *Settlement of Illinois*, 144.

12. Boggess, *Settlement of Illinois*, 139–40, 133. This policy of exemption lasted until 1847. Robert Murray Haig, *A History of the General Property Tax in Illinois*, University of Illinois Studies in the Social Sciences (Urbana: University of Illinois Press, 1914), 3:30, 92.

13. Boggess, *Settlement of Illinois*, 183–84.

14. Solon J. Buck, *Illinois in 1818* (1917; reprint, Urbana: University of Illinois Press, 1967), 278–82; James Hall, *Letters from the West, Containing Sketches of Scenery, Manners and Customs* (London: H. Colburn, 1828), 233.

15. Boggess, *Settlement of Illinois*, 149; Pease, *Frontier State*, 45–46.

16. Herndon, 1:67–68.

17. Pease, *Frontier State*, 174; Boggess, *Settlement of Illinois*, 126–27, 131; Mary Vose Harris, ed., "The Autobiography of Benjamin Franklin Harris, *Transactions of the Illinois State Historical Society* 30 (1923): 75.

18. Charles J. Latrobe, *The Rambler in North America, MDCCCXXXII–MDCCCXXXIII*, 2 vols. (London: Thames Ditton, 1835), 2:217, 253; autobiography for Scripps, *CW*, 4:63, 69; Eleanor Atkinson, "The Winter of the Deep Snow," *Transactions of the Illinois State Historical Society* 14 (1909): 47–62; Thompson Gaines Onstot, *Pioneers of Menard and Mason Counties . . . Including Personal Reminiscences of Abraham Lincoln and Peter Cartright* (Forest City: T. G. Onstot, 1902), 134; Benjamin P. Thomas, *Lincoln's New Salem* (1934; rev. ed., New York: Alfred A. Knopf, 1954), 31; Beveridge, 1:104.

19. Boggess, *Settlement of Illinois*, 131; Herndon, 1:73. Howells, *Life of Abraham Lincoln*, 25, 27–28; Thomas, *Lincoln's New Salem*, 10; autobiography for Scripps, *CW*, 4:64.

20. He had made a lightning trip to his father to inform him of his decision. Beveridge, 1:108.

21. Coleman, *Lincoln and Coles County*, 19, 30–31, 54–55, 63–64; Lincoln to John D. Johnston, 9 and 25 November 1851, *CW*, 2:112–13.

22. There were fewer than two inhabitants per square mile in 1830; Pease, *Frontier State*, 174, 385; Allan G. Bogue, *From Prairie to Corn Belt: Farming on the Illinois and Iowa Prairies in the Nineteenth Century* (Chicago: University of Chicago Press, 1963), 218, 221, 226. Favorable for wheat cultivation, Coles County was mediocre for the production of corn and hogs, which constituted the real wealth of Illinois.

23. Under the weight of the locomotives and the cars, the rail (nailed to a beam) would come loose at the ends to form a "snake-head." If care was not taken to push down the snake-head, it would gouge the floor of the cars, often killing travelers. Samuel Willard, "Personal Reminiscences of Life in Illinois, 1830 to 1850," *Transactions of the Illinois State Historical Society* 11 (1906): 83–84.

24. Testimony of John Hanks, in Herndon, 1:71; notes of James Quay Howard, in Mearns, *The Lincoln Papers*, 1:150 (testimony of George Close, who gives the date of 1829, which is obviously incorrect).

25. Herndon, 1:79; reminiscence of the Canadian journalist Josiah Blackburn, Sacramento *Daily Union* (23 August 1864), reproduced in *Conversations with Lincoln*, ed. Charles M. Segal (New York: G. P. Putnam's, 1961), 336.

26. William E. Barton, "Abraham Lincoln and New Salem," *Journal of the Illinois State Historical Society* 19 (October 1926-January 1927): 79.

27. Thomas, *Lincoln's New Salem*, 29.

28. Herndon, 1:77–78.

29. Barton, "Lincoln and New Salem," 78–79.

30. U.S. Department of Agriculture, *Atlas of American Agriculture, Physical Basis, Including Land Relief, Climate, Soils and Natural Vegetation* (Washington: Government Printing Office, 1936), Part 3: "Soils of the U.S.," maps 2, 4, 5 (section 7), 38, 63.

31. Franklin W. Scott, *Newspapers and Periodicals of Illinois, 1814–1879*, Collections of the Illinois State Historical Library, rev. ed. (Springfield: Trustees of the Illinois State Historical Library, 1910), 6:33.

32. Thomas, *Lincoln's New Salem*, 37; Edward Burlend, ed., *A True Picture of Emigration: or, Fourteen Years in the Interior of North America; being a full and impartial account of the various difficulties and ultimate success of an English family who emigrated from Berwick-in-Elmet, near Leeds, in the year 1831* (London: G. Berger, 1848), 35–43, 51, describes the activities of a merchant in the Quincy, Illinois, region around 1832–35.

33. Burlend, *True Picture*, 46–47; Thomas, *Lincoln's New Salem*, 34.

34. Lord Charnwood, *Abraham Lincoln* (London: Constable and Company, 1916), 62.

35. Springfield merchants' advertisement, quoted by Herndon, 1:87; Paul M. Angle, *"Here I Have Lived": A History of Lincoln's Springfield* (Springfield: The Abraham Lincoln Association, 1935), 36.

36. "Communication to the People of Sangamo County," 9 March 1832, *CW*, 1:5–9.

37. Samuel R. Brown, *Western Gazetteer*, 17–18; Ogden, in *EWT*, 19:55.

38. He gave these reasons to Herndon; Herndon, 1:100; autobiography for Fell, *CW*, 3:512.

39. The term *regulators* refers to a recurring movement in colonial America that brought together poor people of the frontier who wanted to put some order into the chaos of land speculation, the harassment of pettifoggery, and the arbitrary actions of tax collectors. Holland, *The Life of Abraham Lincoln*, 45.

40. R. Carlyle Buley, *The Old Northwest Pioneer Period 1815–1840*, 2 vols. (Bloomington: Indiana University Press, 1951), 2:67.

41. *Sangamo Journal*, 12 April 1832, cited in Buley, *Old Northwest*.

42. Buley, *Old Northwest*, 2:64–65; text of the treaty in Henry Brown, *The History of Illinois, from Its First Discovery and Settlement to the Present Time* (New York: J. Winchester, 1844), 377–80.

43. Black Hawk, *Autobiography of MA–KA–TAI–ME–SHE–KIA–KIAK* or *Black Hawk,* ed. J. B. Patterson (St. Louis: Press of Continental Printing Co., 1882), 56–57.

44. Buley, *Old Northwest,* 2:62–64.

45. William Cullen Bryant, *Prose Writings,* ed. Parke Godwin, 2 vols. (New York: D. Appleton and Co., 1883), 2:20.

46. Autobiography for Scripps, *CW,* 4:64.

47. Herndon, 1:95–96; Bryant, *Prose Writings,* 2:20; *CW,* 1:10–13.

48. Boggess, *Settlement of Illinois,* 207.

49. Buley, *Old Northwest,* 2:70, 77–78.

50. Letter from his old war friend, George M. Harrison, 29 May 1860, in Mearns, *The Lincoln Papers,* 1:248–49; *CW,* 1:509–10.

51. Howells, *Life of Abraham Lincoln,* 39; Latrobe, *Rambler in North America,* 2:258; Rice, *Reminiscences,* 568.

52. Lamon, *Life of Abraham Lincoln,* 135.

53. Autobiography for Scripps, *CW,* 4:65.

54. Charnwood, *Abraham Lincoln,* 62.

55. Herndon, 1:102–4, 106–7.

56. Patrick Shirreff, *A Tour Through North America; Together with a Comprehensive View of the Canadas and the United States as Adapted for Agricultural Emigration* (Edinburgh: Oliver and Boyd, 1835), cited in Angle, *Prairie State,* 129.

57. Autobiography for Scripps, *CW,* 4:65.

58. Michel Chevalier, *Society, Manners and Politics in the United States: Being a Series of Letters on North America* (Boston: Weeks, Jordan and Company, 1839), 449–50. César Birotteau, the title character in a Balzac novel, was a prosperous merchant whose speculations, social ambition, and involvement with unscrupulous financiers led to his bankruptcy.

59. Beveridge, 1:142; Harry Edward Pratt, *The Personal Finances of Abraham Lincoln* (Springfield: The Abraham Lincoln Association, 1943), 16–17; autobiography for Scripps, *CW,* 4:65.

60. Robert Gibson, *A Treatise of Practical Surveying . . . 8th ed. with Alterations and Amendments, Adapted to the Use of American Surveyors* (Philadelphia: J. and J. Crukshank, 1803), v.

61. Herndon, 2:308; autobiography for Scripps, *CW,* 4:64.

62. Howells, *Life of Abraham Lincoln,* 41; Willard, "Reminiscences," 86; *CW,* 1:20–21; Herndon, 1:122–25.

63. Tarbell, *Early Life,* 186; Herndon, 1:123–24.

64. Herndon, 1:122; Luthin, *The Real Abraham Lincoln,* 34; *CW,* 2:543.

65. *CW,* 2:92n; Lamon to Lincoln, 21 November 1854, in Mearns, *The Lincoln Papers,* 1:197; "Opinion Concerning Land Surveys," 6 January 1859, *CW,* 3:348–49.

66. Herndon, 1:133; *CW,* 4:65.

67. Atkinson, "Winter of the Deep Snow," 48–50.

68. Scott, *Newspapers,* 33, 167. The first farm newspaper, linked to the

Democratic *Illinois Advocate,* was the *Western Ploughboy,* which survived only one year (1 January 1831–17 January 1832).

69. David Donald, *Lincoln's Herndon* (New York: Knopf, 1948), 152, citing a manuscript published in the first issue of the *Abraham Lincoln Quarterly* (406–7). Donald suggests that we not take seriously—as did the oafish Herndon—these reflections from a Lincoln tired out after an unpleasant day spent rejecting the demands of office seekers who besieged him in Washington. We will thus take the matter with a grain of salt, but we will take it nonetheless.

70. Edgar Lee Masters, *The Sangamon* (New York: Farrar & Rinehart, 1942), 233.

CHAPTER 4: THE RISE AND FALL OF A PROVINCIAL POLITICIAN

1. Bidwell and Falconer, *History of Agriculture,* 310.

2. U.S., Department of Commerce, Bureau of the Census, *Historical Statistics of the United States, Colonial Times to 1970,* 2 vols. (Washington: Government Printing Office, 1975), 1:27; Paul Simon, *Lincoln's Preparation for Greatness: The Illinois Legislative Years* (Norman: University of Oklahoma Press, 1965), 33; Pease, *Frontier State,* 176–77.

3. Haig, *General Property Tax,* 62, 66–67.

4. Paul W. Gates, *Landlords and Tenants on the Prairie Frontier: Studies in American Land Policy* (Ithaca: Cornell University Press, 1973), 58–59.

5. *CW* 1:7–8.

6. Alfred Brunson, "A Methodist Circuit Rider's Horseback Tour from Pennsylvania to Wisconsin, 1835," in Angle, *Prairie State,* 164.

7. Charles Dickens, *American Notes for General Circulation* (Leipzig, 1842), cited in Angle, *Prairie State,* 212.

8. Pease, *Frontier State,* 178.

9. Cited by Robert W. Johannsen, *Stephen A. Douglas* (New York: Oxford University Press, 1973), 36–37.

10. Calvin Colton, *Manual for Emigrants to America* (London: F. Westley and A. H. Davis, 1832), 125.

11. John Mason Peck, *A New Guide for Emigrants to the West* (Boston: Gould Kendall and Lincoln, 1843), 291–92; William Eldon Baringer, *Lincoln's Vandalia, a Pioneer Portrait* (New Brunswick: Rutgers University Press, 1949), 32.

12. Willard, "Reminiscences," 79–83; Pease, *Frontier State,* 48, 363–82.

13. Lincoln's speech of 11 January 1837, *CW,* 1:65–66. This was, in fact, a personal attack against Usher F. Linder.

14. Simon, *Preparation for Greatness,* 21.

15. Herndon, 1:126.

16. Herndon, 1:127; Ford, *History of Illinois,* 106. The unflattering opinion of Mrs. John T. Stuart is reported by Luthin, *The Real Abraham Lincoln,* 39.

17. Baringer, *Lincoln's Vandalia,* 40; Simon, *Preparation for Greatness,* 18.

For the "turbulent political arena," see Luthin, *The Real Abraham Lincoln,* 40–41, who describes marvellously these "statesmen of great expectorations."

18. Ford, *History of Illinois,* 88.

19. Cartwright, *Autobiography,* 262.

20. Simon, *Preparation for Greatness,* 21; Charles Manfred Thompson, *The Illinois Whigs Before 1846,* University of Illinois Studies in the Social Sciences (Urbana: University of Illinois Press, 1915), 4:27, 52, 98.

21. Simon, *Preparation for Greatness,* 27; Beveridge, 1:166n; *CW,* 1:27–29, 33–35.

22. Miers, *Lincoln Day by Day,* 1:45; Simon, *Preparation for Greatness,* 130; *CW,* 1:41.

23. Simon, *Preparation for Greatness,* 39–40, 53.

24. *CW,* 1:32; Boggess, *Settlement of Illinois,* 141.

25. Beveridge, 1:166; *CW,* 1:43; Gates, *Landlords and Tenants,* 57.

26. *CW,* 1:43.

27. *CW,* 1:45, 49–50.

28. Pratt, *Personal Finances,* 143.

29. Simon, *Preparation for Greatness,* 45–47; *CW,* 1:298.

30. Letter to the *Sangamo Journal,* 13 June 1836, *CW,* 1:48.

31. John H. Krenkel, *Illinois Internal Improvements, 1818-1848* (Cedar Rapids: Torch Press, 1958), 47; Simon, *Preparation for Greatness,* 89; Pease, *Frontier State,* 216–35.

32. Herndon, 1:175. DeWitt Clinton, governor of New York, inspired the internal improvements of that state, most notably the Erie Canal.

33. Michel Chevalier, *Histoire et description des voies de communications aux Etats-Unis,* 2 vols. and 1 atlas (Paris: C. Gosselin, 1840), 256, 259.

34. G. W. Dowrie, *Development of Banking in Illinois,* University of Illinois Studies in the Social Sciences (Urbana: University of Illinois Press, 1913).

35. *CW,* 1:61–69. "Sound money" was the Whig euphemism for plentiful paper money.

36. Simon, *Preparation for Greatness,* 18.

37. *CW,* 1:55–60, 72, 127, 139–40.

38. Brown, *History of Illinois,* 418.

39. Samuel Augustus Mitchell, publisher, *Illinois in 1837 . . . together with a Letter on the Cultivation of the Prairies,* by the Hon. *H. L. Ellsworth* (Philadelphia: S. A. Mitchell, 1837), 20–21, 58.

40. Eliza R. Steele, *A Summer Journey to the West* (New York: J. S. Taylor, 1841), 162. By 1841, the prices were going down.

41. Gates, *Landlords and Tenants,* 69.

42. Pratt, *Personal Finances,* 58–59, 143; *CW,* 1:40. If Lincoln paid the entire real estate taxes for the period, the tax burden represented $4.75, taking account of the variations in the tax scale and supposing a minimum evaluation of the land. Haig, *General Property Tax,* 123; Bogue, *From Prairie to Corn Belt,* 43–44; Allan G. Bogue, *Money at Interest: The Farm Mortgage on the Middle Border* (1955; reprint, Lincoln: University of Nebraska Press, 1969), 3.

43. Pratt, *Personal Finances,* 59. It is not known when the other lot was sold.

44. Contract in Beveridge, 1:213–14.

45. Pratt, *Personal Finances,* 60.

46. Bidwell and Falconer, *History of Agriculture,* 493.

47. *CW,* 1:132–38; Beveridge, 1:253.

48. Letter to John T. Stuart, 1 January 1840, *CW,* 1:181.

49. *CW,* 1:132; Miers, Baringer, and Powell, *Lincoln Day by Day,* 1:64, 99; George M. Stephenson, *The Political History of the Public Lands from 1840 to 1862* (Boston: R. G. Badger, 1917), 33–36.

50. Johannsen, *Stephen A. Douglas,* 36–37, 211, 337–38, 358–59, 435–36, 702.

51. *CW,* 1:190–92.

52. *CW,* 1:67; Gates, *Landlords and Tenants,* 57.

53. Edmund Flagg, *The Far West; or, A Tour Beyond the Mountains. Embracing Outlines of Western Life and Scenery,* 2 vols. [New York, 1838], in *EWT,* 26:333–34, gives the example of the sale of clothes, occurring near Springfield in the summer of 1836.

54. Haig, *General Property Tax,* 37–44, 52–53, 63–67, 78–81.

55. Letter to William S. Wait, 2 March 1839, *CW,* 1:147–48.

56. Haig, *General Property Tax,* 28, 81–82; *CW,* 1:148–49.

57. Chevalier, *Histoire et description,* 2:265; Evarts Boutwell Greene and Charles M. Thompson, eds., *Governors' Letter Books, 1840–1853,* Collections of the Illinois State Historical Library (Springfield: Illinois State Historical Library, 1911), 7:22–23.

58. *CW,* 1:123.

59. *CW,* 1:196–97, 200–201. Noah Johnston was the other commissioner. *CW,* 2:162–87.

60. *CW,* 1:243–44.

61. *CW,* 1:215–26.

62. *CW,* 1:217–18.

63. *CW,* 1:220.

64. Haig, *General Property Tax,* 83; *CW,* 1:394.

65. Chevalier, *Histoire et description,* 2:265. It was the state tax which increased by 50 percent, going from 20 to 30 thousandths.

66. *CW,* 1:252.

67. *CW,* 1:216.

68. Hertz, *Hidden Lincoln,* 329; Stephen B. Oates, *With Malice Toward None: The Life of Abraham Lincoln* (London: George Allen and Unwin, 1978), 57–58.

69. *CW,* 1:159–79. The Sub-Treasury was the body charged with collecting and keeping the revenues of the government after the disappearance of the Bank of the United States.

70. *CW,* 1:291–97; Beveridge, 1:338–45.

71. Gates, *Landlords and Tenants,* 64.

72. See Ruth Painter Randall, *The Courtship of Mr. Lincoln* (Boston: Little, Brown, 1957), 11–28.

73. Herndon, 1:194–95.

74. *CW, ,* 1:320.

75. Boggess, *Settlement of Illinois,* 205–7; *CW,* 1:14n, 2:70–71, 324.

76. *CW,* 1:38, 47–48, 77–78.

77. Frances Milton I. Morehouse, *The Life of Jesse W. Fell,* University of Illinois Studies in the Social Sciences (Urbana: University of Illinois Press, 1916), 5:19.

78. *CW,* 1:203–5, 209; Harry Edward Pratt, comp., *Concerning Mr. Lincoln, in which Abraham Lincoln Is Pictured as He Appeared to Letter Writers of His Time* (Springfield: The Abraham Lincoln Association, 1944), 28; Gates, *Landlords and Tenants,* 151.

79. *CW,* 1:208; Gates, *Landlords and Tenants,* 217–18; Bogue, *From Prairie to Corn Belt,* 88.

80. *CW,* 1:206–207, 249; Gates, *Landlords and Tenants,* 201–17; Bogue, *From Prairie to Corn Belt,* 100; Paul W. Gates, "Frontier Estate Builders and Farm Labourers," in *The Frontier in Perspective,* ed. Walker D. Wyman and Clifton B. Kroeber (Madison: University of Wisconsin Press, 1957), 155.

81. *CW,* 1:221; Gates, *Landlords and Tenants,* 151.

82. Herndon, 2:375.

CHAPTER 5: THE YEARS OF MATURATION

1. R. Gerald McMurtry, "Centre College, John Todd Stuart, and Abraham Lincoln," *Filson Club Historical Quarterly* (Louisville, April 1959), cited in Simon, *Preparation for Greatness,* 17.

2. John J. Duff, *A. Lincoln: Prairie Lawyer* (New York: Rinehart, 1960), 33.

3. Simon, *Preparation for Greatness,* 21, 47.

4. Johannsen, *Stephen A. Douglas,* 26, 31.

5. *CW,* 1:83–84, 198, 95–106.

6. Herndon, 1:111; *CW,* 2:327.

7. *CW,* 1:3, 4, 15.

8. *CW,* 3:344, 4:121; Duff, *Prairie Lawyer,* 45; Albert A. Woldman, *Lawyer Lincoln* (Boston, 1936), cited in *The Lincoln Reader,* ed. Paul M. Angle (New Brunswick: Rutgers University Press, 1947), 91. Lacking specialized schooling, law students at the time studied in lawyers' offices.

9. Blackstone, *Commentaries on the Laws of England* (London, 1765, edition of 1809), Book 2, chapter 1, 8. Locke himself says that "As much land as a man tills, plants, improves, cultivates, and can use the product of, so much is his property." See section 32 of *Essay Concerning the True Original, Extent and End of Civil Government* (Second Treatise of Civil Government), ed. Charles L. Sherman. (New York: Appleton-Century-Crofts, 1937), 22.

10. John P. Frank, *Lincoln as a Lawyer* (Urbana: University of Illinois Press, 1961), 93.

11. Alexis de Tocqueville, *Democracy in America,* 2 vols. (New York: Vintage Books, 1990), 1:278, 273.

12. See John Thomas Richards, *Abraham Lincoln: The Lawyer-Statesman* (Boston and New York: Houghton Mifflin, 1916), especially 104–5. The former president of the Chicago Bar Association emphasizes at length what he sees as Lincoln's conservatism as a defender of property.

13. Frank, *Lincoln as a Lawyer,* 24; Herndon, 1:187; Tocqueville, *Democracy in America,* 1:276, 279, 285.

14. Frederick Trevor Hill, *Lincoln the Lawyer* (New York: Century, 1906), 25, 65.

15. George A. Dupuy, "The Earliest Courts of the Illinois Country," *Transactions of the Illinois State Historical Society* 11 (1906): 47–48

16. Duff, *Prairie Lawyer,* 14–15; Boggess, *Settlement of Illinois,* 173.

17. Whitney, *Life on the Circuit,* 34; Hill, *Lincoln the Lawyer,* 80.

18. John McAuley Palmer, *Personal Recollections of John M. Palmer: The Story of an Earnest Life* (Cincinnati: R. Clarke, 1901), 38–39, 41.

19. Pratt, *Personal Finances,* 26–27, 30.

20. Coleman, *Lincoln and Coles County,* 26, 30, 240–41; *CW,* 1:262–63.

21. Duff, *Prairie Lawyer,* 113–14, 85; Pratt, *Personal Finances,* 40–41, 28; "Stuart and Lincoln Fee Book," cited by Herndon, 1:182; *CW,* 1:279, 290–91.

22. Duff, *Prairie Lawyer,* 46, 175–79. A circuit is the jurisdiction of a circuit judge. In two sessions (spring and fall), the judge, accompanied as needed by lawyers who "rode the circuit," moved from county seat to county seat, where his itinerant court was held.

23. Hill, *Lincoln the Lawyer,* 163–64, 171; Paul M. Angle, *One Hundred Years of Law: An Account of the Law Office which John T. Stuart Founded in Springfield, Illinois, a Century Ago* (Springfield: Brown, Hay and Stephens, 1928), in Angle, *The Lincoln Reader,* 97.

24. Arnold, *History of Abraham Lincoln,* 75–78.

25. Palmer, *Personal Recollections,* 40; Herndon, 2:311.

26. Frank, *Lincoln as a Lawyer,* 6, 67–69; Herndon, 1:185–87; Duff, *Prairie Lawyer,* 63–65, 90–95, 252–53; *CW,* 2:340; Johannsen, *Stephen A. Douglas,* 34.

27. Compilation by Coleman, in *Lincoln and Coles County,* 80–103.

28. Duff, *Prairie Lawyer,* 230; *CW,* 1:270, 283–86, 290.

29. *CW,* 1:123; Lincoln to Speed, *CW,* 1:305–6, 323–24, 328.

30. *CW,* 1:306n, 20n.

31. See G. S. Boritt, *Lincoln and the Economics of the American Dream* (Memphis: Memphis State University Press, 1978), 47; *CW,* 1:335.

32. Letter to Speed, 27 March 1842, *CW,* 1:282.

33. Willard Leroy King, *Lincoln's Manager, David Davis* (Cambridge: Harvard University Press, 1960), 51–52.

34. "Notes for a Law Lecture" [ca. 1 July 1850], *CW,* 2:81–82.

35. Theodore L. Carlson, *The Illinois Military Tract; A Study of Land Occupation, Utilization, and Tenure,* University of Illinois Studies in the Social Sciences (Urbana: University of Illinois Press, 1951), 32:62–63.

36. Henry B. Rankin, *Personal Recollections of Abraham Lincoln* (New York: G. P. Putnam's Sons, 1916), 9–10, 22–23.

37. Pratt, *Personal Finances*, 63–65; contract in *CW*, 1:331.

38. Herndon to Lamon, 6 March 1870, cited in Randall, *Lincoln the President*, 1:46n; Boritt, *American Dream*, 104.

39. Boritt emphasizes this point; see *American Dream*, 99, for his analysis of Lincoln's funeral oration on Clay (*CW*, 2:121–132).

40. *Illinois State Register*, 15 March 1844, *CW*, 1:334.

41. *CW*, 1:311–12. He admitted this implicitly by declaring that it was the consumer of luxury articles who bore the consequences of tariff increases.

42. *CW*, 1:382. Colton and Clay had tried to prove this. Cf. Boritt, *American Dream*, 100–117, who studies in detail Lincoln's positions on the tariff at the time in their relation to the economic situation and the opposing points of view.

43. "Campaign Circular from Whig Committee," 4 March 1843, *CW*, 1:311.

44. Boritt, *American Dream*, 101, 103–4.

45. Boritt, *American Dream*, 102.

46. Boritt, *American Dream*, 116; Carey, "the only American economist of importance," letter to Weydemeyer, 5 March 1852, in Karl Marx and Friedrich Engels, *Letters to Americans, 1848–1895: A Selection* (New York: International Publishers, 1953), 43–46. In the United States, any attempt to revise Marxism eventually ends with the recognition of the superiority of Carey and Lincoln over Marx and Engels. Cf. the apostasy of Earl Browder, former general secretary of the Communist party of the United States in *Marx and America: A Study of the Doctrine of Impoverishment* (London: V. Gollancz, 1959), especially the chapter entitled "Marx and Lincoln," 110–23.

47. Joseph C. Rayback, *A History of American Labor* (New York: Macmillan, 1959), 75–99.

48. "Fragments of a Tariff Discussion," [December 1, 1847?], *CW*, 1:407–15.

49. Speech at Carlinville, Illinois, 31 August 1858, *CW*, 3:78.

50. *CW*, 1:409.

51. Potter, *Impending Crisis*, 27.

52. *CW*, 1:409.

53. The figures in the chart have been rounded off. *Historical Statistics*, 1:898–99; Paul W. Gates, *The Farmer's Age: Agriculture, 1815–1860*, Economic History of the United States (New York: Holt, Rinehart and Winston, 1960), 3:167–69.

54. Robbins, *Our Landed Heritage*, 128–29; Stephenson, *Political History*, 44–90.

55. Stephenson, *Political History*, 71. The Illinois general assembly eventually accepted it. "Campaign Circular from Whig Committee," 4 March 1843, *CW*, 1:312–14.

56. Boritt, *American Dream*, 84–87. But Boritt believes that from 1834 to 1849, Lincoln always had the same ambiguous attitude toward Whig policy on public lands, that he was in a way a frustrated Democrat on this issue.

57. David J. Harkness and R. Gerald McMurtry, *Lincoln's Favorite Poets* (Knoxville: University of Tennessee Press, 1959), 1–83.

58. *CW,* 4:65.

59. *CW,* 1:74–75.

60. This was Clay's expression, which Lincoln repeated at Freeport in his debate with Douglas. *CW,* 3:42, 4:108.

61. *CW,* 1:279.

62. Hill, *Lincoln the Lawyer,* 36; Helen Nicolay, *Personal Traits of Abraham Lincoln* (New York: Century, 1913), 219.

63. *CW,* 1:126, 110–11.

64. Letter to Williamson Durley, *CW,* 1: 347–48, 1:337; Duff, *Prairie Lawyer,* 86, 130–40; Coleman, *Lincoln and Coles County,* 90–95; Beveridge, 1:390–96.

65. Donald W. Riddle, *Congressman Lincoln* (Urbana: University of Illinois Press, 1957), 179.

CHAPTER 6: WASHINGTON AND DISARRAY

1. Beveridge, 1:372–83; Riddle, *Congressman Lincoln,* 5–6; see also chapter 2 n91 of this volume.

2. Letter to the *Courier,* 11 July 1847, in Harry E. Pratt, "Illinois as Lincoln Knew It: A Boston Reporter's Record of a Trip in 1847," *Papers in Illinois History* (Springfield: Illinois State Historical Society, 1938), 139–40.

3. Rice, *Reminiscences,* 598.

4. Pratt, "Illinois as Lincoln Knew it," 139.

5. Miers, Baringer, and Powell, eds., *Lincoln Day by Day,* 1:295; William H. Townsend, *Lincoln and His Wife's Hometown* (Indianapolis: Bobbs Merrill, 1929), 153–54.

6. See Boritt, *American Dream,* 140–41.

7. *CW,* 1:420–22.

8. Frank, *Lincoln as a Lawyer,* 105–10.

9. Those are the words of the Ashmun amendment for which he voted. See 12 January 1848, *Congressional Globe,* 30th Cong., 1st sess., Appendix, 93.

10. *Congressional Globe,* 30th Cong., 1st sess., 94.

11. Hill, *Lincoln the Lawyer,* 154.

12. Frank, *Lincoln as a Lawyer,* 108; see especially *CW,* 1:437.

13. Riddle, *Congressman Lincoln,* 35–40. See the long speech by Robert M. McLane, who came after Lincoln in the debate on the Mexican War, *Congressional Globe,* 30th Cong., 1st sess., Appendix, 101–4.

14. G. S. Boritt, "A Question of Political Suicide: Lincoln's opposition to the Mexican War," *Journal of the Illinois State Historical Society* 62 (February 1974): 79–100; Mark E. Neely, Jr., "Lincoln and the Mexican War: an Argument by Analogy," *Civil War History* 24 (March 1978): 5–24.

15. Herndon, 2:283–84.

16. Riddle, who was the first to underscore Lincoln's great amount of work for his constituents, devoted only a few lines to the encouragement given to American hemp and ascribed Lincoln's attitude to the fact that his father-in-law, Robert S. Todd, had interests in hemp processing. Riddle, *Congressman*

Lincoln, 76. This hypothesis should not be entirely rejected, but the situation of Illinois suffices for explaining the position in favor of hemp growers taken by Lincoln and the other representatives of that state.

17. Gates, *The Farmer's Age,* 116–17, 326–27.

18. Cited by Bogue, *From Prairie to Corn Belt,* 143.

19. Note by Pratt, "Illinois as Lincoln Knew It," 142; Richard Bardolph, *Agricultural Literature and the Early Illinois Farmer,* University of Illinois Studies in the Social Sciences (Urbana: University of Illinois Press, 1948), 21:53, 131–32; *Transactions of the Illinois State Agricultural Society* 1 (1853–54): 126–32.

20. Gates, *The Farmer's Age,* 326; Paul W. Gates, *Agriculture and the Civil War* (New York: Knopf, 1965), 169; Angle, *Here I Have Lived,* 155; Bogue, *From Prairie to Corn Belt,* 228.

21. *Congressional Globe,* 30th Cong., 1st sess., 508, 571, 725; *House Journal,* 30th Cong., 1st sess., 645, 670, 697, 766–77; *CW,* 1:462–63.

22. Boritt, *American Dream,* 337; Rice, *Reminiscences,* 239–40; Riddle, *Congressman Lincoln,* 144, 184; *Congressional Globe,* 30th Cong., 1st sess., 56–57, 64, 103; *CW,* 1:417–519, 2:18–67.

23. Boritt, *American Dream,* 133; *Congressional Globe,* 30th Cong., 1st sess., 57, 307; *CW,* 1:442, 460–61, 464.

24. *Congressional Globe,* 30th Cong., 1st sess., 60, 380, 1071, Appendix, 534; 30th Cong., 2d sess., 25–26, 38–39, 559 (Lincoln).

25. *Congressional Globe,* 30th Cong., 1st sess., 58–59, 1063; *CW,* 1:480–90; Boritt, *American Dream,* 133.

26. *Congressional Globe,* 30th Cong., 1st sess., 755; *CW,* 1:469–71.

27. *Congressional Globe,* 30th Cong., 2d sess., 533; *CW,* 2:26–27; Stephenson, *Political History,* 90.

28. Stephenson, *Political History,* 119.

29. Stephenson, *Political History,* 121–22.

30. *Congressional Globe,* 30th Cong., 1st sess., 550; *CW,* 1:460–61.

31. See *CW,* 1:442; *Congressional Globe,* 30th Cong., 1st sess., 57, 181.

32. Boritt, *American Dream,* 133.

33. *Congressional Globe,* 30th Cong., 1st sess., 434, 550.

34. *Congressional Globe,* 30th Cong., 1st sess., 64, 771, 787, 950, 1049. Several separate cases, among them that of Adams County, Illinois, suffered from this problem, but the cases were settled to the satisfaction of the Illinoisans concerned. *CW,* 1:461, 478–79. It was the law of 20 May 1826. See Thomas Donaldson, *The Public Domain, Its History with Statistics* (Washington: Government Printing Office, 1880), 227.

35. *Congressional Globe,* 30th Cong., 1st sess., 82, 778; *House Journal,* 30th Cong., 1st sess., 820.

36. Riddle, *Congressman Lincoln,* 162–80; Beveridge, 1:435–37, 480–86.

37. Riddle treats both sessions of Congress in the same chapter, and confusion in the mind of the reader is heightened by typographical errors in the notes, where references are sometimes incorrect (indicating the second session instead

of the first, for example, on pages 162 and 164). On the other hand, Riddle seems not to have made a distinction in this chapter between abolitionism and anti-slavery, which led him to characterize Lincoln's attitude as pro-slavery when he refused to vote for the Gott Resolution. The revision of Riddle's revisionism, begun by Don E. Fehrenbacher for the period from 1852 to 1854 in his admirable *Prelude to Greatness: Lincoln in the 1850's* (Stanford.: Stanford University Press, 1962), 21–22, 27, 37, would gain by being extended to the period from 1848 to 1849.

38. *CW,* 2:252.

39. *Congressional Globe,* 30th Cong., 1st sess., 1006–7, 1027, 1062–63, 1074–78.

40. *Congressional Globe,* 30th Cong., 2d sess., 39, 155, 605, 695–97.

41. *CW,* 2:1–10.

42. Letter to Williamson Durley, 3 October 1845, *CW,* 1:348.

43. *Congressional Globe,* 30th Cong., 1st sess., 60, 73, 82, 641; Riddle, *Congressman Abraham Lincoln,* 162–63; *House Journal,* 30th Cong., 1 sess., 860.

44. That is, who helped slaves to escape. *Congressional Globe,* 30th Cong., 1st sess., 672–73, 641.

45. *Congressional Globe,* 30th Cong., 1st sess., 784–85, 180.

46. *Congressional Globe,* 30th Cong., 2d sess., 123, 129 (end of December 1848), 177, 303 (6–19 January 1849); *CW,* 2:19; *House Journal,* 30th Cong., 2d sess., 197, 208, 209. He refused to support continuation of the procedural fight; Riddle, *Congressman Abraham Lincoln,* 169.

47. *Congressional Globe,* 30th Cong., 2d sess., 38, 55–56, 83–85, 216. Giddings's plan called for blacks, free or slave, to take part in the voting.

48. Speech in Bloomington, 26 September 1854, *CW,* 2:237–38; speech in Peoria, 16 October 1854, *CW,* 2:253. Lincoln introduced a petition in favor of the abolition of the slave trade sent by Illinoisans during this session (*Congressional Globe,* 30th Cong., 2d sess., 568; Riddle, *Congressman Lincoln,* 163). Lincoln's resolution is in *CW,* 2:20–22; *Congressional Globe,* 30th Cong., 2d sess., 212.

49. *Congressional Globe,* 30th Cong., 2d sess., 244; *House Journal,* 30th Cong., 2d sess., 242; Riddle, *Congressman Abraham Lincoln,* 172.

50. *House Journal,* 30th Cong., 2d sess., 514–15, 539.

51. Stephenson, *Political History,* 114.

52. *Congressional Globe,* 28th Cong., 1st sess., 103; Stephenson, *Political History,* 116.

53. See his reports of 23 June 1848 and of 27 February 1849, in *House Journal,* 30th Cong., 1st sess., 867–68, and 30th Cong., 2d sess., 536. Among the proposals thus turned down should be noted in particular one from Caleb B. Smith (Whig-Ind.) on 17 January 1848 during the first session (*Congressional Globe,* 30th Cong., 1st sess., 181).

54. *Congressional Globe,* 30th Cong., 1st sess., 21, 284, 648, 715. The death of the senator from Arkansas, Chester Ashley, prevented Breese's bill from getting on the agenda on the day it was supposed to, and he did nothing to revive it.

55. See Harlan Hoyt Horner, *Lincoln and Greeley* (Urbana: University of Illinois Press, 1953), 54–55.

56. *House Journal,* 30th Cong., 2d sess., 536 (House Bill 644).

57. 21 December 1848, *Congressional Globe,* 30th Cong., 2d sess., 85.

58. Granted, we do not know how he voted in the preceding session because no roll call vote occurred. However, the very fact that a roll call was demanded suggests the growing importance accorded to the Homestead question, symbolized by the appearance of Horace Greeley following a by-election during the second session. A roll call vote could take place only with the assent of one-fifth of the members.

59. Clarence H. Danhof, "Farm-Making Costs and the 'Safety-Valve,' 1850–1860," *Journal of Political Economy* 49 (June 1941): 317–59.

60. Rayback, *American Labor,* 99.

61. Rayback, *American Labor,* 98–99; Stephenson, *Political History,* 105–10. See Carter Goodrich and Sol Davidson, "The Wage Earner and the Westward Movement," *Political Science Quarterly* 50 (June 1935): 161–85.

62. Rayback, *American Labor,* 98–99.

63. Arthur H. Cole, *The Irrepressible Conflict* (New York: Macmillan, 1934), 117. Their presidential candidate was Gerritt Smith, *CW,* 1:147–48.

64. Joe L. Norris, "The Land Reform Movement" (Phases of Chicago History, no. 2), *Papers in Illinois History and Transactions for 1937,* 77–79; Johannsen, *Stephen A. Douglas,* 318; Gates, *Landlords and Tenants,* 60; *CW,* 2:178, 4:136; Bogue *From Prairie to Corn Belt,* 88.

65. Stephenson, *Political History,* 126, 161.

66. *CW,* 2:27.

67. Luthin, *The Real Abraham Lincoln,* 109; *CW,* 2:41, 48, 55, 57–60, 67, 93; Mearns, *The Lincoln Papers,* 1:169–86; Thomas Ewing, "Lincoln and the General Land Office," *Journal of the Illinois State Historical Society* 25 (1932):145–46.

68. Butterfield to J. J. Brown, 7 June 1849 and Levi Davis to Butterfield, 9 June 1849, in Ewing, "Lincoln and the General Land Office," 141, 143.

69. *CW,* 2:49–50, 28–29.

70. *CW,* 4:67. See also the autobiography for Fell, *CW,* 3:512.

71. *CW,* 2:232.

72. "Eulogy on Zachary Taylor," 25 July 1850, *CW,* 2:89.

73. "Eulogy on Henry Clay," 6 July 1852, *CW,* 2:121–32.

74. Lincoln doubtless referred here to the 1820 line. *CW,* 2:232.

75. "Eulogy on Henry Clay," 2:123, 132.

76. Autobiography for Scripps, *CW,* 4:67.

77. *CW,* 2:135–159.

78. *CW,* 3:512.

CHAPTER 7: RECONCILIATION

1. Speech by Douglas in the Senate, cited by Potter, *Impending Crisis,* 152.

2. Randall, *Lincoln the President,* 1:121–22.

3. Compiled with the help of *Historical Statistics*, 1:27; Latrobe, *Rambler in North America*, cited in Angle, *Prairie State*, 117; Charles W. Marsh, *Recollections 1837–1910* (Chicago: Farm Implement News Co., 1910), 33; Gustaf Elias Marius Unonius, *A Pioneer in Northwest America 1841–1858: the Memoirs of Gustaf Unonius*, trans. J. O. Blacklund, ed. Nils William Olsson, 2 vols. (Minneapolis: University of Minnesota Press, 1950–60), in Angle, *Prairie State*, 292–98.

4. Letters of Reverend J. P. Thompson of New York, published for the first time by Daniel S. Curtiss, *Western Portraiture, and Emigrants' Guide: A Description of Wisconsin, Illinois, and Iowa* (New York: J. H. Colton, 1852), in Angle, *Prairie State*, 265.

5. Frederick Gerhard, *Illinois as it is; its History, Geography, Statistics, Constitution, Laws, Government, etc.* (Chicago: Keen and Lee; Philadelphia: C. Desilver, 1857), 446–47, 451.

6. Fehrenbacher, *Prelude to Greatness*, 6–7.

7. *CW*, 4:25.

8. Fehrenbacher, *Prelude to Greatness*, 6.

9. F. I. Herriott, "Senator Stephen A. Douglas and the Germans in 1854," *Transactions of the Illinois State Historical Society* 17 (1912): 142–58.

10. The series of facts comes from articles in *Ethnic Voters and the Election of Lincoln*, ed. Frederick C. Luebke (Lincoln: University of Nebraska Press, 1971). The quotation is from Ronald P. Formisano, "Ethnicity and Party in Michigan, 1854–1860," 176.

11. Donald, *Lincoln's Herndon*, 124–25; Carl Sandburg and Paul M. Angle, *Mary Lincoln, Wife and Widow* (New York: Harcourt, Brace, 1932), 196.

12. Masters, *The Sangamon*, 63.

13. *CW*, 5:69, 6:71n, 2:323. He wrote in a letter to Speed, dated 24 August 1855, "I am not a Know-Nothing. That is certain." For that matter, neither was he anti-Know-Nothing.

14. Gustave Koerner, *Memoirs of Gustave Koerner, 1809–1896: Life Sketches Written at the Suggestion of His Children*, ed. Thomas J. McCormack, 2 vols. (Cedar Rapids: Torch Press, 1909), 2:33.

15. *CW*, 3:380; James M. Bergquist, "People and Politics in Transition: The Illinois Germans, 1850–60," in *Ethnic Voters*, ed. Luebke, 213–14; F. I. Herriott, "The Conference in the Deutsches Haus, Chicago, May 14–15, 1860," *Transactions of the Illinois State Historical Society* 35 (1928): 101–91. See Mearns, *The Lincoln Papers*, 1:233–34, Delahay to Lincoln, 14 May 1860, pointing out the activity of "Cottonwood" among the German delegates.

16. *CW*, 2:376, 380, 502, 524, 536; Bergquist, "People and Politics," in *Ethnic Voters*, ed. Luebke, 200, 208.

17. Bergquist, "People and Politics," in *Ethnic Voters*, ed. Luebke, 204–5; Herriott, "Conference," 154–55, 120, 180–81, 187.

18. Herman Schlüter, *Lincoln, Labor and Slavery* (New York: Socialist Literature Co., 1913), 82; Bergquist, "People and Politics" in *Ethnic Voters*, ed. Luebke, 214; Jay Monaghan, "Did Abraham Lincoln Receive the Illinois German Vote?" in *Ethnic Voters*, ed. Luebke, 63. Cited by Karl Obermann, *Joseph Weydemeyer: Pioneer of American Socialism* (New York: International Publishers, 1947), 83.

19. O. Fritof Ander, "Lincoln and the Founders of Augustana College," in Ander, *Lincoln Images*, 7, 11–14.

20. *CW*, 3:486–87.

21. *CW*, 4:211–13.

22. Victor Searcher, *Lincoln's Journey to Greatness: A Factual Account of the Twelve-Day Inaugural Trip* (Philadelphia: Winston, 1960), conclusions repeated by Potter, *Impending Crisis*, 560–61.

23. Cited by Francis Fisher Browne, *The Every-day Life of Abraham Lincoln,* rev. ed. (London: John Murray, 1914), 271. Emphasis in the original.

24. These are the two different versions given by the Cincinnati *Daily Commercial* and the Cincinnati *Daily Gazette;* see *CW*, 4:201–3.

25. Johannsen, *Stephen A. Douglas*, 318.

26. Charles Granville Hamilton, *Lincoln and the Know-Nothing Movement* (Washington: Public Affairs Press, 1954), 9.

27. *CW*, 4:203 (*Gazette* version).

28. Marsh, *Recollections*, 50–55, 65; Black Hawk, *Autobiography*, 57.

29. Donaldson, *The Public Domain*, 229, 355.

30. Brown, *History of Illinois*, 411; Paul W. Gates, *The Illinois Central Railroad and Its Colonization Work,* Harvard Economic Studies (Cambridge: Harvard University Press, 1934), 42:99–103; Bogue, *From Prairie to Corn Belt*, 29–31.

31. Donaldson, *The Public Domain*, 237; Gates, *Illinois Central*, 106.

32. On the transaction see Pratt, *Personal Finances*, 67–69; on Moore, see Gates, "Cattle Kings in the Prairies" and "Frontier Landlords and Pioneer Tenants," in *Landlords and Tenants*, 230, 265–66; *CW*, 2:336; Herndon, 1:100.

33. Gates, *Illinois Central*, 102.

34. Herndon, 2:346; Whitney, *Life on the Circuit*, 64, 399.

35. Pratt, *Personal Finances*, 67.

36. Morehouse, *Jesse W. Fell*, 85–87; John William Starr, *Lincoln and the Railroads* (New York: Dodd, Mead, 1927), 40–45; Paul W. Gates, "The Struggle for the Charter of the Illinois Central Railroad," *Transactions of the Illinois State Historical Society* 40 (1933): 55–60; Charles Leroy Brown, "Abraham Lincoln and the Illinois Central Railroad, 1857–1860," *Journal of the Illinois State Historical Society* 36 (June 1943): 128.

37. Pratt, *Personal Finances*, 66–67.

38. Pratt, *Personal Finances*, 78–82; *CW*, 3:399.

39. Pratt, *Personal Finances*, 82.

40. Morehouse, *Jesse W. Fell*, 29–30.

41. See Willard Leroy King, *Lincoln's Manager, David Davis* (Cambridge: Harvard University Press, 1960).

42. Letter of 17 April 1861, *CW*, 4:336; Duff, *Prairie Lawyer*, 185–86; King, *Lincoln's Manager*, 52–53; Gates, *Landlords and Tenants*, 244, 249.

43. King, *Lincoln's Manager*, 52–53; Whitney, *Life on the Circuit*, 59–60; Morehouse, *Jesse W. Fell*, 26, 85; *CW*, 2:189–91, 538.

44. *CW*, 1:395–405, 3:383; Gates, "Frontier Landlords," 276–92.

45. *CW,* 2:333; Gates, "Cattle Kings," 230.

46. *CW,* 5:339.

47. Gates, "Land Speculator," 57; *CW,* 4:44.

48. *CW,* 4:394.

49. Harris, "Autobiography," 95.

50. Harris, "Autobiography," 99.

51. Whitney, *Life on the Circuit,* 42–43.

52. *CW,* 4:124; Gates, "Cattle Kings," in *Landlords and Tenants,* 179–80.

53. *CW,* 2:298; Gates, "Cattle Kings," 203, 208.

54. Paul W. Gates, "Frontier Estate Builders and Farm Labourers," in *The Frontier in Perspective,* ed. Walker D. Wyman and Clifton B. Kroeber (Madison: University of Wisconsin Press, 1957), 144–50; Charles Leslie Stuart, *Land Tenure in the United States with Special Reference to Illinois,* University of Illinois Studies in the Social Sciences (Urbana: University of Illinois Press, 1916), vol. 5.

55. Harris, "Autobiography," 81; Whitney, *Life on the Circuit,* 63; Gates, "Frontier Landlords," 265–66.

56. Brown, "Abraham Lincoln and the Illinois Central Railroad," 159–61. Lincoln's devotion to the I.C.R. cause should not be exaggerated. See Gates, "The Struggle for the Charter of the Illinois Central Railroad," 55–56, and Herndon, 2:353, 412.

57. See Brown, "Abraham Lincoln and the Illinois Central Railroad"; Starr, *Lincoln and the Railroads,* 40–45, 57–70; Duff, *Prairie Lawyer,* 312–19; Carlton Jonathan Corliss, *Main Line of Mid-America: The Story of the Illinois Central* (New York: Creative Age Press, 1950), 30, 105, 115; *CW,* 2:333–35; Gates, *Illinois Central,* 109.

58. Duff, *Prairie Lawyer,* 265–68.

59. *CW,* 1:395–405; R. M. Sutton, "Lincoln and the Railroads of Illinois," in Ander, *Lincoln Images,* 40–61; Pratt, *Personal Finances,* 48.

60. *CW,* 2:134–35; C. A. Harper, "The Railroad and the Prairie," *Transactions of the Illinois State Historical Society* 30 (1923): 102–10; Carlson, *The Illinois Military Tract,* 107–15; Corliss, *Main Line of Mid-America,* 137; Robert M. Sutton, "The Illinois Central: Thoroughfare for Freedom," *Civil War History* 7 (September 1961): 273–87.

61. Pratt, *Personal Finances,* 38; Duff, *Prairie Lawyer,* 244; reminiscences of T. J. Coffey and of Laurence Weldon, in Rice, *Reminiscences,* 240, 201–3.

62. Herndon, 2:304, 347.

63. Whitney, *Life on the Circuit,* 32; Marsh, *Recollections,* 76.

64. Randall, *Mary Lincoln,* 153–60; David Donald, "Herndon and Mrs. Lincoln," in *Lincoln Reconsidered: Essays on the Civil War Era* (New York: Alfred A. Knopf, 1956), 37–56.

65. Whitney, *Life on the Circuit,* 40–46; Duff, *Prairie Lawyer,* 198–99.

66. Whitney, *Life on the Circuit,* 40–46, 61–62.

67. William E. Barton, *The Soul of Abraham Lincoln* (New York: George H. Doran, 1920), 242–43; Louis Dale Carman, *Abraham Lincoln, Free Mason: An Address delivered before Harmony Lodge No. 17, F.A.A.M., Washington, D.C.,*

January 28, 1914 ([Washington, D.C.], 1914); "Lincoln" in Albert G. Mackey and Robert I. Clegg, *Encyclopedia of Freemasonry*, 3 vols., 9th ed. (Richmond: Macoy Publishing and Masonic Supply Co., 1966); *Proceedings of the Grand Lodge of Ancient Free and Accepted Masons of the State of Illinois* (Chicago, 1857).

68. *Proceedings of the Grand Lodge*, 224; Joseph Hartwell Barrett, *Abraham Lincoln and His Presidency*, 2 vols. (Cincinnati: Robert Clarke, 1904), 1:221. Barrett was a delegate to the convention. Olivier Fraysse, "Chicago 1860: A Mason's Wigwam?" *Lincoln Herald* 87 (Fall 1985): 71–72.

69. Boggess, *The Settlement of Illinois*, 194; *Proceedings of the Grand Lodge*, 224–25.

70. Whitney, *Life on the Circuit*, 67.

71. Abram J. Dittenhoeffer, *How We Elected Lincoln: Personal Recollections of Lincoln and Men of His Time* (New York: Harper & Brothers, 1916), 4, 35; Marsh, *Recollections*, 108–12; William E. Baringer, "Campaign Technique in Illinois—1860," *Transactions of the Illinois State Historical Society* 39 (1932): 249.

72. Murat Halstead, *Caucuses of 1860: A History of the National Political Conventions of the Current Presidential Campaign* (Columbus: Follet, Foster and Company, 1860), 143–44; Mearns, *The Lincoln Papers*, 1:235.

73. Oglesby, remarks gathered by *Century Magazine* 60 (June 1900), in Angle, *The Lincoln Reader*, 263–65. Specifying the precise kind of wood was necessary because they were among the most resistant to rotting. Most rails in 1860 were made of Wisconsin pine brought in by railroad.

74. *CW*, 4:48.

75. *CW*, 1:491.

76. Letter to Anson G. Henry of 19 November 1858, *CW*, 3:339. See also letter from Herndon to Trumbull, 20 March 1856, in Pratt, *Concerning Mr. Lincoln*, 4; letter from Davis to Henry E. Dummer, in Pratt, *Concerning Mr. Lincoln*, 22.

77. Mitgang, *Lincoln as They Saw Him*, 200; Mearns, *The Lincoln Papers*, 1:218.

78. Charles A. Church, *History of the Republican Party in Illinois 1854–1912, with a Review of the Aggressions of the Slave Power* (Rockford: Press of Wilson Bros. Co., ca. 1912), 93; Carl Sandburg, *Abraham Lincoln: The Prairie Years*, abridged ed. (New York: Harcourt, Brace, 1929), 495.

79. Pratt, *Personal Finances*, 71–82.

80. Frank, *Lincoln as a Lawyer*, 41.

81. *House Reports*, 1853, 2–24; *CW*, 2:74, 92–93, 117–21, 133, 159, 162–87, 191, 199–201, 210, 219, 317, 323–25, 330–32, 336–39, 393–97, 423, 427.

82. *CW*, 2:199, 206.

83. *Johnston vs. Jones and Marsh*, *CW*, 2:430–31; Frank, *Lincoln as a Lawyer*, 182–84.

84. *CW*, 2:194; *The People vs. Wynant*. Lincoln was the public prosecutor.

85. *CW*, 3:352–55. Lincoln used the term *wrongdoer* in its technical sense of a person who, according to *Webster's*, "violates the legal right of another to his

damage for which a legal remedy is available: one who commits a tort or trespass."

86. Herndon, 2:323; Whitney, *Life on the Circuit,* 539.

87. Henry Villard, *Lincoln on the Eve of '61: A Journalist's Story,* ed. Harold G. Villard and Oswald Garrison Villard (New York: A. A. Knopf, 1941), 15, 19.

88. Allan Nevins, *The Emergence of Lincoln,* 2 vols. (New York: Scribner's Sons, 1950), 1:261–64; Fehrenbacher, *Prelude to Greatness,* 59–61, 78; Donald, *Lincoln's Herndon,* 112–16; letter of 28 December 1857, *CW,* 2:430.

89. Mearns, *The Lincoln Papers,* 1:208.

90. Speech in Springfield, 26 June 1857, *CW,* 2:405.

91. Speech in Springfield, 26 June 1857. The theme would appear frequently in the debates with Douglas. See, for example, *CW,* 3:145–46. He declared his support for social segregation as stipulated by the laws of Illinois. See also Benjamin Quarles, *Lincoln and the Negro* (New York: Oxford University Press, 1962), and Lerone Bennett, Jr., "Was Abe Lincoln a White Supremacist?" *Ebony,* February 1958, 35, 40, 43. See also *CW,* 1:348, and speech at Cooper Institute of 27 February 1860, *CW,* 3:538–41.

92. Cited in Potter, *Impending Crisis,* 475.

93. Speech in Springfield, 9 September 1854, in *Illinois Journal,* 11 September, *CW,* 2:229–30.

94. Whitney, *Life on the Circuit,* 29.

95. *Transactions of the Illinois State Agricultural Society* 1 (1853–54): 1–10; Angle, *Here I Have Lived,* 211.

96. *CW,* 2:242. Emphasis in the original.

97. Herndon, 2:366; Johannsen, *Stephen A. Douglas,* 211, 337–38, 471, 689. Unlike Benjamin F. Wade, for example, Lincoln never accused Douglas of owning slaves.

98. The phrase is from a letter by George Washington to General Alexander Spotswood, 23 November 1794, which inspired the title of Leslie Howard Owens, *This Species of Property* (New York: Oxford University Press, 1976).

99. *CW,* 2:245, 239, 264.

100. *CW,* 2:267–72.

101. *CW,* 2:266. He would have opportunities to repeat this numerous times.

102. Speech in Springfield, 4 October 1854, *CW,* 2:246.

103. See Douglas's questions, *CW,* 3:177, 213–14, 238. The first statement of this thesis was on 26 June 1857, *CW,* 2:406.

104. *CW,* 2:405. The matter was taken up again in the debates of 1858 (*CW,* 3:16, 249).

105. Speeches by Douglas at Jonesboro and Quincy, *CW,* 3:141, 274–75.

106. Lincoln's speech at Columbus, Ohio, 16 September 1859, *CW,* 3:409.

107. Lincoln's speech at Carlinville, Illinois, 31 August 1858, *CW,* 3:78–79.

108. Speech at Greenville, Illinois, 13 September 1858, *CW,* 3:96; speech at Alton, Illinois, 15 October 1858, *CW,* 3:312.

109. The best treatment of the thesis of natural limits (with a complete bibliography) and its refutation are found in Harry V. Jaffa, *Crisis of the House*

Divided: An Interpretation of the Issues in the Lincoln-Douglas Debates (Garden City: Doubleday, 1959), 387–99; Boritt, *American Dream,* 165–69.

110. Speech at Alton, *CW,* 3:315.

111. Speech in Cincinnati, 17 September 1859, *CW,* 3:459, 462–63.

112. *CW,* 4:7–8, 12–13, 24–26. Emphasis in original. This position was courageous, as Boritt shows, in *American Dream,* 182–83. The ideology of the Republicans was opposed, as a general rule, to strikes. See Eric Foner, *Free Soil, Free Labor, Free Men: The Ideology of the Republican Party before the Civil War* (New York: Oxford University Press, 1970), 25–29.

113. Compare Boritt, *American Dream,* 185, 220–21.

114. Seward's speech in the Senate, 29 February 1860, *Congressional Globe,* 36 Cong., 1st sess., 910–12; Glyndon G. Van Deusen, *William Henry Seward* (New York: Oxford University Press, 1967), 217–20; Boritt, *American Dream,* 186.

115. *CW,* 3:471–82. An excellent economic analysis is given by Boritt, *American Dream,* 185–89.

116. They especially had their hour of glory in the 1840s. See Bogue, *From Prairie to Corn Belt,* 94.

117. Harris, "The Autobiography of Benjamin Franklin Harris," 89–92; Bogue, *From Prairie to Corn Belt,* 102; Morehouse, *Jesse W. Fell,* 39–49.

118. John H. Littlefield in the *Brooklyn Eagle,* 16 October 1887, cited by Herndon, 2:316–17.

CONCLUSION

1. Earle D. Ross, "Lincoln and Agriculture," *Agricultural History* 3 (April 1929): 65; Gates, *Agriculture and the Civil War,* 301–24.

2. Frank, *Lincoln as a Lawyer,* 141–47; letter to Engels, 29 October 1862, in Karl Marx and Frederick Engels, *Selected Correspondence, 1846–1895,* trans. Dona Torr, the Marxist Library (Westport: Greenwood Press, 1942), 29:139–40; "To Abraham Lincoln, president of the United States," in Karl Marx and Friedrich Engels, *The Civil War in the United States,* 3d ed. (New York: International Publishers, 1961), 279–81.

3. *CW,* 6:151–52.

4. Charles Hamilton and Lloyd Ostendorf, *Lincoln in Photographs: An Album of Every Known Pose* (Norman: University of Oklahoma Press, 1985), 30.

5. David A. Nichols, *Lincoln and the Indians* (Columbia: University of Missouri Press, 1978), 10–15, 18–20, 65–75, 187; *CW,* 7:246.

6. Solon Justus Buck, "Lincoln and Minnesota," *Minnesota History* 6 (1925): 355–61; *CW,* 5:396, 493, 537–38, 550–51, 7:160, 515–16; Nichols, *Lincoln and the Indians,* 98–113, 119–120, 123.

7. Nichols, *Lincoln and the Indians,* 183. Nichols analyzes Newton's report to Lincoln in 1862 (184–85) and the president's attitude (186–89).

8. *CW,* 7:47.

9. *CW,* 7:48; Nichols, *Lincoln and the Indians,* 137, 159–60, 184.

10. Herndon, 1:48n.

11. David Donald, ed., *Inside Lincoln's Cabinet: The Civil War Diaries of Salmon P. Chase* (New York: Longmans, Green, 1954), 69. Fuller's slaves fell under the Confiscation Act of 1861.

12. *CW*, 5:328–31.

13. *CW*, 4:532. He was referring to Frémont's proclamation.

14. Lincoln had said to Chase, referring to Constitutional problems tied to issuing paper money (greenbacks): "Why, Chase, I don't intend precisely to throw the Virgin Mary overboard, and by that I mean the Constitution, but I will stick it in the hole if I can." Don Piatt, *Memories of the Men Who Saved the Union* (New York: Belford Clarke, 1887), 108–9.

15. Boritt, *American Dream*, 262; *CW*, 6:457.

16. *CW*, 6:30; John Eaton, *Grant, Lincoln and the Freedmen* (New York: Longmans, Green, 1907), 168; LaWanda Cox, *Lincoln and Black Freedom: A Study in Presidential Leadership* (Columbia: University of South Carolina Press, 1981).

17. W. E. B. Du Bois, *Black Reconstruction in America* (1935; reprint, New York: Atheneum, 1985), 237–324; Kenneth M. Stampp, *Andrew Johnson and the Failure of the Agrarian Dream* (Oxford: Oxford University Press, 1962).

18. Paul W. Gates, "The Homestead Law in an Incongruous Land System," *American Historical Review* 41 (July 1936): 652–81.

19. The figures are for original entries. The homesteader entered his plot at the Land Office, but received his patent only after four years of occupation and proof of improvements. Original entries, therefore, include land that eventually became the homesteader's property, as well as land that reverted to the federal government after four years. Donaldson, *The Public Domain*, 351; *Historical Statistics*, 1:428–30; Gates, *Agriculture During the Civil War*, 287; Gates, "The Homestead Law," 662.

20. Gates, *Agriculture and the Civil War*, 345–55.

21. Ruth Painter Randall, *Lincoln's Sons* (Boston: Little, Brown, 1955), 313, 328.

22. Cyrille Arnavon, "Images françaises du président Lincoln," *Etudes Anglaises* 12 (January-March 1959): 29.

23. Herndon, 3:527–28.

24. Herndon, 3:611. These are the last words of the book.

HISTORIOGRAPHY

1. The phrase is the title of an article by Arnavon, "Images françaises du président Lincoln," 8.

2. Arnold, *History of Abraham Lincoln*, 67.

3. Walt Whitman, "When Lilacs Last in the Dooryard Bloom'd," in *Leaves of Grass and Selected Prose* (New York: Modern Library, 1950), 262.

4. James Russell Lowell, "Ode recited at the Harvard Commemoration, July 21, 1865," in James Russell Lowell, *Poems*, 3 vols. (Cambridge: Riverside Press, 1925), 344.

5. Carl Sandburg, *Abraham Lincoln: The Prairie Years*, 2 vols. (New York: Harcourt, Brace, 1926), 1:49, 163, 449–67, 2:129, 151, 206–10.

6. Lloyd Lewis, *Myths after Lincoln* (New York: Harcourt, Brace, 1929), 405.

7. Roy P. Basler, *The Lincoln Legend: A Study in Changing Conceptions* (Boston: Houghton Mifflin, 1935).

8. See Victor Searcher, *Lincoln Today: An Introduction to Modern Lincolniana* (New York: T. Yoseloff, 1969).

9. David M. Potter, *The Lincoln Theme and American National Historiography* (Oxford: Clarendon Press, 1948), 5.

10. Richard Hofstadter, "Abraham Lincoln and the Self-Made Myth," in Hofstadter, *The American Political Tradition and the Men Who Made It* (New York: Alfred A. Knopf, 1948); Beveridge, 2:272.

11. Isaac N. Arnold, in *The Lincoln Memorial*, ed. O. H. Oldroyd (New York: G. W. Carleton, 1890), 62.

12. William E. Barton, "The Lincoln of the Biographers," *Transactions of the Illinois State Historical Society* 36 (1929): 82.

13. John Locke Scripps, *Life of Abraham Lincoln*, ed. Roy P. Basler and Lloyd A. Dunlap (Bloomington: Indiana University Press, 1961), 7, 46, 53–54, 70–71, 75.

14. William Dean Howells, *Life of Abraham Lincoln*, reprint of the original 1860 edition corrected by Lincoln (Bloomington: Indiana University Press, 1960), xxiii, 45–46, 52–53, 60, 94. The original title of this work was *Lives and Speeches of Abraham Lincoln and Hannibal Hamlin.*

15. William Makepeace Thayer, *The Pioneer Boy, and How He Became President* (Boston: Walker, Wise, 1863); O. J. Victor, *The Private and Public Life of Abraham Lincoln; Comprising a Full Account of His Early Years, and a Succinct Record of His Career as Statesman and President* (New York: Beadle and Company, 1864); see Barton, "The Lincoln of the Biographers," 86–116.

16. J. G. Holland, *The Life of Abraham Lincoln* (Springfield, Mass.: Gurdon Bill, 1866).

17. George S. Boutwell, *The Lawyer, the Statesman and the Soldier* (New York: D. Appleton, 1887); Lucius E. Chittenden, *Recollections of President Lincoln and His Administration* (New York: Harper & Brothers, 1891), and *Personal Reminiscences, 1840–1890 including some not hitherto published of Lincoln and the War* (New York: Richmond, Croscup, 1893); Carl Schurz, *Abraham Lincoln: A Biographical Essay* (Boston: Houghton, Mifflin, 1907); Theodor Canisius, *Abraham Lincoln* (Stuttgart: Abenheimische Verlagsbuchhandlung, 1878); James R. Gilmore, *Recollections of Abraham Lincoln and the Civil War* (Boston: L.C. Page, 1898); Allen T. Rice, ed., *Reminiscences of Abraham Lincoln by Distinguished Men of His Time* (New York: North American Publishing Company, 1886); O. H. Oldroyd, *The Lincoln Memorial* (New York: G. W. Carleton, 1890)

18. Henry B. Rankin, *Personal Recollections of Abraham Lincoln* (New York: G. P. Putnam's Sons, 1916); Francis Fisher Browne, *The Every-day Life of Abraham*

Lincoln, rev. ed. (London: John Murray, 1914); Norman Hapgood, *Abraham Lincoln: The Man of the People* (New York: Macmillan, 1899).

19. [George Barnett Smith], *Abraham Lincoln, Farmer's Boy and President* (London: Society for Promoting Christian Knowledge, 1916).

20. Jay Monaghan, *Lincoln Bibliography: 1839–1939,* 2 vols., Collections of the Illinois State Historical Library, vols. 31 and 32 (Springfield: Illinois State Historical Library, 1943–45).

21. Arnold, *History of Abraham Lincoln,* 67–68, 87, 675.

22. Frederick Jackson Turner, "The Middle West," *International Monthly* (December 1901), reprinted in *The Frontier in American History* (New York: Holt, 1920), 135.

23. Nicolay and Hay, 10:346, 1:44, 77, 81, 109, 104, 123.

24. Nicolay and Hay, 1:131–32, 293, 294–95; Hay to Nicolay, 10 August 1885, cited by Benjamin P. Thomas, *Portrait for Posterity: Lincoln and His Biographers* (New Brunswick: Rutgers University Press, 1947), 103–4.

25. Letter from Beveridge to Frank H. Hodder, 15 December 1925, in Thomas, *Portrait for Posterity,* 250.

26. Louis Obed Renne, *Lincoln and the Land of the Sangamon* (Boston: Chapman & Grimes, 1945), 42–43; Donald, *Lincoln's Herndon,* 131–32, 139, 246–50, 285.

27. Herndon, 1:99, 121, 2:264–65, 412–20, 3:480, 509, 609.

28. Lord Charnwood, *Abraham Lincoln* (London: Constable and Company, 1916), 102.

29. Herndon, 1:172–80, 2:205.

30. Lamon, *The Life of Abraham Lincoln,* 123, 128, 131–32, 147, 193–95, 237, 312, 422.

31. Tarbell, *In the Footsteps of the Lincolns,* 137.

32. William E. Barton, *The Life of Abraham Lincoln,* 2 vols. (Indianapolis: Bobbs Merrill, 1925); Louis A. Warren, *Lincoln's Youth: Indiana Years, Seven to Twenty-One, 1816–1830* (New York: Appleton, Century, Crofts, 1959).

33. Thomas, *Portrait for Posterity,* 209; Charnwood, *Abraham Lincoln,* 11, 73.

34. Herman Schlüter, *Lincoln, Labor and Slavery* (New York: Socialist Literature, 1913), 5, 11, 179.

35. Claude G. Bowers, *Beveridge and the Progressive Era* (Boston: Houghton Mifflin, 1932).

36. Beveridge, 1:115.

37. Beveridge, 2:633.

38. Beveridge, 1:98–99, 174–75, 183–87, 200–205, 236, 245, 253–66, 267, 286, 531, 2:142–80, 229–30.

39. Thomas, *Portrait for Posterity,* 187–88.

40. Masters, *Lincoln: The Man,* 497.

41. "Lincoln: Free Soil Liberal," in V. L. Parrington, *Main Currents in American Thought,* 2 vols. (1927; reprint, New York: Harcourt, Brace and World, 1954), 2:145–53.

42. Masters, *Lincoln: The Man*, 229. Samuel Lincoln, Abraham's ancestor, had settled in Hingham, Massachusetts, in 1637.

43. Luthin, *The Real Abraham Lincoln*, 39–40, 125–30.

44. Harry J. Carman and Reinhard H. Luthin, *Lincoln and the Patronage* (New York: Columbia University Press, 1943); Luthin, *The First Lincoln Campaign*, 220; Luthin, *The Real Abraham Lincoln*, 36.

45. *CW*, 3:5–6.

46. Randall, *Lincoln, the President*, 1:2, 23–24, 125–27, 3:145.

47. Thomas, *Abraham Lincoln*, 21, 66, 79–80, 135.

48. Marx to Engels, *Civil War in the United States*, 332.

48. Boritt, *American Dream*, 79–91.

50. In this chapter, Boritt, *American Dream*, 85, mentions only the fact that Lincoln, by advocating a higher tax on uncultivated land, was attacking speculation.

51. Boritt, *American Dream*, 44–45, 49–50, 156.

52. Boritt, *American Dream*, 155–93.

53. Whitney, *Life on the Circuit*, 64–67, 390–404, 601.

54. Herndon, 3:584.

INDEX

OLIVIER FRAYSSÉ, an alumnus of Ecole Normale Supérieure, graduated from Institut d'Etudes Politiques de Paris, where he majored in economics. He holds a Ph.D. from the University of Paris-Sorbonne. He is currently an associate professor of American studies at the University of Sorbonne Nouvelle.

SYLVIA NEELY is associate professor of history at Saint Louis University. A graduate of Duke University and the University of Notre Dame, she is the author of *Lafayette and the Liberal Ideal (1814–1824): Politics and Conspiracy in an Age of Reaction.*